THE
ASIA
BUSINESS
BOOK

THE

ASIA
BUSINESS
BOOK

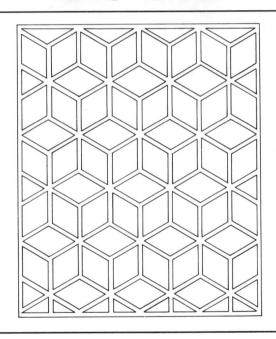

DAVID REARWIN

INTERCULTURAL PRESS, INC.

922875

For information, contact:
Intercultural Press, Inc.
P.O. Box 700
Yarmouth, Maine 04096, USA

Printed in the United States of America.

97   96   95   94   93   92   2   3   4   5   6   7

Library of Congress Cataloging-in-Publication Data

Rearwin, David, 1941–
    The Asia business book : survival and success in the Pacific Rim / David Rearwin.
        p.   cm.
    Includes bibliographical references and index.
    ISBN 0-933662-92-0
    1. East Asia—Commercial policy.   2. East Asia—Commerce.   3. East Asia—Commerce—United States.   4. United States—Commerce—East Asia.   I. Title.
HF1600.5.R4   1991
338.095—dc20   90-22615
                                                          CIP

Contents

THE ASIA BUSINESS BOOK

Introduction

If today's Asian business environment could be summed up in a single word, that word would be *change*. The field upon which the game of Asian business is played is being reshaped in ways that would have seemed impossible only a few years ago and at a rate that has left even experienced Asia hands wondering whether they can keep up. Some businesspeople are more concerned with what the changes will lead to and how they will affect their ability to do business. Others, mostly new arrivals, wonder whether or not Asia is becoming Westernized. This book is one attempt to give at least partial answers to these questions and to examine the Asian business environment in terms of both its origins and its evolution: where it has come from, where it is, and where it may be going.

Asia is destined to be a world leader in industrial, economic and trade growth for the rest of the twentieth century and probably well into the twenty-first. Although increasing numbers of American businesses have been discovering the advantages of doing business there, most of them have found themselves reinventing the wheel at every turn (often through costly and time-consuming mistakes), and many others have simply stayed away because they didn't know how to begin getting acquainted with the realities of doing business in the region. Unfortunately, one of the most frustrating business experiences in Asia is also one of the most common: you do your best to penetrate an Asian market, or set up a joint venture, or meet whatever other goals you and your company have set there. You try, you persevere, you do everything that you can think of, and still you can't get the results that you need. Something is wrong, but you can't quite define it.

It would be nice if you could turn to some sort of playbook that would give you ready solutions for each and every Asian business problem, or to a collection of techniques that you could apply to make things happen in the Asian business world. In the real world, however, business success cannot be reduced to formulas.

What you can do is acquire an orientation that lets you begin looking for solutions to the unique business problems that you will inevitably face in Asia. In the process, you will come to understand not only some of the things that Asian businesspeople and officials tend to do, but also why they do them. The long-term objective is to go beyond technique to develop awareness and attitudes that will enable you to steadily increase your effectiveness in the Asian business context.

The countries discussed in the pages that follow—the People's Republic of China, Hong Kong, Taiwan, Japan, the Republic of Korea, the Democratic People's Republic of Korea and Singapore—have been chosen because they are the most dynamic and important countries in East Asia, or in what is often called the Pacific Basin or Pacific Rim. All too often, the same characteristics that make them so dynamic and so important for international trade and business have created both extremely tough competitors and very difficult business environments. Under these circumstances Western businesses can use all the help they can get.

The countries selected have much in common in addition to their economic and commercial accomplishments. They all derive much of their culture and language from China. Two key areas, Taiwan and Korea, were under the Japanese for most of the first half of the twentieth century, during which time they absorbed a considerable amount of Japanese business culture. With the exception of Singapore, a Chinese island in a sea of Malay and South Pacific cultures, all of the nations look deceptively homogeneous, which has led some Westerners to refer to them as "chopstick cultures." But the locals see themselves as quite different from one another, and Westerners who ignore the differences can run into major problems.

Since conditions are different in each country, the content of each country briefing in part 2 of this book also differs. For example, more space has been devoted to marketing in Japan because of the especially demanding nature of the Japanese market. In the country briefing on Korea, there is more discussion of personalities because they tend to be a more important factor in business dealings there. The section on the People's Republic of China (PRC) reflects the centralized, bureaucratized business environment in the PRC by stressing structural problems. Clearly, almost everything that is true in one of the countries is true to a certain extent in some or all of the others. But in each country some traits—and the challenges they produce—are more pronounced and more significant for business. *The Asia Business Book* has tried to single these out in each case.

The Asia Business Book is based on years of business and consulting experience in East Asia (including participation in dozens of embassy business briefings). It starts with the same practical background that is given to ranking American business and government leaders when they visit East Asia for top-level briefings—and then goes on to give frank evaluations that are normally kept "in house."

In addition, this book draws on the collective experience of hundreds of Western businesspeople who have made the effort to do business in the East Asian context, and on the insights of East Asian business contacts whose experience often spans several cultures. One objective of this book is to help you profit from their experience. The author and editors welcome your suggestions for future editions.

The information provided here has been gathered from a variety of public and private sector sources. Although every effort has been made to ensure accuracy and completeness, neither the author nor the publisher is responsible for errors, omissions, discrepancies or variant interpretations of fact. In Asia, government rulings are often based on special laws, separate regulations, internal administrative guidelines (not available outside the bureaus that create them), and the host-country government's evaluation of the merits of the specific case under consideration. You should

obtain legal counsel during the early planning stages of any investment project (the U.S. embassy in each country can furnish a list
of attorneys, and the American Chamber of Commerce and the
Foreign Commercial Service can make informal recommendations
from among them). Also, consult with counsel before entering into
any binding agreement. In addition, you should contact appropriate host-country agencies regarding proposed agreements and visit
these agencies to discuss any proposal before formally submitting
it for approval.

Finally, a special note to our Asian friends. The information in
this book, including interpretations of Asian history, Asian society
and Asian business culture, comes both from Asian sources and
from Western reactions to the Asian experience. We hope that
every Asian reader will accept this book as a sincere attempt to
make sense out of an environment that can be very perplexing to
Westerners, and in so doing to help all of us develop more harmonious business relations.

PART I

DOING

BUSINESS

IN ASIA

CHAPTER ONE

Asia Briefing

EAST IS EAST

Perhaps the most important point to remember when doing business in Asia is that Asians are not Westerners, nor have they been Westernized. This may sound obvious, but far too many U.S. businesspeople, misled by the glass and chrome office buildings, three-piece suits and fast-food outlets that abound in much of Asia, act as though they were dealing with people from Los Angeles or Cincinnati. Sooner or later, this misperception causes serious business problems.

Part of the confusion comes from the nature of the typical foreign business visit. You fly into a major city, usually the capital, which is one of the more advanced and Westernized urban areas in the country and which may have been intended as a showplace. Both physically and culturally, these cities are often as different from outlying towns as Manhattan is from Gila Bend.

The neighborhood where your Western-style hotel is located is often even more Westernized—after all, the host country is trying to attract foreign business—and the people who work or live there are fairly well habituated to the presence of non-Asians.

Many of the people with whom you meet have been chosen by their companies for their ability to deal with Westerners. These might be called designated alien handlers (a position that to many Asians is about on a par with lion tamer or alligator wrestler), and they will do everything they can—which is a lot—to make you feel at home. This red-carpet treatment will often take place in hotels, restaurants, meeting rooms and entertainment places that have at most a very small place in the life of the average Asian. True, many of the settings, be they *kisaeng* houses or *karaoke* bars, are exotic, but in the company of your hosts you may feel that you are visiting one of the kingdoms of Disneyland with other tourists instead of seeing and experiencing something that should tell you how different Asia really is.

The net result of all this is that many foreign businesspeople come to Asia, have what seem like totally positive and productive meetings (punctuated by unforgettable evenings on the town), and yet fail to attain their objectives. In the short term, it often seems that things are going just as you would like, but then—often so subtly that it's hard to say when it began—things change. The contract that was supposed to be signed has been delayed or modi-fied beyond recognition. Or maybe it has been signed, but the Asian party isn't doing what you believe the agreement calls for. Or perhaps the commitments, concessions or gestures of goodwill that you had been led to expect never materialized. Welcome to the wonderful world of Asian thought and Asian business!

Can you do well in this environment? Absolutely. Thousands of U.S. companies, from America's biggest corporations to small sole proprietorships, are enjoying profitable and rewarding busi-ness relationships in Asia. There is no single procedure or magic formula for success, of course, but all the winners have one thing in common: they keep their eyes and their minds open. They take nothing for granted, they never stand still, and they are willing to change.

There is no playbook on Asian business that can get you through every situation, but there are concepts—Asian concepts—which, if you keep them in mind, will guide you through many a stretch of rough water. Two of the most useful are Japanese Zen and the Chinese *I Ching*. (A third, Confucianism, will be discussed later in the book.)

Many Americans have at least heard of Zen. One major objective of Zen training is a totally open mind that perceives everything equally, without any sort of bias, prejudgment or presumption. In physiological terms, this means that if a meditating Zen practitioner is exposed to a uniform sound—say, a mechanically produced clicking noise, repeated at regular intervals—the neurological response (as measured by an EEG machine) is identical every time. In other words, the practitioner doesn't tune it out, as most untrained people do after a few minutes, but perceives it each time as something new. What this does is to enable the individual to recognize the smallest differences or changes that occur in the environment. You don't have to take up Zen to use the same approach when dealing with Asians. Even if you have seen something done before, don't assume it will be the same the next time. Pay attention. You may see something that escaped your notice on previous occasions, or you may find that there has been a change.

Zen isn't as important in Korea or the Chinese cultures of the People's Republic of China, Taiwan, Hong Kong and Singapore as it is in Japan, but there is another, related conceptual framework that you can use to your own advantage. This is the *I Ching*, whose English name, *Book of Changes*, reflects the Asian attitude that change is a constant. Basically, the concept embodied in this work, which leads to much the same attitude as that acquired through Zen training, is that since every day is the product of different circumstances, one's actions must be changed on a daily basis in order to get the best results.

You simply cannot stand still when doing business in Asia: every business relationship is, in effect, in constant transition. It is fatal to sign a contract, set up an operation, and then turn most of your attention elsewhere in the belief that things will continue to run according to the structure and guidelines that you have created. You cannot put your Asian business in the back of your mind or tune it out. Instead, you have to pay constant attention to every major aspect of the business—and often the minor ones as well.

It's like owning a very fine, high-performance automobile: it will deliver top performance only if it's constantly fine-tuned and adjusted. Let it get very far out of tune and you are looking at some very expensive repairs.

THE PLAYERS AT A GLANCE

The first step in creating or maintaining productive business relationships in Asia is to get a feeling for the overall environment, including countries where you have no intention of doing business. There are at least two main reasons for this. The more you understand the region as an interlocking web of relationships that go back hundreds or even thousands of years, the more clearly you can see things that will affect you in the specific operating environment that you have chosen. In addition, some of the keenest competition that you face in any Asian country or market comes from other Asian countries. The more you know about your Asian competitors, the easier it will be for you to devise strategies and tactics for overcoming some of their natural advantages in the Asian markets you have targeted. With that in mind, let's take a look at the players in the Asian arena.

PEOPLE'S REPUBLIC OF CHINA (PRC)

Official language: Chinese (Mandarin). Other languages: several Chinese dialects, Tibetan, Mongolian, other minority languages. Cantonese, the most widely used nonofficial dialect, is spoken in Guangzhou (Canton) and the surrounding region including Hong Kong.

Population: 1.1 billion.

Size: 3.69 million square miles (slightly larger than the U.S.).

Currency: yuan, renminbi (Rmb).

Capital city: Beijing (9.3 million). Other major commercial/industrial cities: Shanghai (11.9 million), Tianjin (7.2 million), Guangzhou (5.2 million), Shenyang (4.8 million), Wuhan (4.4 million), Chandu (4 million).

Dominant political party: Chinese Communist party (CCP). Other legal parties: none.

Issues: eventual control over Hong Kong (1997), Macao (1999), Taiwan. Foreign military aid to Taiwan. Rapprochement with Taiwan. Resolution of recurring tensions with the Soviets and their allies (Afghanistan, India, Vietnam-Laos-Kampuchea, Outer Mongolia). Stability on the Korean peninsula. Conservation of foreign exchange. Modernization; acquisition of technology. Risk of inflation and economic distortions as the economy develops. Trade deficit with Japan. Lack of internal coordination and infrastructure. Fears of excessive Westernization and liberalization. Race relations and image in the Third World. Lack of definite political and social course. Corruption, profiteering, rising crime rate.

Weights and measures: Chinese, metric.

Electricity: 50-cycle AC, 220–230 volts.

Holidays: January 1; Lunar New Year's Eve and New Year (first and second day of the first moon); May 1; October 1–2. U.S. Embassy and consulates closed on U.S. and local holidays.

HONG KONG

Languages: English, Chinese (Cantonese, Mandarin).

Population: 5.5 million.

Size: 409 square miles.

Currency: Hong Kong dollar (HK$).

Dominant political party: British colony until 1997.

Issues: uncertainty about its future in the PRC. Status of its 11,500 Commonwealth residents. Handling of Vietnamese and Chinese refugees. Financial stability and financial scandals. Flight of local capital. Wheeling and dealing. Overbuilding, weakening of property market.

Weights and measures: English system.

Electricity: 50-cycle AC, 200 volts.

Holidays: January 1; Lunar New Year's Eve and New Year (first and second day of first moon); April 5; Good Friday; Easter Monday; June 14 or 15—Queen's Birthday (day varies); Monday following Queen's Birthday; fifth day of fifth moon (mid-June); Saturday before last Monday in August; last Monday in August; fifteenth day of eighth moon (late September); Chung Yeung Festival (late October); December 25; first weekday after December 25. U.S. Consulate closed on U.S. and local holidays.

TAIWAN, REPUBLIC OF CHINA (ROC)

Official language: Chinese (Mandarin). Other languages: Taiwanese, several Chinese dialects.

Population: 19.5 million (85 percent native Taiwanese, 15 percent mainland Chinese).

Size: 13,814 square miles (Maryland plus Delaware).

Currency: new Taiwan dollar (NT$).

Capital city: Taipei (2.4 million). Other major commercial/industrial cities: Kaohsiung (1.3 million), Taijung (640,000), Tainan (625,000).

Dominant political party: Kuomintang (KMT). Other legal parties: three, two of which are creatures of the ruling KMT and one of which (Democratic Progressive party) is a gadfly formed and then legalized in 1987. New parties permitted under 1987 security legislation theoretically must follow the KMT line on anticommunism and reunification with the mainland.

U.S. representation: Since the U.S. government transferred diplomatic recognition from the ROC to the PRC, there is no U.S. embassy on Taiwan. However, the American Institute in Taiwan (AIT) continues to handle virtually all the functions of an embassy.

Issues: international legitimacy as the government of China. Risk of absorption inherent in rapprochement with the PRC, just ninety miles away. How to manage reciprocal visits and business activity with the PRC and the USSR. Shifting allegiances, including South Korean involvement with the PRC. Troublesome Taiwanese independence movement. Development of internal democracy, rights of native Taiwanese majority. The effects of thirty-eight years of martial law; continuing security laws. Economic competition from Hong Kong, Korea, Thailand. Growing trade surplus, ballooning foreign exchange surplus. Access to U.S. market.

Weights and measures: metric, Chinese.

Electricity: 60-cycle AC, single and three-phase 110/220 volts.

Holidays: January 1; Lunar New Year's Eve and New Year (first and second day of first moon); March 29; April 4; fifth day of fifth moon; fifteenth day of eighth moon; September 28; October 10, 25, 31; November 12; December 25. AIT is closed on U.S. and local holidays.

JAPAN

Official language: Japanese. Other languages: none.

Population: 120 million.

Size: 147,470 square miles (smaller than California).

Currency: yen.

Capital city: Tokyo (metro: 11 million, including Yokohama). Other major commercial/industrial cities: Osaka-Kobe-Kyoto metro (8 million), Nagoya (2 million), Sapporo (1.4 million), Kitakyushu (1 million).

Dominant political party. Liberal Democratic party (LDP). Other parties: several.

Issues: trade surpluses with all countries in the region. Trade surpluses with the West (including the U.S.). Concern over future protectionism in unified European market after 1992. Effect of high value of yen on export industries. Role of military, 1 percent de facto defense budget ceiling and defensive capability. Access to the U.S. market. Status of Korean residents. Anti-Japanese feeling in China and Korea. Aging population. Sunset industries. Increasing *yakuza* (gangster) and school-age violence, changing social values.

Weights and measures: metric; Japanese system (*tsubo,* equal to about 36 square feet) for land and building area measurement.

Electricity: (1) 60-cycle AC 110/220 volts (Osaka and south), (2) 50-cycle AC 110/220 volts (Tokyo and north). Check specific cities before shipping appliances or consumer electronics. Also note that the chemical composition of gas (and technical requirements of gas appliances) varies in different parts of the country.

Holidays: January 1, 15; February 11; March 21; April 29; May 3, 5; September 15, 23; October 10; November 3, 23, 24. U.S. Embassy and consulates closed on U.S. and Japanese holidays. Many Japanese take several days of vacation in mid-August, although there is no official holiday at that time.

REPUBLIC OF KOREA (ROK)

Official language: Korean. Other languages: none.

Population: 40 million.

Size: 38,211 square miles (larger than Indiana).

Currency: won.

Capital city: Seoul (10 million). Other main commercial/industrial cities: Pusan (3.5 million), Taegu (2 million), Inchon (1.3 million).

Dominant political party: Democratic Liberal party (formed in 1990 by merging the two major opposition parties with the formerly dominant Democratic Justice party (DJP). Other parties: several; effective power of opposition parties fluctuates.

Issues: division of the peninsula and reduction of tensions with North Korea. Developing commercial and political relations with mainland China and the Soviet Union. Legitimacy of the present government, tainted by association with former military-dominated regimes. Demand for democratization. Radicalism, anti-Americanism. Overconcentration of population (about 25 percent) in Seoul. Troublesome manpower surplus, exacerbated by a very young population. (Unrealistic official unemployment figures—anyone who worked one day in the preceding month is classified as employed—mask widespread underemployment.) Access to U.S. market. Status of Koreans in Japan. Trade deficit with Japan. Potential for political and economic instability.

Weights and measures: metric; English/U.S. system widely understood.

Electricity: 60-cycle AC, single and three-phase 100/200 volts but converting to 220 volts (all imported appliances must be designed for 220 volts).

Holidays: January 1–3; March 1, 10; April 5, 8; May 5; June 6; July 17; August 15; October 1, 3, 9; December 25. U.S. Embassy and consulates closed on U.S. and Korean holidays.

DEMOCRATIC PEOPLE'S REPUBLIC OF KOREA (DPRK)

(NOTE: Although trade and business opportunities with the DPRK are virtually nonexistent, the DPRK plays such a dominant role in South Korean thinking and political, military and economic strategy that it is important to know something about it.)

Official language: Korean. Other languages: none.

Population: 18 million.

Size: 47,000 square miles (smaller than Mississippi).

Currency: won; not available and not convertible.

Capital city: Pyongyang (1.3 million).

Dominant political party: Communist party. Other parties: none.

Issues: self-sufficiency in military and economic terms. (The DPRK economy is heavily militarized, with 25 percent of GNP going for military purposes. The export of weapons and military training, especially to Africa and the Middle East, is an important part of the economy.) Risk of diplomatic isolation in an era of detente. Question of unification. Legacy of bitter and violent competition with ROK. Problem of succession in world's first Communist family dynasty. Economic stagnation, lack of foreign exchange.

SINGAPORE

Official languages: Chinese (Mandarin), Malay, Tamil, English.

Population: 2.5 million.

Size: 239 square miles (smaller than New York City).

Currency: Singapore dollar (S$).

Dominant political party: People's Action party (PAP). Other legal parties: several, none with effective political influence.

Issues: small economy with recent tendency toward extreme fluctuation. Transition to service economy. Political favoritism. Extreme overbuilding and depressed property market. Unemployment. Slack tourism industry. Controls on domestic and foreign press.

Weights and measures: English system.

Electricity: 50-cycle AC, 220/240 volts.

Holidays: January 1; Chinese Lunar New Year's Eve and New Year (first and second day of first moon); Good Friday; May 23; June 9; August 9; November 1; December 25. U.S. Embassy closed on U.S. and local holidays.

THE "FOUR SMALL DRAGONS"

The People's Republic of China, the giant of Asia, has long fascinated Americans, along with the business and trade potential of such a vast and populous country. Japan, although a distant second in population, is still large relative to other Asian countries and has repeatedly earned respect as an international contender in almost every business and industrial sector. There are four other business environments in Asia, however, that stand out in terms of competition, opportunities and challenges.

Americans love generalizations, and Asians love symbolic numbers and animals, so it's natural that someone should have come up with a concept that satisfies both urges. The "four small dragons" (or "four small tigers")—the Republic of Korea, Taiwan, Hong Kong, and Singapore—are often lumped together because their economies and industrial bases, while far smaller than that of Japan (their combined exports to the U.S. total less than two-thirds of Japan's), have for two decades been the most dynamic and rapidly growing in Asia, and indeed in the world.

Although there are certain similarities among the four, their differences are greater and more important. The ROK has a totally homogeneous population of forty million people. It is a world leader in steel production and shipbuilding and has very rapidly expanded its mainline, finished product sectors like automobiles and computers. The Korean economy has grown so dramatically (in spite of a couple of slack periods) that in 1986 the Koreans turned down a major international loan on the grounds that it wasn't needed. At the same time, however, the ROK has a nagging trade deficit, serious labor problems and the unresolved issue of how to restructure relations with the U.S., Japan and North Korea. At the other end of the size spectrum is little Singapore with 2.5 million citizens, a tiny economy and an ethnic mix that has created internal political problems, but no organized social violence and no major international issues to resolve.

Taiwan, midway between Korea and Singapore in size with nineteen million people, is one of the world's richest countries in terms of foreign currency reserves. Unlike the Republic of Korea, which has firmly established itself as the winner over North Korea in their fierce competition for industrial and economic supremacy and international recognition, Taiwan is fighting a losing rearguard political action against the PRC, which, in spite of domestic political turbulence and unpredictability, has become the de facto representative of the Chinese people in terms of official international recognition. At the same time, the loosening of travel and commercial restrictions has allowed the industrious islanders to gain a firm foothold in mainland manufacturing and trading, often through companies set up for that purpose in Hong Kong. There are major structural differences, too: while the ROK economy is based on huge industrial conglomerates and, like Singapore, still features highly centralized industrial and economic planning, Taiwan is characterized (as is Hong Kong) by large numbers of small businesses operating with little government intervention. Finally, Hong Kong (5.5 million), for all its bustle and hard-driving business style, may well be facing the beginning of the end of its freewheeling capitalist phase. (The PRC, after all, has only promised fifty years of capitalism after 1997, and there is reason to believe that a combination of capital flight and the bureaucratic incompetence and political meddling that hinder business activity in the PRC may smother many businesses even before the fifty years expire.)

Major internal political differences also affect (or have the potential to affect) foreign businesses in each of the four countries. Korea, for example, is utterly lacking in democratic tradition, and the country's recent political history has created neither consensus nor the legitimacy that is so important in Asia's Confucian tradition. Furthermore, a series of violent events ranging from the bloody suppression of the Kwangju uprising in 1980 to the street rioting and physical attacks on students and labor organizers through the rest of the decade have polarized the political spectrum and left scars that will not be easily healed. But Korean politics is never as clear-cut as it may seem to the outside observer. In the past, the government has used the threat of attack from the north to distract fractious political factions from their internecine squabbling; in the future they may be able to get the same result by holding out the promise of rapprochement or even peaceful reunification with the DPRK. This is not necessarily good news for foreign business, however. Historically, the more internal solidarity the Koreans have experienced, the more they have rejected outside influences of any kind. Furthermore, the Koreans have yet to solve the underlying problem of Korean domestic and international political life: how to become accustomed to using compromise rather than confrontation.

In Taiwan, the political problems are of a different nature. There the most radical groups advocate not accommodation or unification with China, but Taiwanese independence, a position that both Taiwan's ruling Kuomintang (KMT) party and the Communist leadership in the PRC absolutely oppose. Other issues include the development of real opposition parties, increased participation by the Taiwanese majority, and a rationalization of the legislative system of representation (which is anachronistically organized around electoral districts on the mainland). The KMT leadership, although ruling under security measures that critics charge are only slightly less odious than the martial law that prevailed from 1949 to 1987, has in fact been much more flexible and less heavy-handed than its Korean counterpart. As a result, there is virtually no violent opposition, and (perhaps because the Chinese as a people have long been accustomed to a variety of international activity) antigovernment sentiment has been remarkably free of antiforeign or anti-American overtones.

Singapore, ruled for over twenty years by Premier Lee Kuan Yew and the People's Action party (PAP), has no such political divisions to worry about. Perhaps for this reason it has been easier for the tiny city-state to keep business separate from politics: while not officially recognizing the mainland Chinese regime, Singapore has long had open trade relations with the PRC. In spite of—or perhaps because of—an active opposition political sector (twenty registered political parties), the government faces no serious challenge to its legitimacy. Economic performance is so good that Singaporeans can be concerned about questions like how to put some local color back into their clean, modern city.

Finally, there is Hong Kong, where politics is of necessity oriented toward the Colony's future under the PRC. A quick glance at any aspect of life and business in Hong Kong in comparison with the situation in, say, Korea, is enough to show that the "Four Small Dragons" are in many ways just as different from each other as they are from Japan or the PRC.

ASIAN TRADE AND BUSINESS RELATIONS

When doing business in Asia, it is important to remember that the Asians have been interacting with each other for centuries in all areas, including business. This means that some of your toughest competition will come from inside the region. At the same time, an understanding of Asian interactions can give you an edge over even the strongest competitor. For example, in China there is both resentment over Japan's past behavior in China (reinforced by Japan's glossing over in contemporary history books of their military activity in China during the 1930s and 1940s) and apprehension at the success the Japanese have had in marketing consumer products over the last few years. Similar sentiments are evident in Korea. Japanese business has a lot to offer both of these countries and enjoys a number of definite advantages (including physical proximity, similar cultural and linguistic background, and long experience in the market), but fear of Japanese domination may offset these advantages. Non-Japanese firms that are aware of intra-Asian frictions and plan their activities accordingly can benefit if they themselves behave in a nonthreatening manner.

Regional Politics

Partly because of the tremendous importance Asians attach to form, symbolism and gesture, Asian history and current international politics are often just as important as economics in determining certain types of business relations and business activity. In addition, a long history of cultural, economic, technological and military contact has given Asians perceptions of each other that can affect your business dealings. For example, many U.S. firms make the mistake of running their Korean marketing operations from Japan, using Japanese agents. From a purely rational, Western business point of view, this seems to make sense: the Korean market for the products in question may well be too small to justify the expense of setting up shop in Korea, Japan is just an hour or so away by plane, Japanese culture seems very similar to Korean, and the Japanese agents you have selected speak fluent Korean. But this seemingly sensible decision ignores both centuries of animosity between the Koreans and the Japanese, and the Koreans' consuming need to be recognized and respected as an independent industrial nation with world-class ambitions. By using a Japanese agent, a U.S. firm may be ruining its chances for success in the Korean market.

Japan, with a present population of about 120 million, has clearly been the dominant country in the region for about a hundred years, and even today the mere notion that Japanese defense spending might exceed the very modest current annual rate of 1 percent of GNP sends chills through all her neighbors. The countries of the region also feel intimidated by Japan's industrial and economic muscle. The 1.1 billion Chinese on the mainland are apprehensive about an incipient flood of Japanese products and services. Although the Republic of Korea (population: 40 million) has a much more developed economy than the People's Republic of China and is far more self-sufficient in both consumer and industrial production, the strength of the Japanese economy (which is about fifteen times the size of the Korean economy) is perceived as a major threat by the Koreans. This perception, which is shared by the other countries in the region and is reinforced by Japan's heavy trade surplus with them all, has led to considerable official discrimination against Japanese products in Korea, the People's Republic of China and Taiwan.

Internal Politics

Relations among the three national groups are further complicated by what the Asians consider to be internal politics. Although Westerners tend to regard Taiwan and the PRC as different countries and to speak of "North Korea" and "South Korea," few Chinese or Koreans confuse regime with nationhood. Although both China and Korea have rival communist and noncommunist governments, the Chinese on Taiwan and the mainland and the Koreans on both sides of the demilitarized zone (DMZ) are united in their respective beliefs that there is only one China and only one Korea. The question, of course, is who should be in control and how is control to be attained.

It is important to keep in mind that neither China nor Korea has a significant tradition of democratic government, a loyal opposition, or a truly peaceful means of transferring power. Much of their history, like that of the rest of Asia, has been dominated by the concept of limited good or zero-sum (the more you have, the less I have; if you win, I lose). The principal political doctrine in both societies is one of absolute legitimacy, which means that one party or group is right (and therefore politically, historically and morally justified) and the other is wrong. This absolute view of political relations is perhaps the main reason why it has been so difficult for the communist and noncommunist sides (both Korean and Chinese) to sustain any sort of meaningful dialogue and why the government of Taiwan has a stated policy of "three no's" (no negotiation, no compromise, no contact) vis à vis the mainland.

The sharp contrast with Germany is worth noting. There the two regimes of the divided country, in spite of serious political problems ranging from the Berlin Wall to the killing of both East and West Germans by East German border guards, maintained an active dialogue and remained relatively free of the constant threat of armed conflict that has dogged both the Chinese and the Koreans. This willingness to communicate, which was a major factor in the dramatic opening of East Germany in late 1989, has been slow to develop in China and Korea.

The issue between the adversarial regimes contending for power in Korea and in China is more a matter of rivalry and legitimacy than communist or capitalist ideology. The "anticommunist" Republic of Korea, for example, would love to have extensive commercial relations with the PRC, but the PRC, which could benefit greatly from increased trade and technology transfer with the ROK, has moved slowly to avoid offending its (theoretical) allies in North Korea. Likewise, although significant numbers of people on Taiwan profit from substantial direct and indirect trade (running over two billion U.S. dollars a year by the late 1980s) with the PRC, the government on Taiwan hesitates to appear too approving of such trade for fear of legitimizing the mainland regime. And so it goes.

Trade and Competition

Asians are deeply political, but as PRC trade with the ROC and the ROK shows, they are even more concerned with commerce and industry. Japan, which boasts by far the largest and most advanced economy, is the most influential player in this arena. But in several sectors (including steel, shipbuilding, automobiles, personal computers and consumer electronics) the Koreans, who have made overtaking Japan a national cause, have given the Japanese a run for their money, and in some industries have even pulled ahead. In some sectors they have been aided by the politics of certain Western countries which have given unrestricted access to Korean products while narrowing the entryway for the Japanese.

The big question, of course, is whether or not the ROK can overtake Japan in high-tech areas like electronics, biotechnology and aerospace. One Korean strategy involves leapfrogging the usual stages of industrial and technical development by recruiting researchers and experts from high-tech companies in the U.S. and elsewhere. Many Korean companies (apparently aided by the government) have also obtained foreign technology through reverse engineering or direct acquisition of proprietary information.

Nevertheless, Japan still runs substantial trade surpluses with the countries in the region and is continually urged by Korea and the PRC to take steps to correct the situation. In the case of the PRC, the problem is mostly structural: there is very little that the PRC can sell to Japan, while Japan is the most economical supplier of a host of goods and services that the PRC needs in order to modernize and to satisfy consumer demand generated by partial liberalization of the PRC's economic system.

With Korea, there seems to be more exclusionary intent on the Japanese side. Japanese tariffs, for example, which are only 3 percent overall, average about 10 percent for the types of products exported by Korea; when Japan reduced tariffs in 1985, only twenty-four Korean products were on a list of almost two thousand items covered. And almost half of Korean exports to Japan fall under some sort of import restriction. Finally, Japan steadfastly refuses to sell or license technology the Koreans need to move up the ladder in manufacturing and exporting.

As a result, the ROK threatens to place special tariffs on Japanese goods, to restrict entry to imports from Japan, and to decrease depreciation rates on Japanese machinery purchased by Korean manufacturers. In addition, the Korean Ministry of Trade and Industry (MTI) plans to provide incentives for Korean firms to substitute locally made machines, parts and components in several industrial sectors. These measures are in addition to market restrictions (including a total ban on the import of Japanese motion pictures) that are already in place against the Japanese. In spite of Korean resistance the Japanese continue to hold or increase their share of Korea's imports (Japanese trading companies handle over 10 percent of the total), and Japanese parts and components make up a significant percentage of the value of Korean VCRs and other products that are exported from Korea to the U.S. and other Western markets.

The PRC, while running a sizable trade deficit with Japan, runs a surplus with Southeast Asia. (Most of its trade with the Republic of Korea is still unofficial and hard to quantify.) This surplus, like Japan's surplus with the PRC, appears to be structural. As a result of the modernization program begun in 1978, the PRC has bought more manufactured goods and increasingly sophisticated products overseas (often from Japan) and has begun to produce more quality manufactured goods for export. As a result, PRC imports from developing countries (especially producers of primary products) have fallen significantly in recent years while exports to those same countries have risen.

From the fall of 1985 to the spring of 1987, the Japanese yen underwent a series of rapid appreciations against the dollar that totaled about 50 percent. This was good news to the "Four Small Dragons," whose currencies are generally closely pegged to the dollar. Almost immediately, Japanese imports from these countries showed sharp increases in dollar terms. (Fortunately, yen debt exposure, which became more costly as the yen rose, isn't large enough to be a problem for any of the Asian countries discussed.)

The bad news, of course, was that the dollar cost of the Japanese materials, parts and components used by Asian manufacturers increased at the same time. Nevertheless, the change in yen value appeared to help most of Japan's neighbors boost their real economic growth. Meanwhile, Japanese companies competing with Korea and Taiwan in products like electronic parts, cameras, textiles and eyeglasses were sent reeling, with some going into bankruptcy. Although a combination of factors, including pressure from the United States, forced Taiwan and Korea to allow some appreciation of their currencies, they still maintained a substantial advantage against the Japanese yen.

Just as important is the long-term, regular appearance of imports from Korea, Taiwan and Hong Kong in quality Japanese retail outlets, which could lead to a permanent change in Japanese buying patterns and perceptions. In the first year of the yen's rise, Japanese imports from Taiwan were up 18 percent from a year earlier while imports from the ROK increased by 21 percent, and Hong Kong enjoyed a phenomenal 44 percent jump.

The rise in Asian imports, coupled with the yen's increased ability to buy land, labor and equipment in other Asian countries, means that Japanese manufacturers are also looking at new Asian locations for manufacturing investment. As a result of the yen's rise, Asian trade and investment offices in Tokyo began receiving substantially higher numbers of inquiries from Japanese firms interested in manufacturing offshore. The increased movement to other Asian manufacturing bases could lead to Japanese offshore Asian production of big-ticket items like automobiles for import into Japan, which would materially alter present trade and industrial patterns in the region.

ASIAN LINGUISTIC RELATIONS

The Asians' use of languages, both Asian and Western, reveals quite a bit about their attitudes toward each other and toward the West. In general, although Western languages (primarily English) are studied as a requisite for college entrance, their actual use is limited mainly to situations in which an international flavor is called for, and little attention is paid to accuracy or appropriateness of meaning. With Asian languages, the situation is quite different. Japanese and Korean have a common origin and are very similar even today, but few Japanese or Koreans can read or speak each other's language. This fact is both a cause and a result of centuries of animosity. With Chinese, however, the situation is very different.

In much of Asia (ranging from Korea all the way down to Vietnam) the Chinese language played much the same role that Latin did in Europe. For centuries all educated Asians studied Chinese, and Chinese was even used as the official language in many government and legal documents throughout the region. This tendency to regard Chinese as an elegant mode of expression has persisted to this day, so much so that the extensive use of Chinese characters in brochures, announcements, posters and other forms of publicity is still considered a sign of quality and refinement. It is important for Western businesspeople to keep this in mind when ordering translations of business cards and other printed matter for use in Asian markets. The use of Chinese characters can impart prestige.

Another reason that Chinese characters are still widely used outside of China is practicality. When the Japanese and Koreans first made contact with China, they encountered hundreds or even thousands of concepts, inventions and discoveries that did not yet exist in their own countries. To express these new ideas and describe these new things, they were forced to use Chinese words because their own languages lacked adequate vocabulary. In fact, since the concept of a written language was also new to them, they learned Chinese writing, which they used both to record the new Chinese vocabulary and to express in writing the existing words of their native languages. Once the thousands of Chinese loan words had become part of both the Japanese and the Korean languages, it made sense to keep writing them in their original Chinese form even after Japanese and Korean alphabets (*kana* and *hangul,* respectively) were developed. This inclination was reinforced by the fact that both Japanese and Korean have many homographic homonyms (words that are spelled and pronounced identically but have different meanings), which makes it much more practical to use a mix of Chinese characters and kana or hangul to avoid confusion.

In addition, the use of Chinese characters means that any literate person (over 95 percent of the population of the region) can understand at least the general meaning of signs, instructions and brochures—even in another Asian language—provided they are written in Chinese characters. As a result, the extensive use of Chinese characters in advertising and related areas is a real benefit to Asians visiting or doing business in each other's countries. The more easily tourists or businesspersons can read, the more easily they can function. Yet, in Korea, Japan and China alike, recent linguistic trends and policies will make tourism more difficult and hinder the flow of business communication.

The Koreans, who are intensely proud of their scientifically based alphabet created by court linguists several hundred years ago, have undertaken several official campaigns to eliminate or drastically reduce the use of Chinese characters in all forms of written communication. The late Korean president, Park Chung Hee, for example, did away with the teaching of Chinese characters in Korean schools for several years, a move which deprived the better part of a generation of the ability to easily understand business communication with their Asian neighbors. In Japan, although the study and use of Chinese characters has been encouraged officially, the desire to be fashionable or trendy (as opposed to cultured, elegant or literate) has caused a proliferation of Japanese kana which is crowding out Chinese characters in advertising and popular magazines. The People's Republic of China has taken the most drastic step of all; there the authorities have changed the appearance of the traditional Chinese characters to such a degree that many of them are no longer recognizable to anyone in Korea, Japan, Taiwan or other ethnic Chinese outside of the PRC. The fact that the largest countries in the region have all made linguistically isolationist moves is evidence of their ethnocentric mindset.

It is worth noting that in Japan, where Confucian theory is less important than in China and Korea, recent language changes have largely been generated by the business community despite government policy. Conversely, the official language policies in the other two countries have subordinated business to other interests, demonstrating that business still does not receive the same attention and respect that it does in the West or in Japan.

Business realities may force changes in Asian language trends because it is becoming evident even to the Asians that ease of communication is vital to market access and business operations. However, more realistic policies will probably be slow in coming. In the early 1980s the Korean government, although it had allowed Chinese character study to return to the classroom, decided that Chinese characters should be eliminated on all public signs (including street signs, public advertising and the signboards on shops, stores and restaurants), and government teams began replacing all road signs and calling on private businesses to inform them that their signs must be changed.

This policy undoubtedly benefited the sign-painting industry, but it made no economic sense at all, especially in view of the fact that Korea had eagerly sought and won the right to host the Asian Games in 1986 and the Olympic Games in 1988. By drastically reducing the public use of Chinese characters, the Korean government inadvertently discouraged many potential Asian visitors to the games. This language policy typifies the nationalistic, ethnocentric mentality of Asian countries in general, as well as the ability (which is exercised freely and often) of Asian governments to impose arbitrary standards and restrictions on business for other than business motives.

Although not courting international events (or even thinking in international terms) at the time, the government of the PRC created similar handicaps for China by drastically simplifying the written form of Chinese characters after the communist victory in 1949.

Some simplified forms of Chinese characters are in use in Japan and Korea (and even in Taiwan), but many of the characters modified by PRC bureaucrat-scholars were altered so radically that they became totally unrecognizable to anyone familiar only with the traditional forms. Although the stated reason for the change was to simplify the characters and make them more accessible to the masses, the new system has the politically useful effect of making it impossible for younger Chinese, who are not taught how to read the traditional characters, to understand any propaganda, history or other written material from outside the PRC.

Since the PRC's opening to foreign business in 1979, the commercial problems created by this policy have become evident. As a result, official PRC business and trading agencies have begun making extensive use of traditional Chinese characters in their advertising and literature, and there is talk of revising the writing system to bring it more or less in line with the forms used in neighboring Asian countries. For now it remains merely talk, and students in the PRC are still being taught only the simplified characters.

Trends in language are important because they reveal general truths about Asian attitudes toward business and toward contact with outsiders. In Asia a wide array of considerations, including politics and ethnocentrism, still prevail over Western-style pragmatism in many situations. All too often one hears a Western businessperson, trying to second-guess Asian business contacts or an Asian government agency, exclaim, "They wouldn't do that; it wouldn't make good business sense." Maybe not, but in many cases Asians regard other factors as more important. When doing business with Asians, one must analyze possible courses of action in the light of Asian priorities rather than Western business logic.

ASIAN POINTS IN COMMON

Demographics

All Asian countries are crowded, in part because none of them has more than about 18 percent or so of arable land. The PRC is about the same size as the United States, but much of it is deserts or mountains; the populations of Japan, Korea, Taiwan and Hong Kong are crowded between the mountains and the sea. This crowding has doubtless contributed to the self-contained personality that has often been described as "inscrutable" in the West.

Isolation

Japan and Taiwan are island countries, Korea (known since ancient times as the "hermit kingdom") is a peninsula, and mainland China is cut off from most surrounding countries by such barriers as the Himalayas and the Gobi Desert. Although the Japanese are often characterized (including by other Asians) as having an "island mentality," their attitudes are not entirely unique: the Chinese and the Koreans historically followed fairly similar isolationist and antiforeign policies and are in many ways even more xenophobic today. It is worth remembering that, in each country, Western powers had to force the authorities to allow the entry of Western ships and the establishment of trade relations and that Western domination (including outright colonization) has reinforced the Asians' initial reluctance to open their countries to the West.

Language

Despite the divisive effects of politics and nationalism, the Chinese language has had essentially the same unifying effect on Asia that Latin had on much of Europe. Just as it is relatively easy for an educated French person to learn Spanish or for a Portuguese to understand Italian, Koreans, the Japanese and the Chinese can all learn each other's languages without undue difficulty. Even though the Japanese and the Koreans developed their own writing systems, they still make extensive use of Chinese characters for writing words of Chinese origin. In the area of business and trade, about 90 percent of the vocabulary is the same in all three languages (although the pronunciation varies from one language to another). Recognizing the potential in this situation, representatives from

Vietnam, Japan, China and Korea met in Japan in 1986 to discuss ways to apply their common linguistic base to trade and business.

Ethnicity

Although racism among Asian ethnic groups can be pretty harsh (witness the Vietnamese treatment of ethnic Chinese, some of whose families had been in Vietnam for generations), Asians feel much closer to each other than they do to non-Asians. Non-Asians, for example, are all lumped together as "foreigners" (and other, less complimentary terms), but other Asians are almost always referred to by nationality (Korean, Japanese, Chinese). "Asia for the Asians," one of Japan's slogans during the Second World War, may still have some resonance today. At the same time, each major Asian ethnic group is fond of proclaiming its uniqueness and homogeneous racial makeup.

Sense of Accountability and Responsibility

When a Taiwan Chinese pilot diverted his cargo jet and defected to the PRC in the spring of 1986, the director of Taiwan's Civil Aeronautics Administration (Taiwan's top aviation official) took full responsibility for the incident and submitted his resignation. So did the board chairman and the president of China Airlines (CAL). The year before, the president of Japan Airlines took full responsibility and resigned after the crash of a JAL Boeing 747, even though Boeing admitted negligence in repair of the aircraft some time before the crash. This acceptance of accountability at the top levels of both government and private administration, unheard of in the United States, is reflected in business thinking as well. Asians expect a high degree of personal accountability at the top levels of the U.S. companies they deal with. If things go wrong, circumstances may be the culprit from the American point of view, but if you are prepared to accept the responsibility in a sincere manner, it can do wonders for your future business relations.

Religion and Philosophy

Confucianism and Buddhism have had a profound effect on the thought and social practices of all Asian countries. One result of this influence has been a historical tendency to relegate business and commercial activity to the bottom of the social hierarchy—the opposite of the tendency in much of the West. Although the support given to business by Japan and Korea might lead one to conclude that business has finally come into its own, closer examination reveals that attitudes and social standing are still evolving. In Taiwan, for example, the native Taiwanese are allowed to succeed in business, but they are generally excluded from the political process that determines how business will be conducted. Throughout Asia, business is subject to a high degree of control by government, and businesses are supposed to work for the good of the country. One common complaint voiced about foreign businesses is that they are in Asia to make money; Asian executives, even from very profitable Asian firms, will look you in the eye and claim that their companies' main goal is to help their country. Asians obviously recognize the need for businesses to make money in order to survive, but they still look askance at any firm that openly makes profitability the primary objective.

The Influence of Confucianism

When doing business with Asia, you are bound to hear a lot of comments about Confucianism and "Confucian society." It is important to know what these terms mean, both in theory and in practice.

Confucius, a Chinese who lived in a time of great political disorder around 500 B.C., developed a theoretical road to peace and harmony based on tradition and order in society and on "correct" attitudes in the individual. (This terminology was later echoed in the concept of "correct thought" stressed by Mao Zedong.) Confucius postulated that all human relations came from five basic relationships: ruler-subject, father-son, elder brother-younger brother, husband-wife, elder friend-junior friend. Implicit in this structure are three ideas: the superiority of the ruler, the superiority of age and the superiority of males. The duty of those on the bottom is to respect and obey those above them, while those on top must show wisdom and set a good example.

Three governing principles emerge from Confucian thought: *li, te* and *wen*. Li includes ritual and the notion of a "correct" way to do things. Te holds that the power to rule comes from competence, sincerity and goodness, thus implying that bad rulers may be legitimately overthrown. Wen stresses the importance of learning and the arts as a means of improving the individual, which at one time contributed to the rise of a scholar class which controlled the administration of the Chinese empire.

In practice, the modern manifestations of Confucianism have led to many interesting attitudes and actions. Rulers, believing in their innate superiority, have tended to be arbitrary and autocratic. The opposition, firm in their conviction that rulers they consider "bad" are meant to be overthrown, can be disloyal, extremist and violent. Belief in male superiority has led to everything from limited job opportunities for Japanese and Korean women to female infanticide in the PRC. Students, secure in their chosen role as keepers of knowledge and members of a privileged caste, are often ignorant, arrogant, xenophobic and visionary. In fact, since the last century, Asian students have consistently had a disproportionately large role in Asian politics, as evidenced by their role in the fall of the Chinese Nationalist government in 1949 and of Korea's Syngman Rhee in 1960, by the former power of the Zengakuren in Japan and the Red Guards in China, and by the student-inspired political turmoil in the Republic of Korea today.

In business, the goal of harmony, order and the maintenance of proper relationships means that legal action is viewed as the last resort of unworthy people who are incapable of living and acting as they should. Thus, judges and the business community in general take a dim view of both parties to a suit, regardless of the merits of the case. This attitude can have particularly serious repercussions for Americans, who tend to make liberal use of attorneys; a more productive approach is a close association with government officials, who occupy an honored position in the Confucian scheme of things. At the same time, Confucianism's overriding stress on form, order and relationships, which often implies the assignment of everything to well-defined categories with no exceptions allowed, can lead to maddeningly detailed bureaucratic formalism, which Westerners often confuse with obstructionism.

Confucianism was most deeply rooted in China, where it remained the official basis for the training of all public officials from 130 B.C. until 1912, a span of over two thousand years. Its influence in Korea and Japan, while less pervasive, was nevertheless quite strong, as is seen by the emphasis on (1) formality and ritual, (2) an often exaggerated respect for authority figures (including older male family members, government officials and university professors), (3) an almost blind faith in education and written documentation (regardless of content), and (4) a stratified and fairly rigid social order with a great emphasis on "face."

DIFFERENT CHOPSTICKS

There are few things in life more frustrating than trying to function in a situation that appears familiar but isn't. It's like waking up in a hotel room that is the mirror image of the one across the hall where you stayed on your last visit. You get out of bed and run into a wall because in this room the door is on the opposite side. It's unnerving to say the least.

Doing business in one Asian country and trying to transfer the experience and method to another can be equally unnerving. On the outside, they can be astonishingly similar, but when you try to import the hard-earned understanding and expertise that you've acquired in one country and apply it in another, it mysteriously fails to work. You get responses and results far different from what you anticipated. I once accompanied a seasoned European diplomat, fresh from a successful, long-term assignment in China, when he first went to Korea. At first, he was all contentment. He was obviously pleased to see so many familiar features and to be assigned to a country exhibiting many of the developmental characteristics of the post he had just left. This would be a piece of cake.

But as the day wore on into evening, his tension and frustration mounted exponentially. Finally, he turned to the rest of us to vent his feelings.

"How can they do this?" he fairly shouted. "They've got it all wrong!"

And what was "it"? Everything. Those of us who had been transferred to Korea from Japan could empathize. So much the same, and yet so different. This experience can cause far greater culture shock than simply leaving one's own country for an Asian destination. At least in the latter situation, you expect things to be different.

Westerners have a tendency to overgeneralize about the Orient—an error that can cause serious problems in business. Although there are undeniable similarities in attitudes, thought patterns and business practices, these often appear to be greater than they are.

When considering the differences between Asians, it is instructive to see how the Asians describe themselves and each other. We will focus on the three main ethnic, linguistic and cultural "neighborhoods" in what might be called the Asian village: Chinese, Japanese and Korean.

If you ask an Asian to explain how these three groups differ, the answers are sometimes long and colorful. A Korean Ph.D., educated in Japan and China, describes the basic difference between the Chinese and the Japanese in terms of two social clubs. Imagine that in each club, one member misbehaves or breaks the club rules. Unable to get the offender to mend his ways, the club expels him. The outcast is pushed out the front door and the members gather at the clubhouse window to watch as he trudges toward the sidewalk. Up to this point, the scene in both Japan and China is quite similar.

Suddenly, in each neighborhood a mugger appears and attacks the lone ex-member. Now national differences come into play. The Chinese, according to this parable, will merely watch while their former associate is assaulted. After all, it serves him right. He broke the rules and deserves this misfortune. The Japanese reaction, however, is quite different. The Japanese club members rush out and overpower the would-be assailant. Because the mugger is an outsider who has no business in the neighborhood, he will not be allowed to interfere with anyone there. However, this attitude does not affect the internal situation. Once they have defeated the mugger, the members return to the clubhouse, leaving their former colleague alone on the sidewalk.

Does this parable imply that foreign businesspeople, like the foreign colonialists who earlier forced themselves on various sectors of Asian society, are unwelcome intruders in the Asian village? Perhaps. But an equally important message is that the differences among Asian groups are substantial, a fact that the foreign businessperson ignores at his or her peril. At the same time, a knowledge of the differences can work to the foreigner's advantage. For example, some Western businesspeople report that it seems easier to work with Chinese companies against Chinese competition than it is to team up with Japanese companies to the exclusion of other Japanese. In at least some cases (to continue the metaphor) nonmembers find it easier to deal with the Chinese club.

How about the differences between the Japanese and Koreans? An Asian businessman offers an interesting interpretation of the reverse psychology that often leads Westerners and Asians alike to conclude that Koreans are difficult to deal with.

The Koreans, he explains, have spent much of their history as underdogs, either under attack or actually subjugated by more powerful neighbors. This collective experience has led them to identify with the weak and resist the strong. At the same time, they have a consuming need to continually improve their own position against what they perceive as a constant external threat. In business this means, among other things, that attempting to dictate or make a power play on a Korean may provoke almost self-destructive resistance. It may also mean that even the appearance of too much strength on the part of a Western company will cause the Korean to sow the field with mines and continually encroach on any positions won by the other side. This behavior leads many Westerners to conclude that it's impossible to really conclude a deal with a Korean. In the words of one experienced Korea hand, in Korea a contract is the starting point for negotiations.

The Japanese, on the other hand, are seen by this same Asian business source as just the opposite. Because of their isolation (and perhaps a "divine wind" or two), they were never conquered in historic times. Moreover, their strategic location enabled them to prey on neighboring countries, first as pirates and then with naval armadas and invading armies. Their high success ratio in these adventures, coupled with their ongoing glorification of stoicism, skill and fighting spirit as embodied in *bushido* (warriors' way, the code of the samurai), led them to despise weakness and glorify strength. This analysis seems to fit the historical Japanese tendency to gravitate toward big business rather than the entrepreneurship favored by many Westerners. Could it also lend support to Western assertions that Japanese business practices are predatory or confirm the impression of small businesses that they may not get enough respect in Japanese business circles? There is no proof, but perhaps this line of thought is worth considering.

If you ask Chinese business contacts to explain what makes their culture different, you may find that a high percentage will respond that the Chinese are self-directed, self-centered or even selfish. This seems incompatible with common Western ideas about Asians' alleged lack of concern for the individual. What it means, some Chinese explain, is a lack of concern for other individuals, especially those outside the immediate or extended family. This interpretation of Chinese attitudes brings us back to the anecdote about the club. The social bonds are in place but not so tightly that they can't be broken.

In some cases the differences among Asian nations have created undercurrents of conflict and hostility that Western businesspeople should be aware of in order to be effective in their business dealings. It is also useful to consider some of the causes of the differences.

Geopolitical and Historical Factors

One of the major causes (perhaps the most important one) of both Asian similarity and Asian diversity is an unusual geopolitical situation: a massive, culturally and politically mature nation (China), bordering on a rugged peninsular people (the Koreans) and interacting with a very independently oriented chain of islands (Japan). Until the advent of Western transportation technology, Korea was the most convenient route for travel between China and Japan. As we noted earlier in this book, Korea was for centuries the conduit through which Chinese thought and technology, as well as significant numbers of both Chinese and Korean immigrants (some of whom were political refugees and members of threatened dynasties), flowed from the mainland to the Japanese islands. In addition, the two massive Mongol invasions of Japan, the first of which did considerable damage on the southern island of Kyushu and the second of which was largely destroyed by a typhoon that the grateful Japanese interpreted as *kamikaze* or "divine wind," both passed through Korea and used the southern end of the peninsula as a forward staging area for their invasion fleets.

The Japanese, in turn, have used the Korean peninsula to get at China. In the sixteenth century (1592–1597), Toyotomi Hideyoshi, one of Japan's greatest political and military figures, sent some 200,000 men to invade Korea after the Koreans rejected Japanese requests for right of passage to attack China. This military adventure, which ended in a negotiated withdrawal, wreaked tremendous suffering on the Korean people and is a basic cause of the deep resentment that many Koreans still feel toward Japan.

Another negative factor in relations between the two countries is the Japanese occupation (1905) and annexation (1910) of Korea, the pretext for which was again China. The Japanese, whose experience with the Mongols had led them to view the Korean peninsula as "a dagger pointed at the heart of Japan," were uneasy when the Korean government, following a centuries-old tradition, called for Chinese military assistance to put down a traditionalist rural uprising in 1894. At the same time, Japan's persistent competitive attitude toward China turned the entry of Chinese troops into Korea into a golden opportunity to "teach the Chinese a lesson." The Japanese did this by attacking the Chinese in several places in Korea and China, leading to China's defeat and effective Japanese control of Korea. This control was turned into full-scale military occupation at the time of Japan's victory over Russia in 1905, and Korea was formally annexed in 1910.

In spite of continuous Korean resistance, this colonial situation continued until the end of World War II. During the war the Koreans' hardship multiplied as tens—perhaps hundreds—of thousands of Koreans were forcibly relocated to Japan and other parts of the Japanese Empire to provide manpower, often in difficult and dangerous jobs. Today, partly as a result of this relocation, there are about 800,000 Koreans living in Japan (mostly in the Osaka area), whose ambiguous political and social status remains a sore point between the two countries.

Current relationships among China, Korea and Japan are complex and paradoxical. The Koreans, while justifiably unhappy about Japan's role as colonial exploiter before and during World War II, strangely bear no discernible ill will toward the Chinese who, by entering the Korean War (1950–1953) on the communist North Korean side, prolonged the war, contributed to the toll of one million Korean lives lost, and perpetuated the division of the country. (In fact, rather than blaming the Chinese, many Koreans today blame the United States and Japan for the division of the peninsula.) And although the Chinese, through their continuing support for the communist regime in North Korea, helped create the need for the large defense outlays that have diverted Korea's resources from economic development, the Koreans are more likely to express resentment at the Japanese because Korea serves as Japan's de facto front line of defense while the Japanese spend less than 1 percent of GNP on their own military. At the same time the Koreans, like all other non-Japanese Asians, react with alarm at suggestions by Americans and by Japanese conservatives that Japan increase military spending and assume a more forward defense posture.

The Chinese, like the Koreans, want Japanese technology and assistance in developing their natural resources and industrial base. At the same time, they have powerful collective memories from the 1930s and 1940s, when over twenty million Chinese are said to have died as the result of Japan's invasion and occupation.

Today, many Chinese fear that the waves of Japanese investment and products sweeping over China will succeed where the Japanese military failed.

Japan, although dwarfed by China in size, manpower and military might, has often tended to feel like a hardworking and ambitious younger brother who, by virtue of having achieved more visible material success, has earned the right to correct the ways of the older brother (China), who educated him in infancy. Today, however, Japan's main business in China is business. As in Korea (where, in spite of having to keep an absolutely invisible profile, Japanese companies sell more and have more investments than anyone else), the Japanese are in a good position because of their geographic proximity, their understanding of local thought and the similarity of their written language.

Business Structures and Practices

Because of the Japanese occupation and colonization, many older Korean leaders were educated in Japan, and significant portions of the country's infrastructure and business system are built on Japanese foundations. In addition, since the Koreans never went through the forced democratization and social upheaval created by MacArthur and the Occupation in Japan, many aspects of Korean political and business organization are like authoritarian relics of a Japan that no longer exists. For example, the giant Korean industrial conglomerates (*chaebol*) are very similar to the prewar Japanese *zaibatsu* (the word, although pronounced differently, is written in both languages with the same Chinese characters), and their day-to-day operating style, in which decisions and directives flow from the top down, lacks most of the consensus building and upward flow of ideas that is now central to most major Japanese companies.

At the same time, centuries of closer and friendlier Korean contact with China have created family systems, architecture and patterns of business behavior that are much closer to the Chinese way of doing things. For example, the Chinese tradition of making business staffing decisions on the basis of strong extended family ties rather than professional competence led one of Korea's biggest conglomerates, whose divisions were run by the husbands of the founder's half-dozen or so daughters, into bankruptcy in the early 1980s.

Confucianism and Business

Other more general differences among the ways of doing business in China, Korea and Japan also arise from history and culture, including Confucian thought. The Confucian system which originated in China became dominant both in China and in Korea. An important feature of this system, which emphasized harmoniously paired relationships (husband-wife, ruler-subjects, and so on), was its exaltation of intellectual activity and its respect for authority, combined with a rejection of business and commerce as lowly forms of human activity bordering on necessary evils. The Confucian goal of harmony, combined with the tendency to look down on business activity (which may help explain some of the virulent anticapitalism observed during much of the PRC's history) plays an important role in Chinese and Korean business life. For example, a judge hearing a business-related civil suit tends to look at both parties with a jaundiced eye—in the first place because they have failed to maintain a harmonious relationship and in the second because their dispute is part of business, which to some degree is still not a totally acceptable activity.

Conversely, in Japan, where Confucian ideals were significantly modified by Buddhism, Shintoism and a complicated system of group relationships that developed during a long feudal period, the merchant class gained political power and full respectability some 120 years ago. Although the Japanese share with the Chinese and the Koreans an exaggerated respect for academicians and government officials, business has long been the mainstay of the country. As a result, the relationship between business and government is highly symbiotic: government provides leadership while business provides the support, organization and economic cohesion that has made the postwar Japanese government far and away the most stable in the region. Korea, in contrast, is characterized by much more pushing and pulling between business and government, the latter playing a much more authoritarian role in determining what business is allowed to do.

It is probably fair to say that Japan, while paying less lip service to Confucian ideals, adheres to them far more closely than does either China or Korea. For example, the central Confucian value of harmony is realized to a much greater extent in the smoothly integrated Japanese society (including business) than in the other two cultures. Perhaps more importantly, in Japan the reciprocity of the paired relationships that are so important to Confucian theory is actually put into practice across the board. Subordinates are loyal because superiors are fair and reasonable. Workers and their unions cooperate with management because management has a sense of responsibility for them. In contrast, the Koreans and the Chinese (particularly academicians and those at high levels of management and government) are fond of talking about Confucian-style relationships, but in practice they tend to convert them into one-way streets, with loyalty and obedience flowing upward and little fairness or sense of obligation flowing down in return. Instead, there is a tendency toward autocracy and a high-level imposition of policies and practices that ignore the aspirations and desires of those below. The basic inequality of this type of power relationship can create considerable political risk for business by forcing political, economic and social pressures to build and explode in a series of crises rather than allowing them to stabilize continuously.

Differences in the flow of power and responsibility also produce very different approaches to day-to-day business operation. In many Korean companies, for example, those in top management are the last to arrive at the office, and workers and staff are supposed to remain at their workstations until after the boss goes home. In Japan, a high percentage of business executives feel strongly that they have an obligation to provide inspiration and leadership by setting an example; accordingly, they are often the first at the office or plant (often going in early to the factory floor to keep in touch with manufacturing reality by getting their hands dirty), and they stay until most or all of the other staff have gone home for the night. In addition, they shun conspicuous differences of dress and often wear the same plain overall or work jacket used by everyone down to the warehousemen. In China, this type of egalitarianism seems to have first appeared when, during the Cultural Revolution, the People's Liberation Army eliminated insignia for officers—an experiment which has since been abandoned.

Many observers believe that these basic differences in attitude are combined with varying degrees of attention to detail, with the Japanese (as demonstrated by the overwhelming qualitative superiority of much of their industrial production) being the most conscious. According to one, only half-humorous analysis, the basic difference among Japanese, Korean and mainland Chinese businesses can best be seen on a factory tour with a company president of each nationality. On coming to a piece of scrap on the factory floor, the Japanese CEO will stoop, pick it up, and throw it away. In a like situation, the Korean CEO will order someone else to get rid of it, and the mainland Chinese CEO (or the socialist equivalent) won't bother with it at all. This is clearly a stereotypical oversimplification, but it may contain a grain of metaphorical truth that can be helpful in your business dealings.

Postwar Factors

American intervention (or, in some cases, the lack of it) in the aftermath of the Second World War played an important part in altering the features on the map of Asian business. Before the war Japanese industry could be described, as one Japanese industrialist who was there expressed it: cheap and dirty. The cult of frugality and minimalism that had been created out of centuries of living on an island with a very sparse and limited range of natural resources had been reinforced and extended by the Spartan samurai ethic of *bushido* and a Prussian distaste for ornamentation. Added to this was the fierce elitism of prewar Japanese militarism. The prewar industrial worker labored under sweatshop conditions of insufficient heat and ventilation, poor light, and inadequate safety.

After the war, the Occupation forced changes on Japanese society that also changed the business world. Today, if Japanese executives want the staff of their firm to purify their souls by undergoing a suitably rigorous ordeal, they are forced to turn to outside consultants who dutifully dish up a mix of boot camp, hell week and survival school. The in-house capability to provide trial by fire is gone.

In Korea, democratic intervention stopped at the front door. After all, the U.S. was liberating the people of an occupied nation, not imposing Western-style political concepts on a conquered enemy. After the defeat and expulsion of the occupying Japanese and the de facto division of the country, the Koreans were told, in essence, that they were free to be democratic. It was highly unrealistic, however, to expect a nation with no democratic traditions or institutions to somehow discover them in the aftermath of occupation, war and internal division; and inevitably, freedom failed to bring democracy. Ironically, in fact, it meant a continuation of the militaristic, authoritarian model that Japan had implanted during thirty-five years of colonialism.

For Korean business, the result was a perpetuation of miserable working conditions in factories and unrestricted growth of giant conglomerates that swallowed up small businesses like hungry leviathans in a school of fish. As the 1980s drew to a close, the Korean work week was the longest in the world, and Korean workers toiled under conditions that produced the world's highest industrial accident rate. Combine this with an average wage on the low end of the scale in industrialized Asia (about three-fourths the weekly wage of Taiwan and about one-third that of Japan) and it becomes clear that the Korean economic miracle may be in serious trouble unless business and society undergo the same sort of real democratization that was forced on Japan at the end of the war. Worker strikes and student violence attest to the current demand for change.

Changes in the balance of power can generate violent conflict in both Japan and Korea, but the differences in the two nations' business and industrial realities are evident in the nature of the episodes that occur. In the mid-1980s, the Japanese government decided to privatize the Japan National Railway (JNR) system, which was awash in a rising tide of red ink. In typical postwar

Japanese fashion, all parties to be affected were consulted and the final decision was announced only after agreement was reached. Labor leaders representing JNR workers were involved in the process.

The announcement was greeted by violence on the part of militant radicals (who, ironically, wanted the government to stay in the railway business although they tended to oppose government activity in other business areas). Stations were firebombed in Tokyo and Osaka, control cables were cut on the *shinkansen* or "bullet train," and other acts of vandalism occurred. The greatest violence, however, was reserved for the labor leaders who had agreed to the deal. In apparently well-coordinated attacks, the radicals assaulted a number of them as they slept in their homes, and several deaths resulted. This labor violence in Japan was apparently violence from the bottom up, against labor leaders who collaborated with the employer opposition.

In Korea, much of the hardball, premeditated violence in labor disputes still comes from the top down, just as it did in prewar Japan. As late as 1989, the media reported that a band of a hundred company "goons" launched a surprise night attack on a large meeting of union leaders near Ulsan that left a score of unionists injured, several of them seriously. According to reports, the company even allegedly hired an experienced consultant to organize and oversee the reported assault.

Some theorists explain the differences between Japan and Korea in terms of timing. They point out that Japan has been industrializing and modernizing ever since Commodore Perry's visit while Korea began only after the Second World War. They see this late start, rather than the perpetuation of prewar Japanese attitudes, as the reason for the roughness in Korean society; their thesis is that Korea is still going through the swashbuckling, bare-knuckle, undemocratic phase observed in the industrial sectors of all developing nations. Although this argument contains an element of truth, it ignores the unbroken postwar tradition of heavy-handed authoritarianism whose violence can be directed against those near the top of the business world, as was the case in the early 1980s when a Korean business executive in Seoul was allegedly beaten to death by government investigators who were trying to extract an admission of illegal land dealing by the conglomerate where the executive was employed.

A look at Taiwan provides additional evidence that a late start in development is only part of the reason for different business environments. When the communists took control of mainland China in 1949, the fleeing KMT army, accompanied by hundreds of thousands of supporters, swarmed across the Formosa Straits and set up a self-styled government in exile on the island. The threat of invasion helped maintain authoritarianism, including a world-record thirty-eight years of martial law. This structure was imposed on an essentially agrarian economy which had been left largely undeveloped during some fifty years of Japanese rule.

In spite of late development and a physical, social and political environment that remained highly militarized well into the 1980s, Taiwan has evolved into a relatively open society. A major reason is that the KMT swept away prewar Japanese social and political patterns on Taiwan just as MacArthur did in Japan. Only in Korea were they left relatively intact.

On the mainland, the necessities of consolidating the revolution, weeding out and destroying potential opponents, and reversing the downhill slide of a society battered by centuries of poverty and decades of war left the Chinese no time to create a free and open environment for any activity, including business. It is significant, however, that even such disasters as the Great Leap Forward and the Cultural Revolution involved the decentralized action of large numbers of people far removed from the top of the political hierarchy. More recently, the process of opening the economy has allowed a surprisingly rapid movement toward local and individual initiative and the rise of smaller enterprises. On the mainland as on Taiwan, a high percentage of Chinese are still individualistic entrepreneurs at heart, and it is not uncommon to meet PRC bureaucrats who dream of starting their own businesses. This type of individual can be easier to deal with than the somewhat more rigid and impersonal officials that one often encounters in Korea and Japan.

Business, the Individual and the Family

Besides geography, history and Confucianism, what other factors might explain the many differences among Chinese, Japanese and Korean attitudes and behavior? Common sense indicates that it is not unreasonable to consider the way children are raised in each of the three cultural areas.

In many respects, Chinese child-raising practices are not all that different from what one finds in the West. One major difference has been the tendency to favor male children, which has meant that in many families the males have been overindulged. At the same time, traditional deference to older male family members (including father, uncles and older brothers) instills hierarchical discipline that usually compensates for early permissiveness.

In the PRC, tradition has been distorted by the one-child policy instituted by the government as a means of population control. Since medical technology now makes it easy to determine the sex of an unborn child, many couples are said to abort female children in the hope that the next pregnancy will result in a male. In the future, the most important human factor affecting the PRC may be the large numbers of children of both sexes who are their parents' only offspring and who spend most of their waking hours in state nursery schools. Because they have no siblings and because their working parents have only a few hours with them each day, there is a tendency for parents to spoil them at home. And experts fear that institutional child-care settings do not provide an adequate environment for developing a full range of social interactive skills. Before too long, Western businesspeople will be dealing with the new generations of workers, managers and leaders raised under these conditions.

In Japan and Korea the situation is somewhat different. Although child-raising practices are of course in continuous evolution, the Japanese tend to allow young children (up to the age of five or six) to do more or less as they please during their free time. However, a high percentage of children as young as two years of age spend several hours a day in classes designed to give them a head start in the ferocious competition to get into a top university—

and thence into a good job with a major corporation. The price of chasing this prize for some eighteen or twenty years is high; the positive side is that Japanese children learn to be obedient and to follow instructions.

At home, the absence of overt discipline is compensated for by the presence of example: Japanese couples tend to be polite, quiet and cooperative, and the children learn these behavior patterns by observation and imitation. The process is capped by a sudden change in treatment at about the age of six; at this time the parents, often in startlingly brusque fashion, require that the previously somewhat babied child start contributing to various household chores and duties and assume greater responsibility in all areas of family life. Many Japanese who have experienced this abrupt change recall it as a major adjustment.

In many Korean families, the child is king. Koreans are quick to point out that they love children, and their affection often takes the form of almost total permissiveness. Adults' laissez-faire attitudes extend to the point of allowing children to engage in dangerous behavior like playing in traffic (the traffic death rate for children in Korea is several times higher than that of the United States) or handling the presumably loaded assault rifle of one of the Korean soldiers on patrol near a U.S. installation.

Korean children are given wide latitude at home, including a high degree of freedom to work out their sibling disagreements among themselves in whatever way they see fit. The net result is often a might-makes-right situation in which the larger and stronger children (predictably males after a certain age) can physically dominate and even abuse younger and weaker ones. All too often this pattern is perpetuated as the child grows older. In the Korean military, officers and noncoms engage in violence to recruits, and soldiers forcibly impose their will on civilians. On the street, the police seem quick to resort to force to attain their goals. (Paradoxically, the riot police are often models of restraint even in the face of stonings and firebomb assaults that often leave their fellow officers severely wounded.) Similarly, in Korean companies management may treat workers harshly or even (as in widely publicized cases toward the end of the 1980s) with violence. All of this takes place in a society which has spent all but a few years of this century under foreign domination, in war, or under the Korean military.

The product of this environment is a highly adaptable hardball player who will use indirect or manipulative means when the competitor appears stronger but who can also become ruthless if the opportunity presents itself. Of course, such a temperament exists in Western business as well, but many Western businesspeople feel that it may be more pronounced in Korea.

Whatever the underlying reasons, business in each of the three main cultural areas is affected by the family and related social systems. We have already mentioned the family orientation of one Korean company, where the primary qualification for being a division head was marriage to one of the owner's daughters. This case, while somewhat extreme, points to the importance of the extended family or clan—particularly male members—in both Chinese and Korean life and sheds some light on the effects of this system and thinking on business.

The Chinese and Koreans tend to see things first in terms of their personal objectives, secondly in relation to the desires of their superiors and older male family members, and only lastly in the context of a larger organization (be it a company or society as a whole). In Japan, there is a high degree of respect for and deference to one's *senpai* (those who graduated earlier from the same school, entered the same company earlier, and so on), which foreigners sometimes confuse with the influence enjoyed by older male family members in Chinese and Korean society. The Japanese system, however, is intrinsically different because it is based on organizational and societal relationships rather than on family ties. One result of this is that the freewheeling entrepreneurs found in Chinese society (including the PRC) and the sometimes flamboyant, high-profile corporate leadership seen in Korea are almost totally absent in Japan, where it is considered very bad taste to stand out from the group.

And the chopsticks? They also say quite a bit about national and ethnic tendencies. In China, chopsticks are often made of bamboo or plastic so that they can be used over and over. The

Japanese find this unsanitary, so they normally provide disposable wooden chopsticks, which says something about their priorities and character. The chopsticks with a colorful past are the metal ones commonly used in Korea. According to tradition, early Korean royalty used silver chopsticks (and bowls) as a protection against assassination: the silver was believed to turn black on contact with poison. Today's metal chopsticks, of course, are no longer made of silver, but perhaps their continued use reminds the canny Koreans that in their often rough-and-tumble business world, eternal vigilance is the price of survival.

DEALING WITH ASIANS

Dealing successfully with Asians can be a challenge, but often it is simply a matter of common sense. Unfortunately, common sense cannot be taught, so in spite of the spate of books written on topics like "the secrets of doing business with the Japanese," Western businesspeople continue to sabotage their own efforts. An example will show what I mean.

An American trade mission in Japan has scheduled stops in Tokyo and Osaka. After the group's arrival in Osaka from Tokyo, the mission director informs local contacts that a couple of the mission members have decided not to come to Osaka and that someone should cancel all the business appointments that have been arranged for them for the following day. An American might not be aware that the Japanese look askance at anyone who breaks commitments or drops out of a group before that group has completed its mission, but anyone with common sense knows that breaking appointments at the last minute is inconsiderate and bad business.

To avoid hurting your own cause, take the trouble to screen your actions for content that may give a wrong impression or, worse yet, cause your Asian contacts to take offense. Perhaps the most common errors in behavior involve humor. Although Asians do, of course, have a highly developed sense of humor, it is usually markedly different from Western humor. In particular, Asians tend to be rather literal-minded, so that what might be a joke to a Westerner will be taken seriously by an Asian. And this perceptual problem is often compounded by language barriers.

In one unfortunate situation, an agricultural representative from the United States reacted jokingly to some small-sized potatoes that he saw in an Asian country by remarking, "At home, we throw away potatoes like that." His intent was to let his hosts know that his state could provide potatoes of larger size and of more uniform quality; the effect, however, was not only insulting, but it also left his contacts with the mistaken impression that Americans were wantonly wasteful. Needless to say, neither of these perceptions was conducive to further business.

Misguided attempts at humor can be compounded by other cultural attitudes. Asians naturally attach more significance to events and facts closer to their cultures, and as part of their tendency toward traditionalism, they often have longer collective memories and more consistent interpretations of things that Western minds may find blurred by the passage of time. And unlike Americans, they do not tend to commercialize, trivialize and "humorize" events whose original impact was serious. Instead, they maintain their original perceptions.

Against this background, the actions of some Western companies with major business interests in Asia are virtually incomprehensible. For example, one U.S. international service company ordered and distributed to employees and others headbands bearing the characters for the Japanese word kamikaze. Here was an item virtually guaranteed to offend almost anyone in Asia. To the Japanese, the concept of kamikaze, whether in reference to the storms that sank most of an invading Mongol fleet in 1281 or to the Japanese pilots who hurled their planes against the armor of American dreadnoughts toward the end of the Second World War, is loaded with significance, all of it serious. To other Asians, anything related to Japan's role during the period of Japanese domination of the region brings back painful memories. For a company intent on doing business in Asia to do something so offensive seems incredible, and yet this sort of thing happens in one way or another on a regular basis. To nurture your Asian business, get in the habit of thinking before you speak. As the Chinese say, "Take the wrong road, retrace your steps; say the wrong word, live with regret."

When dealing with Asians, it is important to remember that in spite of their many similarities they are not all alike, any more than all Europeans or all Americans are alike. Any general statements about Asian thought, behavior and business practices refer only to averages or major tendencies, and are not hard-and-fast rules that apply to every individual case. Generalities are useful, however, both as guidelines for your own behavior and as a benchmark against which to measure your business associates in the Asian world.

In many respects, Asian thought and business behavior are a continuum with Japan at one end, China at the other, and Korea in the middle. This is due partly to centuries of history in which Korea was the bridge between China and Japan and partly to the more recent imposition of Japanese business structures and practices on Korea during the period (1910–1945) when Korea was a Japanese colony. Because of Taiwan's even longer period under Japanese rule (1896–1945), one might expect to find the same situation there, but the Nationalist (Kuomintang) Chinese exodus to the island in 1949 was a countervailing factor that ensured a more typically Chinese approach to business and political affairs.

Even though important differences exist, the common historical and cultural legacy of Asian countries has created at least an equal number of important similarities. For Western business, one of the most problematic is situational ethics.

Situational Ethics and Asian Pragmatism

Situational ethics means that abstract moral concepts like right and wrong, or truth and untruth, depend on the circumstances, rather than being absolute. Behavior that is acceptable in one situation may be unacceptable in another. Both morally and legally, individuals and governments have no compunctions about changing the rules at any time to fit a new set of circumstances (including newly discovered needs or newly defined objectives on the part of the Asian in question). Unfortunately, the process seems to be a one-way street: if changing conditions lead the Asian government or partner to request, demand or force a new deal, well and good—but all too often this rationale fails to work in favor of the non-Asian foreigner. At times, the Asian attitude leads to actions that shock and outrage Westerners, who have different criteria for judging behavior; at other times it makes it absurdly easy for Westerners to be deceived because they have trouble foreseeing (or believing) that their Asian contacts could blithely violate written agreements without the slightest embarrassment or remorse, or unilaterally redefine an entire business relationship (often without advising the Western business partner involved) simply because it no longer suited them.

Perhaps the most common mistake made by foreign businesspeople is for them to allow the Asian partner to acquire the technology, management, contacts, distribution network, or whatever it is that makes the business go, and then disassociate from the foreign partner in order to shut him out and compete with him. The techniques for accomplishing this are different, of course. As one wag put it, a Japanese partner may shut you out by changing the locks on the office when you are out of town, a Korean will talk you into letting him change the locks, and a PRC government official will hire a locksmith and send you the bill.

Although Asian and foreign commentators alike wax eloquent about the importance of relationships in the Asian business world, it might be more appropriate to speak of personal contact rather than relationships. Often, what foreigners may perceive as close relationships (implying a significant degree of trust, good will and moral obligation) are actually a series of business and social contacts based on personal desires and objectives of the moment that may be terminated or severely modified as soon as they have served their purpose. Entertainment and social get-togethers, for example, may lead a Westerner to believe that a friendship has been created when the Asian sees only a series of business-related parties and related behavior that are simply a requirement for doing business. All too often, the Asian businessman with whom you believe you have a good relationship may not hesitate to terminate that relationship if offended or if a better opportunity comes along.

At times it appears that Westerners may receive more cavalier treatment than would an Asian. Even the Japanese, who are famed for their adherence to commitments, can indulge in abrupt turnabouts when Westerners are involved. There are, of course, many Asian businessmen who live by a very strict code of honor (although not a moral code in the Western sense) and who will go to great lengths to keep their end of any bargain, but in general Asian business is fiercely competitive and is often viewed by the participants as a military campaign whose objective is total victory. Partly because the name of the game is survival and partly because a business alliance with a foreigner carries less weight than one with a compatriot, you should keep in mind that your Asian business or trading partner may not be nearly as committed as you would like to think.

Asians, then, do not have the same sense of moralism found in the West, and in business they are highly pragmatic. Their objective is success, and they have no inhibitions about taking as much advantage as possible of business situations of all kinds. At trade shows, for example, representatives of Asian firms often blithely ignore "no cameras" signs and exhibition guards and take photographs of competitors' products. At industrial seminars you may see members of the audience leaping up to try to photograph the speaker's flip chart or even attempting to photograph slides being projected on a screen. Asian business visitors on plant tours have been known to wear special shoes with porous, gummy soles that pick up chips and filings of paints and metal alloys so that the wearer's firm could later analyze them.

These and other tactics are more than just annoyances. Asian hardball is effective no matter what the stakes, and as the following cases show, the game involves a wide range of tactics.

Imagine yourself as an expatriate manager for a major U.S. accounting firm. Your company has entered into a joint venture with an Asian firm, in part because host-country restrictions on foreign companies made it difficult to enter the market in any other way. The local staff seems friendly and cooperative, and your host-country counterparts treat you with respect, but everyone seems so incompetent. Nothing goes right. At first you try to educate them, but as the months drag on and nothing improves, you find your patience wearing thin. The home office is losing patience even faster than you are, and after a year your job is on the line. Finally, your company withdraws from the market, leaving your former joint-venture partner with the expertise, the records and the client base.

On your last night in town, your head assistant takes you out to dinner. After a couple of drinks, you broach the subject.

"Tell me, Mr. Wang, where did I go wrong?"

He fills your glass, you both drink and he answers, "You did nothing wrong. We were all under strict orders that nothing you tried was to succeed."

You look at him in shock. "Even down to not replacing the toilet paper in the bathrooms?"

"Yes, even that."

The object, of course, was to create frustration that would lead to the foreign company's withdrawal. Mission accomplished.

This next true anecdote has at least a grain of humor: a retired U.S. sporting goods executive who invested hundreds of thousands of dollars in an importing and distribution venture with an Asian partner finds himself locked out of the premises and his inventory sequestered by his partners. But in many cases it is hard to find anything funny. A Fortune 500 company loses millions when it is forced to withdraw from a joint venture because the host-country government withholds needed permits. As soon as the foreign company is out of the picture, the former partner, which has acquired the foreign company's share of the joint venture at a fraction of its real value, smoothly obtains the permits from a sympathetic (and apparently collusive) Asian ministry. An American who has spent his adult life building a business in an Asian country teams up with a local company to attract a major U.S. partner and quickly finds himself on the outside looking in. Western expatriate executives whose companies have disagreements over local contracts suddenly find themselves unable to extend their visas. The game can get rough.

A question that Western businesspeople often ask of Asians is "Do you do this to each other?" or perhaps more to the point,

"Can you succeed in doing this to each other?" The best answer to both questions is probably something like "Not as often." When both parties are from the same (or similar) cultures, they are far less likely to get into dangerous situations without realizing it. At the same time, the ethnocentrism inherent in each Asian society (remember that each country is a highly homogeneous ethnic and linguistic group with strong traditions of belief in its own cultural superiority) makes it easier for them to justify extreme tactics against foreigners. In this they are not too different from many Western ethnic groups who have far smaller visible differences among them.

Asian business is often characterized by a single-minded pursuit of business advantage (which includes joint-venture control, market share, and so on) as opposed to Westerners' profit orientation. This tendency, combined with the Asians' generally inward-looking psychological orientation, their thought patterns that diverge from Western logic, and their consistent underestimation of Western business (and government) resolve, makes them inclined to press their luck too far. Eventually, reality forces them to perceive and correct the mistakes, but in the meantime operating, or even surviving, can be awfully difficult for Western business.

Beginning in 1979, for example, Singapore permitted business costs to soar (by allowing sharp increases in government-controlled cost factors, including obligatory employer contributions to employee benefits) and ignored the warnings of concerned foreign businesspeople until foreign investment plummeted and the economy took a nosedive in 1985. The Korean government did much the same thing in 1983–1984 when its repeated refusal to pay attention to the concerns of foreign business (including a capricious regulatory environment and a lack of protection for intellectual property rights) resulted in a sharp decrease in new investment. In 1985–1986 it appeared that the PRC, which had driven labor and other costs beyond reasonable limits and had shown little concern for foreign exchange and other legitimate foreign business requirements, was following the same path.

In each country the result of this type of miscalculation is large and often abrupt policy swings as the host-country government tries to get as many golden eggs as it can without killing the goose. The foreign business community can (and does) present its position through meetings, position papers and protests, but all too often the complaints are ignored until conditions become unbearable. This is not only frustrating, it causes a loss of efficiency and profitability as well.

The failure of Asian countries to learn from each other's experience makes problems all the more frustrating to foreign businesspeople, whose inability to alter the course of events often seems to leave them with only two possibilities: withdrawal (often involving large write-offs) or patient endurance (which implies living with continuous problems and uncertainty) in the hope that conditions will improve. Luckily, there are effective ways to cope with Asian business practices and Asian government policies toward business in general and foreign business in particular.

Responding to Asian Business Behavior

In your business dealings with Asians, it is important to be more vigilant than would normally be necessary at home and to have controlled, aggressive tactics planned in advance. Be prepared for the unexpected. Many Americans, when caught off guard by Asian business behavior, tend to compound the problem by reacting impulsively and even emotionally. Before you begin any Asia-related business activity, take some time to ask "what if?" Think through several scenarios, and prepare plans of action for each one. You can protect your business interests in Asia but not by being indecisive or emotional, or by resorting to legal action.

Some Westerners make the mistake of being too passive, perhaps in the belief that anything else would be considered rude. This attitude is too extreme. If you do not appear to be willing to protect your interests, why should your Asian competitors do it for you? If you are faced with overt commercial or industrial espionage, do not hesitate to be as assertive as necessary. At trade shows, politely but firmly refuse to allow known competitors to pick up your brochures and catalogues, and stop anyone with a camera from pointing it in the direction of your booth or bringing it into a product seminar. Factory visits by Asian business contacts can present a more delicate problem if you need to maintain good relations with the visitors. Since many Asians seem to equate an invitation to visit your production facilities with a license to acquire proprietary information, you may want to eliminate factory visits altogether as many Asian companies wisely have.

How should you deal with contractual relationships? In Asia, a contract rarely has the same significance that it does in the West; often it is merely the starting point for negotiations. To many Asians, the execution of a contract merely formalizes a mutual desire to do business, and they may sign without carefully reading the contents. Before the ink is dry, they may come back to you requesting (or demanding) new concessions or revisions to fit changing circumstances. Be forewarned, however, that an accommodating attitude on your part will rarely be reciprocated. Instead, you are likely to find yourself on a one-way street of continual encroachment by your Asian business partner or by the host-country government. To avoid this, follow a policy of never giving anything away for the sake of goodwill. If you make a concession, always get a meaningful one in return.

Legalism, as we said earlier, is definitely not the best way to counter the Asian tendency to reinterpret, redefine, and change the rules. More than one foreign company has created a seemingly watertight contract only to find later on that their insistence on nailing down every possible detail had alienated the Asians, who subsequently made a pastime out of looking for loopholes or of living up to the letter, but not the spirit, of the agreement. It is usually far better to spell out the points that are vital to you, then prepare to continually negotiate the rest and stay alert to signs of trouble.

In case of disputes, again it is better to avoid the common American tendency to resort to legal action. American laws, under the U.S. Constitution, exist for two main reasons: to protect its citizens from each other (from crime, violations of civil codes and contract law, and so on) and to protect its citizens from the government (which is why we have the Bill of Rights). In Asian countries, however, the function of law, to one degree or another, is to make it easier for the government to rule and to control society, including business. Government is a given, and the law is merely the mechanism through which it operates. For this reason, foreign companies and managers operating in Asia are often subject to unpleasant surprises that would be unheard of in the U.S. or Europe. In Korea, it may be the discomfort of tax harassment or the shock of ex post facto regulations on business. In Japan, it is more likely to be continuous changes in administrative procedures and the addition of layer upon layer of new regulations which may render your business activities difficult or impossible. In the PRC, there are arbitrary government fees, rule changes, and the sudden failure to get permission for something you have done many times before. Everywhere, it is often very difficult to get a prior opinion on the permissibility of a proposed course of action because the bureaucracy and regulatory systems are not transparent but operate on the basis of internal administrative guidelines that are unavailable to anyone outside the bureaucratic structure. (Why should they be, when their purpose is not to inform but simply to regulate?)

Given this background and attitude on legal matters, it is not surprising that the courts (including arbitration boards) are usually very poor places to get satisfaction or relief in case of disputes with business partners or with the government. Instead, you are better off to try reasonable discussion supported by personal contacts. From the moment you begin thinking about business involvement in Asia, start identifying people in government and business (including your potential partners, trade associations, regulatory agencies and other groups) who appear relatively sympathetic, understanding or tolerant of the role and needs of foreign business in general and of yours in particular. Take the time to cultivate the acquaintanceship of these people, as would a lobbyist. To do business anywhere in Asia, you should have a respectable entertainment budget. Use it to build relationships. At all times, remember that as a foreigner you are often at a significant potential disadvantage in Asia; in fact you have very little leverage. You can make more progress by being polite and framing your objectives and desires in terms of requests or suggestions rather than by being demanding, blustering or otherwise overtly aggressive. Quiet persistence and reasoned arguments work far better than loud insistence or displays of emotion.

If your own efforts don't produce results, turn to the U.S. embassy commercial section. They are responsible for knowing who the key players are in government and how to deal with them, and often the mere fact that the U.S. government is interested in a case will induce the host-country authorities to regard it in a more favorable light. The American Chamber of Commerce (AmCham) is another valuable source of information; contact them early on for help in identifying important local business and government figures. AmCham members have all been through the process of trying to do business in the host country, and they have learned a lot in the process.

Perhaps because many Americans believe that going directly to the top man is the most effective way to get action and because they often seem so ready to listen to Asians' claims of having an inside track, they tend to become enthusiastic about agents or potential partners who represent themselves as having friends in high places and who produce important people's business cards to prove it. Of course, since everyone in Asia exchanges business cards with practically everyone he or she meets, going through thousands of business cards per year in the process, the possession of someone's business card means nothing. More importantly, the Asian business world has become so complex and sophisticated that even the approval of a highly placed acquaintance is rarely enough to get a permit or to speed a proposal through the bureaucracy. One reason is that Asian governments and major business and industrial groups have very definite ideas about what is good for business and the local economy. Projects that match these ideas will have no problems; those that do not will often require great amounts of time, patience and perhaps U.S. embassy intervention. Finally, people with enough clout to make things happen don't talk, they produce. Believe what you see, not what you hear.

Perhaps because they separate business from moralizing, Asians are much less emotionally involved in business than are many Americans, who often confuse good treatment with friendship. Asian businesses understand the value of entertainment and are extremely skillful at using it to advance their cause. An amazingly high percentage of foreign businesspeople, who have allowed themselves to be swayed by lavish parties and constant smiling attention, are shocked at the change in treatment once the contract has been signed. As one dismayed businessman lamented about a group of Asian business contacts, "Because they were so nice to me, I made the mistake of thinking that they liked me." Maybe they did like him (he's a very likable guy), but it didn't stop them from doing what they wanted without much regard for fairness toward him.

Because of such experiences, it appears to many foreign businesspeople, that doing business in Asia is a long series of unpleasant surprises. Just when things are going well, your Korean partner insists on renegotiating the contract, or the Japanese government creates a new product safety standard, or the Chinese decide to put new restrictions on foreign exchange transfers.

The only way to deal with these business conditions is to maintain a vigilant skepticism. If you cultivate caution and frequently reassess your position in each of your Asian business relationships, you can avoid going through an experience that is all too common to Western companies and individuals doing business in Asia: love at first sight—when a rush of friendliness, concern, and good times bathe everything and everyone in a golden glow of international camaraderie and potential success—followed by a backlash in which governments appear impossible, partners unpredictable, and markets illusory. You can do business in Asia, and you can succeed, but only if you remain objective and alert and avoid emotional swings between enthusiasm and frustration or despair.

American business and political perceptions of the PRC provide a good example of the kind of psychological roller coaster you should avoid. When the U.S. finally recognized the PRC, thousands of U.S. businesspeople, drawn by visions of a billion smiling Chinese all buying even just one of anything, packed their bags and headed for Beijing, only to throw up their hands and come home when things took longer than expected and the Chinese reversed decisions on major import and investment projects.

Shortly thereafter, widespread publicity for Deng Xiaoping's modernization program and accompanying trade and business policies sparked a second wave of enthusiasm, based in part on the belief that China was turning capitalist. By the mid-1980s, however, many Western investors were again questioning the viability of continued operations because the behavior of Chinese authorities, in particular their insistence on minimizing outflows of foreign exchange, did not correspond to the Americans' desires.

A more realistic and rational appraisal of China would enable U.S. businesses to make better decisions and avoid a lot of frustration. China, still extremely underdeveloped, is run by pragmatic developmentalists, not capitalists, and any moves to woo Western industry are strictly for the purpose of developing the country's productive and technological capabilities. Western business should remain aware that the Chinese (like most other Asians) are using the West as a source of markets, capital and technology for economic and industrial growth and that they are not concerned with making the relationship reciprocal or in providing the "level playing field" that Western politicians and government officials keep clamoring for. The Chinese will give as little as they must to get what they need, a fact which adds a whole new dimension to the popular Chinese saying, "First friendship, then competition." If you relax too much during the friendship phase, you may be shocked to find how rough things can get when the competition starts.

Finally, never forget that as a Westerner you are a foreigner and, therefore, not a member of any of the national "clubs" or of the broader "Asian club." In Korea, for example, you are not only not Korean (and therefore ineligible for a whole line of treatment available only to Koreans), you are also not Japanese or Chinese (which would qualify you for still other types of treatment). As a foreigner (i.e., a non-Asian), you must operate under an entirely different set of unspoken rules and often you must overcome Asian assumptions about the strong and weak points of Western business.

On the other hand, as we have said previously, past and present rivalries among the Asians can generate opportunities for Western business. For example, Japan's substantial trade surpluses with

Korea have led the Koreans to impose discriminatory restrictions on Japanese products while the Japanese tariff structure discriminates against Korean products. These and other restrictions on trade within Asia create openings for alert Western firms to increase sales.

ASIAN THOUGHT AND BUSINESS

Asian thought processes vary from one country to another, of course, but there are general characteristics that set them all apart from Western thinking, several of which can cause problems for Western businesspeople.

· *Essentially unquestioning and uncreative attitudes*
The attitude of acceptance may be due to Asian educational systems (which tend to rely heavily on rote learning and which use examinations as mechanisms not to gauge progress but to screen out successively larger numbers of students at each educational level), the generally hierarchical nature of Asian societies, reverence for tradition and "legitimacy," or other factors. Whatever the reason, Asians do not engage in as much mental exploration as Westerners. They tend not to question, analyze or go beyond the facts at hand. Circumstances or conditions that Westerners might tend to question are treated as givens simply because they exist, and often an Asian will become confused or embarrassed if a Westerner insists on probing too deeply into the reasons for decisions or actions. In a similar vein, Asians often do not indulge in creative speculation, nor do they engage in extensive thinking about new and unusual approaches to business situations.

These Asian characteristics make many business relationships difficult for Westerners. In the first place, the Western party to a transaction may lack an understanding of the givens in a business or social situation and may find it impossible to get an explanation, simply because the Asian cannot comprehend how anyone could question the foundations that everyone in his or her society takes for granted. In addition, Westerners tend to assume that a buyer, client or business contact will respond creatively to information received. In dealings between Westerners, if one party provides information on a product or proposal, the other party will normally grasp the implications and possibilities, including benefits to himself or herself. When dealing with Asians, however, it is sometimes necessary to go further and to paint a more complete picture. For example, it may not be enough to demonstrate that a product is superior. It may be necessary to outline various situations in which it can be used.

· *Tendency to state or request confirmation of the obvious*

The characteristic of stating the obvious, which appears to be the opposite of inscrutability, can also be inscrutable in itself. Many Westerners find themselves at a loss for words when confronted with statements like "Can you eat Japanese food?" (after the foreigner has finished, with evident relish, a four-course meal), or "You can eat with chopsticks?" (after the foreigner being interrogated has skillfully grasped everything in sight with them). Perhaps the finest expression of the Asian tendency to state the obvious is found in the phrase "tourist souvenir," which is dutifully emblazoned on most of the souvenir items in every tourist spot throughout Asia.

· *Minimal awareness of originality*

Partly because of Asian reverence for tradition and conformity, the Western Renaissance notion of originality tends to be absent from the Asian thought process. One troublesome result of this fact is the general lack of respect among Asians for intellectual property rights. Because originality is poorly understood and generally undervalued, it is difficult for many Asians (including those with degrees from American universities) to accept Westerners' insistence on the sanctity of patents, copyrights and other inscrutable Western notions.

·*Extreme ethnocentrism*

In most of Asia, as was mentioned earlier in this chapter, there is an almost absolute identification of nation with race and linguistic group. This is quite different from North America, Europe, Latin America and Africa: few people would consider Norwegians and Danes (or Bolivians and Ecuadorians, or Nigerians and Liberians) to be of different races. Not so in Asia. By citizenship, ethnic group and language a Korean is a Korean, a Japanese a Japanese, a Chinese (even an overseas Chinese) a Chinese. This identification of nation, race and language leads to insular thinking, which creates another set of challenges and opportunities for the Western businessperson.

ASIAN THOUGHT AND ADVERTISING

One of the easiest and most fascinating ways to examine Asian thought processes is by studying advertising. Although Japanese and other Asian advertisers have created some of the most sophisticated and esthetically pleasing (from a Western point of view) ads to be found in the U.S. today, back home in Asia their advertising is quite different. By observing it you can get a feel for how different Asian thought processes are from your own.

Holistic Thinking

One evident aspect of Asian home market advertising is the tendency toward holism rather than Western logic. Instead of aiming directly at a conclusion or building toward it by progression, Asian thought moves toward its objective in a sort of spiral. To determine the Asian objective one has to figure out where the center of the spiral is (or is most likely to be). Unless the Western businessperson understands this, he or she is likely to conclude only that Asians bring up all sorts of facts and observations that are unrelated to the main point. In reality, of course, Asians are very clear about what they are trying to achieve. For example, a Westerner who asks a simple, direct question that in Western terms requires only a yes or no answer may receive a long, rambling response that appears to avoid the question entirely. The key in this type of situation is to stop listening for the direct answer you originally anticipated and concentrate on the information that you are actually receiving; somewhere in it is an answer. Your mission is to triangulate, as it were, to get a fix on the central point of the answer. The answer may circle around this central point, or it may follow a number of seemingly unrelated lines. Your job is to calculate the center of the circle or the focal point of the lines of thought. It is often difficult to make this kind of shift in orientation, but there is no alternative except frustration.

As in conversations and business dealings, Westerners examining Asian advertising find an unsettling mix of non sequiturs and redundancy, with a high percentage of elements with no apparent message-carrying function that are included as a matter of form or for no apparent reason at all. In Japan, for example, visuals tend toward montages that are often blurred, sometimes seemingly unrelated, and with only the most tenuous relationship to the message conveyed by the text. If you ask a Japanese what the message is, in many cases he or she doesn't have any better idea than you do, at least not in analytical terms. But the advertising works because it communicates with the consumer's holistic mental process.

The common American practice of using visuals to imply identification with some aspect of the good life (i.e., scenes that convince consumers that drinking Old Catfish makes for good times or that driving a Turbo 440-A means instant popularity with the opposite sex) has yet to catch on in a big way. On the other hand, when this sort of connection is made, it is often by stating directly what a U.S. ad would leave implied ("You can be popular like me if you use Moonbeam contact lenses").

The use of nonfunctional forms, the omission of connecting detail and the reverse tendency to state the obvious are deeply rooted in Asian thought processes and ways of looking at reality. In traditional Asian art, a picture was required to have a balance between symbolic elements ("yin" and "yang"), and only a limited number of styles, techniques and materials were considered appropriate for a given subject. Since the overall impression was more important than detail, large areas of a picture might be left untouched; at the same time, a painted scene whose subject was perfectly obvious might be explained in writing ("picture of a river with a man fishing in the spring while cherry blossoms fall").

The same tendency to alogical, holistic thought can lead to the most unlikely (from a Western point of view) juxtapositions of elements in other promotional areas. At some Chinese trade shows you can find cement mixers next to costume jewelry, and product catalogues from the various Chinese trade offices may feature slinky, sweater-clad fashion models on the same page with diesel engine parts or roller bearings. In Japan, where the urge to analyze, classify and organize seems stronger than elsewhere in Asia, catalogues and product exhibitions are usually carefully broken down by category as they would be in the West. Nevertheless, Japan seems to generate the most surprising mixtures of seemingly unrelated elements in billboard, poster and other media advertising.

Perhaps because the Japanese economy (and with it the Japanese advertising industry) is the most developed in the region, Japanese advertising seems to reveal more facets of Asian and Japanese thought. In particular the lack of appreciation of originality, which is behind a large percentage of intellectual property rights problems in Asia (if a society sees no value in originality, why should they protect it and pay royalties for it?), leads to an incredible uniformity in advertising. In the first place, activities and products are seasonal, and the appropriate seasons start at very precise times. Thus, all ski resort advertising will appear virtually on the same day all over the country and will be taken down in unison a few months later. The same is true for temples and other famous spots (Asians have a proclivity for designating "famous spots"), beach resorts, and so on.

A related phenomenon, which also points out the Asian's opposite need for order, structure and formalism in society (if not in thought), is the fact that each category of place, product or attraction has a corresponding type of advertising associated with it. In many cases, the deviation from the norm is so slight that one has to look at an ad twice to make sure it is really different from its neighbor. In Japanese advertising, for example, there is a genre that uses famous temples to promote particular products and services. In addition to using the same temple motif, these ads all feature an identical layout: photo of the temple (full color), main message written horizontally underneath, poetic expression written vertically down the left side of the picture, and on the right side of the picture, a separate vertical photo (stripped in) of a rock or stone (all famous temples apparently being endowed with at least one famous rock or stone). This formula is reproduced with such precision that a casual glance at the inside of a railway car during the temple-oriented advertising season can lead an unsuspecting Westerner to believe that he or she is suffering from multiple vision.

Language in Advertising

Asian attitudes toward society, business and communication, as well as their general thought patterns, are often revealed through their use of language in advertising and product promotion. In clothing and accessories, a few words of English (and, to a lesser extent, French) are considered stylish. This is nothing unusual; after all, from time to time Western designers have been known to decorate their creations with a Chinese character or two. But in spite of the fact that Asians make far more extensive use of English as a key element in advertising and elsewhere, they often show amazing disregard for correct spelling (as in "University of Frorida" on a logo), and from a Western point of view the meaning of the English words is often utterly unrelated to the context in which they are used. In many cases the words make no sense whatsoever, and the more English is used, the stronger this tendency seems to be. In Japan, for example, it is common to see incomprehensible advertising slogans like "The freshful your. To with!"

In both Japan and Korea, one encounters innocent-looking young women with blouses and sweaters bearing slogans like "milk here" or "combination bra and dickie" across the chest. These same young women (all of whom, it should be remembered, have studied English for years) would be appalled at the thought of displaying the same message in their own language, but apparently virtually anything goes in English. At any rate the double standard applied to language in much of the region reveals how far removed most Asians are from anything that occurs outside of their own cultural context. The same extremely ethnocentric mindset is seen in the linguistic relations among Asian countries.

Careful consideration of the Japanese use of English in advertising and product promotion can reveal a lot about the Japanese mentality. Unfortunately, few Westerners seem prepared to approach this important subject with an open mind. An American sporting goods executive on a business trip to Osaka wondered aloud about the name "Ings" on a chain of sporting goods stores. Could it be Chinese? He was familiar with the Chinese name "Eng." When an American expat responded that perhaps the name had been taken from the English verbal ending "-ing" to denote action (as in running, jumping, playing), the visitor was visibly irritated. Couldn't the expat at least give him the courtesy of taking his question seriously?

Later, the two Americans met with the Japanese in charge of purchasing for the chain. Triumphantly eying his companion, the visiting fireman put the question to the Japanese executive: what was the origin of the store name?

"We wanted an active name," came the reply. "You know, running, jumping, playing. . . ." In short, sometimes things make more sense than you might think. It's all a matter of perspective.

Your marketing efforts can be helped considerably if you learn to drop your preconceived notions of what messages the words and images are supposed to convey and how they are supposed to convey them. You may not want to go as far as the Japanese manufacturer who came out with a car called "Lettuce" (denoting freshness, crispness and a healthy lifestyle), but you should keep in mind that regardless of the market, Asians, including the Japanese, are going to keep thinking their way, regardless of how strange it may seem to foreigners.

Images of the West

Perhaps more than in other Asian advertising, the Japanese reveal the difficulty Asians have in deciding how to deal with Western products, trends and people. The following standard themes tend to appear in Japanese advertising: sexy-but-innocent (often tending toward Lolita types) in outdated cheesecake or calendar-girl poses, classic (samurai, Noh, and the like), powerful (Marlboro man), or nature-oriented. Western-type products or lifestyles, however, are usually presented as humorous, bizarre, or slightly menacing. In some cases equating the West with "funny" may represent a failed attempt to capture the casual, joie de vivre approach common in much U.S. advertising; in others it appears to reflect a perception of foreigners as outlandish (a word which, by the way, originally meant "foreign" in English). If a foreign language text is used in these ads, it is often (deliberately?) incomprehensible, just as foreigners and their ways still are to most Asians.

Korean advertising, as perhaps befits a country on the threshold of developed-nation status, makes heavy use of vague statements of a brighter future. Couched in the same rather ponderous language common in Japanese advertisements, the text of many of these ads resembles the blurred montages often found in Japanese visuals: the message is a collection of isolated sentences or phrases with little or no conceptual relationship between them. Visuals, in turn, often do little to enhance the message and frequently appear to be at cross-purposes with it. One electronics manufacturer's ad, for example, recently featured a stylized tandem bicycle (hardly a symbol of the high-tech progress pointed to in the text) as the central theme while another company's billboard in downtown Seoul showed a prehistoric nuclear family, dressed in ragged animal skins, staring awestruck at an array of consumer electronic products. Advertisements like these, with an intended impact that is often difficult for a Westerner to grasp, are a useful reminder that Asian thought processes and business practices do not correspond to what a Western businessperson might expect.

In the People's Republic of China, the holistic and often surrealistic view common in Korea and Japan gives way to pragmatism and the hard sell. In an economy of scarcity, there is little need for subtlety in advertising, and even in advertising aimed at foreigners, the message is usually simple and direct: "Buy this; it's good" (aimed at consumers) or "Let's make money together" (for commercial and industrial buyers). In keeping with this utilitarian approach, models and poses are often more suited to tractor sales or a women's army brigade than for consumer goods. But in some areas they are learning to adapt the message to the market.

Advertising reveals how superficial and misleading the apparent westernization of Asian business can be. Because of traditional Asian attitudes and beliefs, Asian attempts to westernize their advertising often produce mixed results even in Japan. For example, Asian companies have for centuries had logos based both on Chinese characters and on abstract or semi-abstract designs derived from traditional Asian art motifs; traditionally these logos have been characterized by uniformity or similarity of overall design. Over the last decade or so, Asian companies and their ad agencies have attempted to create logos that are more contemporary and look more Western. The traditional Asian lack of emphasis on originality, however, has produced a remarkable similarity in the logos. In Japan, for example, so many logos are based on the circle—segmented, overlapping, or what have you—that from a Western perspective they fall short of contributing to a strong company or product identity.

Japanese advertising may indicate the direction that the Koreans and the Chinese will take. The Japanese, who have the most developed economy and the most experience in sophisticated marketing, are the most skilled at adapting their advertising style to the target audience. In the U.S., their ads are marvels of sleek artistry; in Japan, they're visually vague (even confusing) and verbally explicit; in the PRC (where Chinese requests to reduce Japanese visibility indicate how effective the ads have been in stimulating demand for Japanese products), they usually stick to basics such as montages of consumer products. In Korea, the political necessity of keeping a low profile makes Japanese ads virtually impossible to find. This variety proves that some Asians, at least, are keenly aware that there are big differences in thought and perception not only between Asia and the West, but also among different parts of Asia. If the Koreans and the Chinese develop this level of awareness and communication skill, Western business is going to find itself facing even stiffer competition than at present.

ATTITUDES TOWARD WESTERN BUSINESS

Your business dealings in Asia are taking place in a context that will condition Asian responses to your actions. Often, your business contacts' attitude toward you is entwined with established attitudes toward Western business in general. On a personal level, Asians quite naturally tend to judge Western behavior in comparison with their own. On a group level, their collective historical experience with the West takes precedence, and, unfortunately, their experience has not been entirely positive.

To many Asians, American society appears extremely permissive, and the people produced by American society seem terribly undisciplined and self-indulgent. Virtually every Japanese in a large company has survived ferocious competition and expended incredible effort to get into a major university, which is virtually the only route to the best and most secure jobs. His Korean and Chinese counterparts have lived through similar experiences. The grinding preparation for the workplace may start as early as two years of age if the child's parents are ambitious. Compared to Americans, Asian schoolchildren put in longer hours in school, study more after school, and spend a greater portion of the year in class: the Japanese school year, for example, is approximately sixty days longer than the American. Mainland Chinese who grew up during the Cultural Revolution may have done their studying late at night after putting in a twelve-hour day of backbreaking manual labor; many Chinese and other Asian children living in the United States spend their after-school hours (and sometimes Saturdays) in special classes, learning the language of their parents' country.

After graduation, they keep up the pace: most Asians, even the prosperous Japanese, work at least half a day on Saturdays, and they show an almost universal willingness to meet with a foreign buyer or business partner at night or on weekends. In Korea, the workweek (already longer than in the West) has gotten longer over the last few years. And the learning goes on. In Taiwan and Hong Kong, taxi drivers cruise the streets listening to English-language cassettes so that they can deal better with English-speaking customers and eventually move on to a better job; managers and executives throughout the area make a far greater effort to learn Western languages than do their Western counterparts. It isn't just the Americans who are too laid-back. French business representatives who speak no Asian language and very little English (which, like it or not, is the major non-Asian business language in the region) may come to Asia a couple of times a year and wonder why their efforts don't meet with more success.

Perhaps the Westerners' weakness comes from their awareness of "quality of life," a term that still has little meaning in most of Asia. Whatever the reason, the Asian perception is that we are not trying hard enough. One Asian, when asked the difference between Americans and the Japanese, replied that if the American makes a major mistake on Friday, he will start to correct it on Monday while the Japanese—like many other Asians—will take care of it over the weekend. Over the course of a year, it is only natural that the American should fall behind, and that the farther back he falls, the less respect he deserves in Asian eyes.

For these reasons, many Asians (Japanese or not) find it absurd that American government officials have seriously suggested that one solution for the U.S. trade imbalance with Japan is for the Japanese to work less, save less and spend more. Notions like this have generated reactions ranging from amusement to contempt.

When they look at Americans, many Asians see a more dangerous form of self-indulgence: a lack of solidarity that on occasion becomes outright disloyalty. Many Asians raise an eyebrow when they see American businesses joining forces to compete with other American businesses, especially if it appears to be for short-term gain. The Japanese, for example, were amazed that the major U.S. television networks competed fiercely against each other in bidding for the broadcast rights to the Olympic Games in Seoul in 1988; Japanese television bid as a bloc and obtained rights for tens of millions of dollars cheaper than the U.S. broadcaster. In many cases, of course, U.S. antitrust laws prevent American companies from cooperating the way Asian companies do, but what Asians often perceive is an American willingness to put profits or one-upsmanship ahead of the long-term interest of the entire group.

More disturbing to Asians is what they perceive as fragile loyalty shown by U.S. officials and executives. To Asian eyes, too many Americans are willing to switch sides in competitive business situations, becoming negotiators or lobbyists for the opposing side and bringing the game plans with them. This not only offends many Asians' sense of loyalty, it also makes them question the entire social and business context that can produce such fragile allegiances. Specifically, it raises a troubling question in their minds: can one rely on American businesspeople when their corporate and government leaders (many of whom move back and forth between the business and political realms) seem so untrustworthy? All of this makes it harder for you to do your job in the Asian context.

In many respects, Asians seem to take business and business obligations a lot more seriously than do most Westerners. As a result, the range of excuses that they are prepared to accept may be far more limited than what Western businesspeople are used to. As one Japanese importer complained in private after a U.S. supplier blamed a late delivery on a series of unexpected setbacks that included a hurricane-induced train wreck, "I'm not doubting one word of his story. I'm sure that he couldn't supply the product from his usual sources. But if I were in his place, I would have sourced somewhere else—anywhere else, even at a loss—in order to fulfill my obligation and build the business relationship."

Your interactions with Asians are also taking place within a historical context. Western businesses in Asia should keep in mind that every Asian country was initially forced to do business with the West against its will, often with results that were detrimental to significant sectors of Asian society. Although present-day Asian political and business leaders realize the importance of trade, investment and technological exchange with the West, they look at it differently from most Westerners.

In the PRC, for example, the establishment of trade and technological ties with the West is strictly a matter of expediency. Having learned through the disastrous experience of the Great Leap Forward that a totally independent approach was impractical and having tried and failed to get what they needed from the U.S.S.R., the Chinese now intend to further China's development by obtaining Western technology and management know-how, recasting it in a Chinese mold, and using it for China's eventual entry into the ranks of the advanced nations. They have no intention of creating the kind of close and generally reciprocal trade relations that Western countries tend to have with each other. Instead, the Chinese objective is to acquire the skills necessary to develop Chinese industry, reduce imports and increase exports.

The situation in Korea, Japan and Taiwan is similar. The Koreans are eager for Western investment but only as a means of creating employment, developing their own industry through infusions of Western capital and technology, and projecting a modern image that will help them gain international stature and recognition as they increase exports. The Japanese, with only half the U.S. population and virtually no natural resources, have created the world's second largest productive capacity and are driven to excel and, in particular, to surpass the United States. Although the Japanese have shown a remarkable willingness to accept Western ways (from colonialism and gunboat diplomacy to multinational marketing), they have done so to beat the West at its own game, not to convert to Western values or become a member of the Western world. Their objective is (to use the military terminology one sometimes encounters in Japanese business circles) total victory. Taiwan has followed similar trade and investment policies that have created what are probably the world's highest per capita foreign exchange reserves: over US$60 billion for a population of only 19.5 million people.

Asian countries compete fiercely with each other, but they share an understanding of the meaning of the competition and the rules that govern it. Perhaps because of this mutual understanding, and certainly because they share a common cultural heritage (including similar experiences with the West), when two Asian countries do business together, they often shut out Western companies. A case in point is the PRC's Bohai Bay petroleum development project, a Sino-Japanese joint venture which has largely excluded Western companies from bidding on various aspects of the project, even though they seemed likely to deliver equivalent products and services at lower cost. This tendency is not due to pure xenophobia, of course, for factors like linguistic similarity, geographic convenience and cultural similarity (which eliminates the nervousness and unpleasant surprises that both sides may experience in East-West business relations) also play a part. Western companies can definitely further their cause by acquiring cultural awareness and linguistic capabilities through the hiring or training of qualified Western staff and management. It is important not to simply rely on Asian staff and managers; although they have a thorough understanding of their own culture, they often do not understand or agree with the objectives of a Western company. In addition, they may be unduly influenced by their attitudes toward other Asian countries.

Western business should also study the competition, not only from a technical and business standpoint but also in terms of the historical, political and economic tensions in the region in order to take advantage of the rivalries and imbalances between various Asian nations. For example, since Japan runs trade surpluses with all the countries in the region, politicians and economists in those countries are natural allies for a foreign company competing with the Japanese. Or if the Japanese fear the transfer of technology to Korea, Western companies may be able to sell that technology to Korea on more favorable terms. They might also find out why the Japanese are reluctant to give the Koreans access to proprietary information.

INTELLECTUAL PROPERTY RIGHTS

Partly because of economics and, as we mentioned earlier, partly because of historical attitudes toward the value and ownership of concepts, designs and expression, foreign businesses face significant intellectual property problems in every Asian country.

The question of intellectual property rights protection in Asia is heavily conditioned by the ways in which the United States deals—or fails to deal—with it. Although the U.S. is by no means the only country concerned with intellectual property rights issues, its position as the world's largest market and the closest large

Western country to Asia gives it far more leverage than other Western countries have in the region. In fact, the U.S. government's role in the intellectual property rights issue is so pervasive and so representative of the way other business and trade-related matters evolve that it is worth a few lines of discussion.

Asian countries, like others around the world, know that one of the great weaknesses of the U.S. in international negotiations is an inability to perform consistently over time. For a number of political and psychological reasons, the United States has relatively little collective patience with long-term problems and the protracted negotiations that go with them. American politicians need favorable headlines before the next election, and the American public has little interest in the technical details that must be dealt with in complicated international matters. They tend to want action now so that they can turn their attention to something else. As a result, the U.S. government will often avoid calling attention to problems overseas or getting seriously involved in them unless it appears that they can be resolved quickly. This allows Asian countries to continue to follow trade and industrial policies long after they have been given notice that U.S. industry or the U.S. government considers those policies to be unfair. The Asians have learned that the U.S. government relegates discussions (or in the preferred jargon, "consultations,") of problematic issues to such a low priority level that talks may be dragged out for years without fear of any serious consequences.

Another time-related problem involves personnel. The U.S. government is plagued by high turnover at the top, with individual mobility and collective position shuffling creating a perpetual expertise and awareness gap. New appointees, who have their own agendas and who need to make a considerable commitment to master the details of intellectual property rights issues, are often too busy looking at their next career move to become terribly concerned or involved. In fact, today's State or Commerce Department official is likely to be tomorrow's well-paid pro-Asian lobbyist, which makes commitment all the more difficult. It is hard to win a long game when your main strategist takes the playbook and joins the other team.

The chronic lack of high-level attention to the problem, coupled with the desire for high personal visibility, has hindered what few initiatives have come from upper levels of government. For example, a highly touted interagency "strike force," whose formation was announced by the U.S. Trade Representative's office in the 1980s, spent months reinventing the wheel (and, not coincidentally, generating reams of politically useful publicity because of their supposedly aggressive initiative) by researching intellectual property problems that had been reported on in detail by U.S. embassies for years. Once the project had been milked for headlines, it dropped from sight.

At lower levels, changes in staffing patterns or specific assignments mean that it is rare for the U.S. to send the same negotiating team twice. Often, staffers and midlevel officials who have uncovered issues and followed them from the start, acquiring irreplaceable expertise along the way, are shouldered aside by ambitious superiors whenever a topic acquires a high enough profile to attract potentially career-enhancing attention. All this leads to poor preparation and inexperience which Asian negotiators are understandably quick to exploit.

As if this weren't enough, the U.S. Congress is notoriously mercurial and easily distracted by a variety of domestic issues (many of them of local, rather than national, significance). These domestic issues quickly push intellectual property concerns, which are harder for constituents to understand and get excited about than simpler issues like jobs and competition from cheaper or better foreign products, to the background.

The net result is that when the U.S. wants to discuss intellectual property rights (or trade issues), Asian countries can stall almost indefinitely, provided that they promise to take action. When and if U.S. countermeasures (reduction of the generalized system of preferences (GSP) benefits, for example) appear imminent, the Asians can simply produce draft legislation (rarely enacted into law) that gives little more than the appearance or the promise of protection. Then the American bureaucrats and politicians hold press conferences to announce that the problem has been solved, grateful voters return the politicians to office, and the politicians in turn fund the bureaucrats for another year. Meanwhile, America's trade position (and possibly your specific business sector) continues to erode.

At the same time, some U.S. government officials are generating ill will for you by making large waves in areas where they believe they can garner publicity to promote their own careers.

Asian attitudes and approaches to intellectual property are a good example of the perceptual gulf that often separates business in Asia from business in the West. To begin with, the entire concept of private property and its sanctity is essentially a Western idea, not an Asian one. Likewise, in Asia the boundaries between the public and private sectors are ill-defined and constantly shifting. This fact, if not clearly understood, can cause Western businesses to make errors of interpretation or to flounder around trying to get their bearings. Is a consulting firm in Canton public or private? What is the true scope of the firm's authority? In Japan, does the inability of U.S. businesspeople and U.S. government officials to determine whether or not a given entity is public or private mean that the Japanese are being devious? Does it justify frustration, irritation, calls for retaliation? The amorphous ownership and control of key projects that are potentially worth billions in business to U.S. firms are often described by baffled Americans as subterfuge designed to keep qualified U.S. (and other foreign) firms out of the market when in fact it is totally in keeping with Asian views on private property in general.

Problems of private property and public domain are especially troublesome in the area of intellectual property rights. Asians' stubborn insistence that "ideas are free" goes back a long way and permeates the entire society. Asian art, for example, has never had the concept of originality and uniqueness of authorship and design that entered Western art during the Renaissance. Works have long been copied freely, and modern artists pride themselves in making perfect copies, for sale, of styles or specific works of ancient masters. Names, even company names that would be considered valuable property and would fall under trademark laws in the West, are legally difficult to protect in much of Asia. In Korea, for example, anyone could call a company "Hyundai" without fear of legal action by one of the country's largest industrial groups of the same name.

As a result of these attitudes, most existing Asian intellectual property laws have large loopholes that often provide more protection to what the Western businessperson considers a violator than to the property owner from a Western perspective. In both Japan and Korea, for example, it is perfectly legal for anyone to register any name and trademark from anywhere in the world, regardless of how well known it is or who owns it, as long as the mark in question has not yet been registered in-country. Later, when the Western "owner" of the mark wants to do business in these Asian countries, he is forced to buy (angry Westerners say "buy back," but remember that as far as Asia is concerned, there is no Western ownership involved yet) the mark in order to use it in-country.

What Westerners perceive as defects in Asian intellectual property laws also have roots in the Asian predilection for form over content. When Asian countries introduce superficially Western-style legal systems, they tend to faithfully reproduce them (more copying, but at Western insistence, which shows how contradictory and confusing Westerners can be) as symbolic structures, but in practice they pay full attention only to those sections that are of greatest interest to them. Thus, if having a supposedly Westernized legal code means including sections on intellectual property rights, the Asian will dutifully do so, but often without intending that they be enforced. Like so many things in the Asian world, such laws exist because proper form requires it, not because they are expected to add substance.

Because they do not share Western enthusiasm for the general concept of intellectual property, many Asians in business and government sincerely see nothing wrong with appropriating needed ideas (including plans, formulas, processes, and so on) for their own use. Even Asians who have accepted the general need for protection appear to have trouble perceiving the true worth of software, hardware, pharmaceuticals, and other items that may have required tens of millions of dollars from concept to product. The resulting offhand treatment of intellectual property can lead to actions that from a Western point of view are astounding, such as a proposed Japanese government regulation that would have required not only compulsory licensing of foreign software to Japanese companies, but would also have required the foreign authors or owners to make available the basic operating instructions for the programs, thus literally giving away the most valuable part of the package.

In countries less prosperous than Japan (i.e., the rest of Asia), Asians' casual attitudes toward intellectual property are buttressed by economic arguments formulated with their own peculiar Asian logic. One of these is the "rich older brother" argument, according to which the U.S. (in particular) is a wealthy sibling who can surely spare some crumbs from the table; another is the "poor student" argument which states that Asian students, the key to Asian development, cannot afford the books they need to educate themselves and to build a prosperous and stable society if they have to pay for authorized editions. The mention of students is a reminder that politics is also a factor in intellectual property rights issues. In some countries, the presence of both powerful vested interests and anti-Western or anti-American sentiment (typically strongest among students) makes it politically risky for the authorities to push too hard for reform, even though the long-term effect would be to strengthen local industry.

The threat to intellectual property rights is very real, and unauthorized use of proprietary processes, products and information costs U.S. industry hundreds of millions of dollars a year. As with many other aspects of business in Asia, the best approach is persistence, patience and firmness. Since Asians undeniably do understand economics in much the way as Westerners do, comprehensive explanations of the reasons behind the cost and value of intellectual property are often a great help. (In some Asian countries, the American Chamber of Commerce has done admirable work to produce lucid, documented explanations of the economic and industrial benefits to host countries that provide adequate, effective intellectual property protection.) Conversely, threats or visible displays of anger are almost invariably counterproductive because of Asian respect for composure and at least the appearance of harmony.

MAJOR HISTORICAL EVENTS

To understand the behavior of Asians, it is useful to get a feeling for their collective experience; therefore, we close this chapter with an outline of Asian history and some general historical trends. The phases which begin below overlap, and the rough beginning indicated for each is only a general guide. Also, over the centuries covered by these phases, a number of general historical trends and national or cultural characteristics emerge clearly:

1. The rise of Japan and relative decline of China, with Korea in flux between them.
2. Selective internationalization on a broad scale, usually led by Japan.
3. The inability of Russia to gain a substantial foothold or dominance in the region despite geographic proximity and a constant influence on events.
4. Rapid and extensive U.S. involvement after a late start and a tendency toward confrontation.
5. The strength of nationalism in each country, coupled with persistent resistance to non-Asian interference.
6. Asian perseverance and adaptation to changes that might have destroyed other, less self-confident cultures.

Because of the rivalry between the countries of the region, historical objectivity is practically nonexistent. The history writers of one country may claim to have proof that a certain event took place while those of another country (that might lose face if the claim were accepted as true) will insist just as convincingly that the event in question never happened or that it happened differently. For example, some historians in Korea argue that, in early times, Koreans from the kingdom of Puyo invaded southern Japan and settled there. The Japanese version is that in times of internal strife on the Korean peninsula, Korean nobility and others took refuge in a hospitable Japan. The truth is virtually impossible to ascertain, even though some physical evidence exists.

The tendency of each group to rework and reinterpret facts to increase its legitimacy and improve its image is not restricted to ancient history. The most famous recent controversy over history arose in the 1980s when the Japanese Ministry of Education made a persistent effort, spanning several years, to have history textbooks rewritten to remove or water down unfavorable references to Japan's invasions of China and Korea before the Second World War. This tampering with the record evoked a storm of protest in both countries, as well as in Taiwan, Hong Kong, and in Chinese and Korean communities in the United States. To put it in a Western perspective, the reaction of these groups was comparable to the reaction of world Jewry to claims that the holocaust never took place. Another recent example involves an ancient stone monument in what is now Manchuria (PRC) that bears inscriptions relating to Japan and Korea. In spite of a PRC archeology team's finding that the monument is an authentic, unaltered original, the Koreans stoutly maintain that the ancient Chinese characters (which are carved in stone) have been changed to make the Japanese look good and the Koreans come out second best. Westerners can (and do) smile at some of these disputes, but to Asians they are serious, emotionally charged issues, and Westerners dealing with Asia should respect them.

Although each Asian country vigorously promotes its own version of the history of the region, an objective look at that history supports the broad pattern of main trends indicated below.

* * *

PHASE I

Cultural transfer is a dominant theme. Although the level of development is too low to undertake massive invasion attempts, both China and Japan periodically try to establish footholds in Korea.

16th-11th century B.C.: China: Shang Dynasty. Earliest proven dynasty.

660 B.C.: Japan: supposed founding of Japan by first emperor, Jimmu Tenno. (Some Koreans maintain that the first emperor of Japan was of Korean origin—something no Japanese would ever admit.)

500 B.C.: China: Confucius (551–479 B.C.). Long period of turmoil ("Warring States").

400 B.C.: Korea: start of Korean nation with ancient Chosen,* in northern Korean peninsula and Manchuria. Border conflicts with Chinese.

221–207 B.C.: China: Qin Dynasty unites China for the first time. Concept of all non-Chinese as barbarians who should pay homage to—and be enlightened by contact with—the Chinese.

206 B.C.-A.D. 220: China: Han Dynasty establishes pattern of modern Chinese state. Confucianism becomes official basis of government for two thousand years. Contact with Roman Empire.

57 B.C.-A.D. 935: Korea: Shilla kingdom on east coast.

37 B.C.-A.D. 668: Korea: Koguryo kingdom starts in Manchuria and Siberia and encroaches on Shilla.

18 B.C.-A.D. 660: Korea: Paekche kingdom on west coast.

A.D. 350–400: Korea (Paekche) opens conduit for Chinese culture to Japan.

A.D. 350: Japanese Empress Jingu sends expedition to Korea, establishes small colony. Koreans drive Japanese out in A.D. 400.

514: Chinese medicine introduced to Korea.

---

* The name of Chosen for Korea has become politicized in modern times. Many South Koreans resist modern use of the name because it was the Imperial Japanese word for Korea; paradoxically, the equally nationalistic North Koreans refer to the peninsula as Chosen. This, in turn, charges the word with contemporary geopolitical overtones.

550: Japan: Korean and Manchurian population exceeds 100,000. Buddhism and Chinese medical knowledge arrive from China (direct and via Korea).

618–906: China: Tang Dynasty. Golden age of culture and government. Contact and trade with many nations. Korea, Japan and Tibet send missions to China to learn Chinese ways; adoption of Chinese writing system.

645: Japan creates copy of Tang system.

668: Korea: Shilla kingdom, with Tang military aid, defeats Paekche and Koguryo. Tang keeps Koguryo's Manchurian territory; Tang troops remain in Shilla's expanded Korean kingdom.

676: Korea: after eight years, Shilla finally forces withdrawal of Tang Army.

692: Korea establishes medical school based on Chinese texts and methods.

700: Japan: over one-third of Japanese nobility is of Korean or Chinese descent.

841–845: China: weakening and under attack from Turks and Tibetans; Tang government destroys temples of Buddhist and other non-Chinese religions.

906: China: end of Tang Dynasty.

918–1392: Korea: increasing class and urban-rural divisions and fall of Tang lead to rise of Koryo Dynasty (center near Pyongyang). Continuous attempts to retake old Koguryo Manchurian areas from China. First tangential contact with West (hence the English name, "Korea," a corruption of Koryo). Chinese/Mongol invasions. Buddhism and Confucianism flourish.

1185: Japan: beginnings of samurai, *hara-kiri* (ritual suicide by disembowelment; more formally called *seppuku*), *shogun* as institutions.

PHASE II

Increased economic and logistic capability leads to increased trade and invasions.

1206: Mongolia: Genghis Khan unites the Mongols after a twenty-year struggle.

1211: Mongols begin invasion of China, capture Beijing by 1215.

1271–1368: Mongols establish Yuan Dynasty, exclude Chinese from government. Marco Polo visits court of Mongol Emperor Kublai Khan (grandson of Genghis Khan).

1274: Kublai Khan invades Japan (Kyushu) via Korea. Storm forces a withdrawal.

1279: Kublai Khan finishes Mongol conquest of south China. Increased trade with Russia and Europe.

1281: Kublai Khan invades Kyushu again. After fifty-three-day battle, typhoon (kamikaze or "divine wind" from the Japanese viewpoint) wipes out invasion fleet.

1294: China: death of Kublai Khan; beginning of Mongol disintegration.

1368–1644: China: Ming Dynasty. China goes into isolation as Europe approaches age of exploration and conquest. Trade with Korea and Japan continues.

1392–1910: Korea: Chosen era, Yi Dynasty. Like Ming in China, strong nationalism, isolationism. Anti-Buddhism, pro-Confucian policy. Periodic incursions by both China and Japan.

1405–1433: China: brief period of intense exploration by Ming—fleets to India, Persia (Iran), Arabia, Africa, South Seas, perhaps South America.

1400s–1500s: Japanese traders and pirates work China's coast and rivers. Japanese pirates become a problem for Korea.

PHASE III

Resistance to Western penetration as the West, entering the age of discovery, conquest and colonization, tries to encroach on Asia.

1516: China: first Europeans (Portuguese) after Marco Polo arrive by ship.

1542 or 1543: Japan: first Europeans (Portuguese) arrive by ship-wreck.

1549: Japan: first Christian missionary (Spanish Jesuit Francis Xavier).

1557: China: Portuguese allowed to establish trading post at Macao. They help the Chinese fight Chinese and Japanese pirates.

1592: Japanese ruler Toyotomi Hideyoshi invades Korea on his way to attack China. As in the Korean War some 350 years later, China intervenes, stages massive counterattack across the Yalu River in 1593. Korean admiral Yi Sun Shin invents ironclad "turtle ship," with which he decimates the Japanese support fleet. Japanese withdraw to defensive perimeter in southern tip of peninsula.

1597: Hideyoshi stages second invasion of Korea. Hideyoshi dies in 1598, Japanese withdraw. Korean Admiral Yi is killed in sea battle.

1600s: Europeans persistent in attempts to trade with Orient.

1609: Japan begins trade with Holland.

1613: Japan begins trade with England.

1620–1662: Formosa (Taiwan) ruled by Holland.

1637: Japan is closed. Japanese caught leaving or reentering the country are subject to execution. Only Dutch and some Chinese allowed to trade.

1640: Japan: Portuguese send delegation, which is executed and their ship burned.

1644: China: Manchus invade, set up Ch'ing Dynasty (1644–1911). Following Manchu invasion, birth of "Triad Societies," formed to fight the Manchus in south China. Manchus quickly expand empire to include Mongolia and Tibet (precedent for PRC in 1951) but continue isolationist policies.

1685: China finally lets Europeans use isolated port of Canton for trade. China develops trade surplus.

1773: China: British begin selling Indian opium in China to redress trade imbalance. Emperor tries to stop opium dealing in 1800 but fails.

1791: Japan: first U.S. attempt at trade is rejected.

1805: Japan: Russian attempt at relations is rejected.

PHASE IV

European Industrial Revolution gives West tools to practice power politics on a global scale. West expands in Asia by gunboat diplomacy and outright colonialization.

1839–1860: China: four "Opium Wars," each won by England and each settled by an unequal treaty forcing more trade, missionaries, and European presence in China. Treaty of 1842 ends Second Opium War, giving Hong Kong to England.

1851–1860: China: Taiping ("Heavenly Peace") Rebellion and takeover of south China in name of Christianity, human equality, and agrarian and tax reform. Western powers help Ch'ing counterattack and win by 1864.

1853: Japan: U.S. Admiral Perry's fleet ("black ships") enters Tokyo Bay, gives shogunate an ultimatum to open up for trade and coaling stations. In same year, Russian Admiral Putyatin's fleet approaches Japan in attempt to get commercial treaty.

1854: Japan: Perry and Russians both return. Perry gets treaty for trade, supplies, U.S. consulate. Russians leave empty-handed. British Admiral Sterling also arrives with fleet, gets supply treaty.

1855: Japan: treaty opens three ports to Russian ships, gives southern Kurile Islands to Japan, northern ones to Russia. Japan and Russia to share Sakhalin Island. Japan grants extraterritorial rights to Russians.

1856: Japan: first U.S. consul (Townsend Harris) arrives. Negotiates extraterritoriality in following year.

1860s: Japan: strong xenophobia and military clashes with foreign navies.

1860: China: Russia annexes zone in East Siberia. Aided by Western powers, Ch'ing Dynasty counterattacks Taiping Rebellion and wins by 1864.

1862: Indochina: France annexes Cochin China (Vietnam) from China.

1866: Korea: first U.S. attempt at trade is rebuffed when Koreans burn the U.S. ship (the *General Sherman*) and kill the crew.

1867: Indochina: France establishes protectorate of Cambodia (Kampuchea).

PHASE V

Japanese acquire Western technology and tactics. Traditional Orientalism, practiced by China and Korea, is defeated.

1868: Japan: Meiji restoration. Fall of the shogunate, end of samurai class. Start of mass education, citizen army, political parties. Rapid assimilation of Western technology. Stated goal of becoming a world power.

1868–1897: Japan: industrialization. Raw material imports increase by factor of five; exports of finished goods increase by factor of twenty. Beginning of *zaibatsu* (large, diversified industrial conglomerates: Mitsubishi, Mitsui, Sumitomo, Yasuda).

1872: Koreans reject Japanese attempt to force trade relations. Japanese faction favors punitive expedition, but plan is rejected.

1874: Japan sends expedition to attack natives on Formosa (Taiwan) to get better treatment for Japanese seamen.

1875: Japan gets Kuriles from Russia in exchange for all of Sakhalin Island.

1882: Korea: U.S. forces opening of trade and diplomatic relations.

1882: U.S. Congress passes Chinese Exclusion Act, leading to increased immigration from Japan (see 1924).

1883–1885: China: France ends Chinese domination in Indochina via war. French get full control of Vietnam, Laos, Cambodia (Kampuchea). British end Chinese control in Burma.

1894: Korea: Tonghak ("Eastern Learning") peasant rebellion, traditionalist Asian overtones. Korean king calls in Chinese troops. Japan demands Chinese withdrawal, sinks Chinese troopship, declares war.

1895: Japan defeats China, gets Formosa (Taiwan) and Pescadores, Port Arthur and Liaotung Peninsula, Chinese nonintervention in Korea. Within a week, Russia, France and Germany force Japan to give back Port Arthur and Liaotung Peninsula, which Russia soon takes over for herself (1898).

1896: Korean Queen Min assassinated in Seoul with complicity of Japanese Minister Miura Goro. Korean king sheltered in Russian Embassy in Seoul. Miura is convicted in Tokyo but given no penalty.

1898: Spanish-American War gives U.S. the Philippines, greater Asian presence.

PHASE VI

Japan becomes a world power player.

1899–1900: China: Boxer Rebellion. Ch'ing rulers unite with Boxers to throw the foreigners out. Siege of foreign legations, including U.S., at Peking. Japanese troops play a major role on "foreign" (non-Asian) side.

1902: Japan signs alliance with England, partly to keep Russia out of Korea. British assist in formation of modern Japanese navy.

1904–1905: Russo-Japanese War begins when Russian troops enter Korea across the Yalu. Japan occupies Seoul, attacks Russian fleet in Korea and Port Arthur. Japan defeats Russian Far East Army in Manchuria, destroys Russian Baltic fleet in Tsushima Straits. Japan gains Liaotung Peninsula again (see 1895), and the southern half of Sakhalin Island and has a free hand in Korea.

1904–1905: Japan takes effective control of Korean governmental affairs.

1905: China: Dr. Sun Yatsen forms Alliance for Chinese Revolution to end the Ch'ing Dynasty and modernize China.

1907: Russo-Japanese secret pact divides Manchuria.

1910: Japan annexes Korea. Korea remains Japanese colony until 1945.

1911–1912: China: revolution and proclamation of Chinese Republic under Sun Yatsen. Formation of Kuomintang (KMT). Republic quickly disintegrates. Japan becomes a threat. Tibet and Outer Mongolia gain independence from China.

1914–1918: World War I. Japan, financially strapped ever since the war with Russia, prospers by selling industrial products to European Allies and their colonies, thereby further boosting Japanese industry.

1914: China: Japan, as British ally, captures German possessions in Shantung.

1915: China: Japan issues "Twenty-one Demands," basically trying to force the Chinese into the same situation as the Koreans in 1904–1905. China agrees to most of them, including Japanese control in Shantung, southern Manchuria, and Inner Mongolia.

PHASE VII

Marxism and militarism sweep the Orient.

1917: Russian Revolution.

1918–1922: Japan, with Western backing, invades Siberia and northern Sakhalin Island to help White Russians and expand territory.

1919: Versailles Peace Conference recognizes Japan's rights in Shantung, China. Chinese boycott Japanese goods. Anti-Japanese, antiforeign sentiment grows in China.

1921: China: founding of Chinese Communist party (CCP). But Soviets support KMT as more viable to resist the Japanese and other foreigners.

Outer Mongolia: creation of People's Republic of Mongolia, the world's second communist state, with Russian military assistance.

1922: Washington Conference: Japan agrees to withdraw from Shantung, and does so. Naval armaments ratio among Japan, U.S., U.K. set in Pacific.

1923–1927: China: Soviet advisers help KMT, promote CCP-KMT cooperation. But in 1927, Chiang Kaishek massacres CCP members. Red Army founded.

1923: Japan: Kanto earthquake and fire razes Yokohama and half of Tokyo. Rumors that Korean nationalists are involved in a plot leads to massacre of Koreans in Japan.

1924: U.S. Congress prohibits Asian immigration into the U.S. (The shoe of foreign exclusion is now firmly on the other foot. See 1882.)

1925: Japan gives back northern Sakhalin to Soviet Russia.

1928: China: clash between Japanese troops and Chiang Kaishek's KMT Army. In separate incident, Chinese warlord of Manchuria (Chang Tsolin) is assassinated by Japanese army officers in Manchuria. Chang's son, Chang Hsuehliang, allies himself with the KMT.

1930s: Japan: series of militarist plots, assassinations and attempted coups in Japan. Military begins to take effective control of the country.

1931: "Manchurian Incident": Japanese Kwantung Army, without authorization, attacks Chinese and seizes Mukden, then all of Manchuria. Puppet government of "Manchukuo" is set up in 1932.

1932: Shanghai: Japanese Navy and Army defeat regional Chinese Army after six-week battle.

1933: Inner Mongolia: Japan invades and occupies.

1936: Japan signs Anti-Comintern pact with Nazi Germany.

1937: China: after an armed confrontation at the Marco Polo Bridge in Wanping, Japan begins full-scale war. Nanking captured and pillaged, as many as 300,000 civilians killed. U.S. warship bombed and sunk by Japan.

1938: Japan and Russia fight at Korean/Manchurian/Siberian border.

1939: Japanese defeated by Russians at border of Manchuria and Outer Mongolia.

1940: Japan joins the Axis. Forces French and British to close Yunnan and Burma routes into China, cutting off KMT and CCP supplies.

1941: Japan signs Neutrality Pact with Soviet Union. Japan bombs Pearl Harbor and U.S. enters W.W. II against the Axis.

1941–1945: Japanese involvement in World War II, while gaining resentment for Japan in Asia, destroys myth of Western invincibility and superiority. Hundreds of thousands of Koreans forced into Japanese army and labor battalions in Korea, Japan, Manchuria, and elsewhere. Thousands of them (along with many Japanese civilians) stranded in Soviet areas at end of war.

1945: Soviets break pact, declare war on Japan, enter Manchuria, occupy much of Korea. Later withdraw to thirty-eighth parallel at behest of U.S. War ends with atom bombs dropped on Hiroshima and Nagasaki.

    Korea: country divided into U.S.-U.S.S.R. administrative zones at thirty-eighth parallel.

    China: Soviets undercut CCP, support Chiang Kaishek and KMT and recognize Chiang's authority in Manchuria against CCP. U.S. also aids KMT.

1945–1951: Japan, for the first time in history, is occupied by a foreign power, the U.S. The Occupation, coming on the heels of a crushing defeat (also Japan's first), stuns the nation but lays the foundation for modernization and contemporary democracy.

1948: Korea: Syngman Rhee (Yi Song Man) becomes president.

1949: China: KMT defeated by CCP. Chiang Kaishek takes nation's gold reserves and flees to Taiwan, joined by several hundred thousand troops and nearly two million civilians. KMT takes over island, rules by martial law until 1987.

1950–1953: Korean War. As in 1593, Chinese intervene, force stalemate. Japan used as rear base by U.S.-U.N. forces. Like World War I, Korean War gives major boost to Japanese economy, industry.

1951: Japanese Peace Treaty signed in San Francisco. Soviets refuse to sign; neither KMT nor PRC invited. Japan loses Formosa (Taiwan), Korea, southern Sakhalin, the Kuriles. Soviets keep four small Japanese islands. U.S. Occupation ends on main home islands (U.S. forces still control Okinawa).

    PRC invades Tibet.

PHASE VIII

New balance in Asia requires adjustment. This period witnesses growth of industry, trade, technology.

1953: PRC opens trade relations with Japan (cuts them in 1958 because of Japan's continued close cooperation with Taiwan).
    Korea: end of Korean War.

1954: Vietnam: fall of French stronghold at Dien Bien Phu. U.S. financing of 78 percent of French effort.

1958: PRC: start of "Great Leap Forward." Leads to havoc in PRC economy, death by starvation of thirty million Chinese.

1959: PRC: rebellion in Tibet put down with great violence and loss of life.

1960: PRC splits with Russia. Khrushchev withdraws all Soviet assistance.
    Japan: massive student demonstrations against Japan-U.S. Security Treaty.
    Korea: massive student demonstrations against fraudulent elections lead to the fall of Syngman Rhee. Later that year, Park Chung Hee takes over.

1964: PRC: first nuclear bomb test.
    Japan: Summer Olympics in Tokyo, "bullet train" inaugurated.
    Vietnam: increasing U.S. involvement. Bombing starts in 1965. U.S. invasion of Cambodia in 1970.

1965: Korea and Japan normalize relations.

1966–1976: PRC: Cultural Revolution, Red Guards, Mao's "Little Red Book." PRC detonates its first hydrogen bomb in 1967. Border clashes with Russia. China provides safe rear area and limited support for Vietnam.

1970s: Japan becomes world's second largest economic power.

1971: Taiwan ousted from U.N., replaced by PRC.

1972: Nixon visits PRC without advance notice to Japan; shocks Japanese. Japan recognizes PRC the same year, cuts relations with Taiwan.
    Japan: U.S. returns control of Okinawa.
    Vietnam: U.S. forces withdraw.

1974: Japan: World War II holdout, Lt. Onoda, arrives after finally surrendering in the Philippines, saying Japanese have gotten soft.

1975: Vietnam: communist forces conquer South Vietnam.
    Cambodia (Kampuchea): Communist Khmer Rouge conquers the country.

1976: PRC: death of Mao Zedong and Chou Enlai.

1977: PRC: Deng Xiaoping gains power after two earlier brief stints near the top of party hierarchy (and a couple very close to the bottom). Gang of Four, led by Mao's widow, goes on trial in 1980–1981.

1978: Cambodia: Vietnam invades and quickly conquers country.
    China: U.S. recognizes PRC (diplomatic relations established January I, 1979), withdraws recognition from Taiwan.

1979: PRC begins to open the country to foreign business. PRC attacks Vietnam in response to Cambodia invasion, mistreatment of ethnic Chinese.
    Taiwan: Violent repression of native Taiwanese and protesters by KMT.
    Korea: Assassination of President Park Chung Hee.

1980: Korea: General Chun Doo Hwan takes over the country. Martial law declared. City of Kwangju in open revolt. Hundreds, perhaps thousands, killed in army suppression partly commanded by Chun. U.S. complicity charged by opposition.

1983: Korea: most of ROK cabinet killed in Rangoon, Burma, by bomb planted by North Koreans. Chun arrives late, escapes harm.

1984: Hong Kong: Great Britain agrees to return the colony to the PRC in 1997.

1987: Macao: Portugal agrees to return the colony to the PRC in 1999. (Portugal had offered to relinquish Macao in the mid-1970s, but the PRC declined the offer.)

People's Republic of Mongolia and U.S. establish diplomatic relations.

TOWARD THE TWENTY-FIRST CENTURY

Uncertainties abound. The Korean peninsula is still divided; ROK politics are highly turbulent and unstable; the PRC is still trying to reconcile Marxism and development; Taiwan has internal problems; the future of Hong Kong is anything but secure; and what may be structural flaws have appeared in once seemingly invincible Japan. Nevertheless, Asia takes a leading international industrial role because of export-oriented industrial and trade growth and technology transfer.

Japan: Massive trade surpluses with the U.S., the European Economic Community (E.E.C.), Western Europe, Korea, and the PRC create friction; equally massive investment in the U.S. arouses unease in some U.S. political sectors.

Japan, Korea, Hong Kong, Taiwan: Intellectual property rights still a problem.

Japan, Korea: Restrictive import policies create friction. U.S. militancy on trade matters increases, generating Asian backlash.

PRC: Contradictory attitudes and policies on foreign trade and investment lead to fluctuations in trade and the economy, and there are problems with inflation. Hard-line reaction against social liberalism and political pluralism affects budding business contacts with Taiwan and South Korea.

Korea: Increasingly militant and violent political activism, linked with anti-U.S., anti-Japanese, antiforeign sentiment of radical elements. Inconclusive talks with North Korea (DPRK) on relaxation of tension and on possible cooperation.

CHAPTER TWO

Business
Behavior

RULES OF THE GAME

I t might seem obvious that Asia's historical and social development has given rise to business behavior that is very different from what one might expect in the U.S. or Europe. But if you watch countless Western businesspeople blunder through a variety of embarrassing and counterproductive business encounters, you realize that the message has yet to sink in. Luckily, it is not necessary to read volumes on the subject or imitate every nuance of Asian behavior in order to act in an acceptable manner. By simply observing a few basics, you can make your Asian business experience more pleasant and productive.

Throughout Asia, business behavior tends to be more structured than in the United States, or even in Europe. Although it would be absurd to try to "act Japanese" (or Chinese, or Korean), business activity can be much more effectively pursued when Asian social and business norms are observed by both individuals and groups. Here are some key rules of the game.

1. Don't show impatience or lose your temper.

In Asia, perhaps the one truly mortal sin is to show anger. A multitude of other failings, from disorganization to drunkenness, can be forgiven if circumstances warrant, but a show of anger usually means irreparable damage to a business or personal relationship. Asians revere balance, harmony and self-control, and a loss of temper offends them deeply by violating all three, while on a personal level it inflicts an irrevocable loss of face on all concerned. At times you will be irritated, exasperated and frustrated, and by Western standards you may have every right to show it. Don't.

Remember that many of your customs, attitudes and behavior are as odd to Asians as theirs are to you. Learn to accept a different type of logic (some guidelines are given below), eliminate any sense of urgency and keep calm. Don't create time pressure by setting short-term deadlines for yourself. Be ready to come back as many times as it takes to attain your objectives, and be prepared to reexplain points you have already gone over a dozen times. Try to keep your travel schedule flexible so that you can stay in Asia an extra day or two if necessary (your Asian contacts may try to generate time pressure by maneuvering you into a final negotiating session just hours before your return flight is scheduled to depart). Don't be surprised or annoyed if an agreed-upon schedule is changed without prior notification, or if at the last minute you are asked to do something that you had been told wasn't necessary. You can always decline the request, of course, but do so graciously. Keep in mind that you are free to adopt the same noncommittal silences, slow decision-making processes and other negotiating styles that the Asians use.

2. Don't aggressively push your point.

Aggressive behavior will usually cause you to lose the Asian's respect. In addition, a display of aggressive behavior may delude you into thinking that you are winning when in fact the Asian is merely making a strategic withdrawal to avoid your determined charge and to leave you overextended. You are better off if you remain calm, give the other party plenty of time to state his case, and gently return to the points that are most important to you. The worst thing you can do is to threaten. Nothing puts an Asian off faster than threats of embassy intervention, congressional inquiry, or legal action; in fact, there is an out-and-out contempt for the American habit of reaching for an attorney as though he or she were a six-gun. This doesn't mean you can't use the embassy, of course. But it is better to just go ahead and do so rather than talk about it. It's the same with complaints to your congressperson: since few Asians worry about foreign congresspersons or senators (just as you have little or no concern for theirs), there is no point in threatening to bring your congressional representative into the picture. Probably the least effective and most overworked American tactic is the threat of legal action. Both because of the status of law and lawyers in Asia and because of the difficulty and expense of trying to engage in a suit in a foreign country thousands of miles away, few if any Westerners have ever advanced their cause by taking it to the courts in Asia. It is better to be a bit more patient and careful when going into business relationships and to rely on calm, patience and interpersonal skills to get through problem spots.

3. Don't expect Western logic.

It has been attributed to diet, genetics, left-right brain linkage, the writing system, the education system, and a host of other factors—but whatever the reason, the thought processes of Asians are very different from those of Westerners. You will encounter refusals with no apparent reason, leaps of logic (or illogic) that lead to totally impossible conclusions, willingness to follow a course that clearly leads nowhere, cheerful acceptance of mutually contradictory statements, and a literal-mindedness that forces you to ask exactly the right question in order to get useful information. At the same time, Asians often display marked resistance to providing background and explanations if a phenomenon doesn't exist—for example, explaining why there is not a market for widgets. And you will have to wrestle with different idiosyncrasies in each country: Koreans, for example, may appear obdurate for refusing to take "no" for an answer, while the Japanese may wear you down with their seeming inability to *give* "no" for an answer.

When you encounter traits that seem baffling, the only wise course of action is to be patient, and observe. You will need to go beyond simple passive acceptance to get results, of course, but it is unwise to try a frontal assault. Rather than point out the flaws in logic, ask for the specific information or action you want without trying to prove why it makes sense (to you). In this way, you can deal with, or even take advantage of, the Asian readiness to work with two sets of mutually exclusive facts. After all, you are not bound any more than they are to behave as though there were only one reality to any given situation. As one rather cynical (but very successful) Western entrepreneur in Asia puts it, "It's their story; let them tell it the way they want to." His approach is to take an Asian contact's version of things into account without allowing it to dominate his course of action.

At the same time, remember that Asian thinking tends to reach a given target either by moving in a spiral or by generating a holistic image centered on a general (and often rather amorphous) concept rather than a clearly discernible line of thought. In this respect, it differs from Western thinking in the same way that the Korean game of *paduk* (which is the same as Japanese *go*) differs from the Western game of chess. In the Asian board game, no individual piece or area of the board is more important than any other, and the object is to envelop as much of the board as possible rather than dominate crucial sectors and directly attack the opponent's pieces, as in chess.

4. Always carry business cards in the host-country language.

The widespread, almost compulsory use of business cards in Asia is well known but poorly understood in the United States. All too often, American businesspeople regard this practice as an amusing idiosyncrasy to be humored but not taken seriously. Strike one! In contrast to the highly individualistic social and business system in the U.S., Asian societies are based on structure, and the business card is the best way for them to see how a new business contact fits into that structure. Whether surrounded by the myriad ranks and titles in Japanese companies or tucked away in the Byzantine labyrinth of the bureaucratic hierarchy in the People's

Republic of China, the Asian with whom you do business is precisely identified by position and group affiliation. Your business cards (printed both in English and in the local language) should provide your contacts with equivalent information. Otherwise, they will spend over half their mental energy and attention trying to figure out how and where to pigeonhole you instead of concentrating on whatever business proposal you are trying to promote.

The way in which business cards are presented (or, in the case of the U.S., not presented) reveals the differences in structural relations in the U.S. and Asia. A typical first meeting between two American businesspeople begins with a verbal introduction and a handshake, often followed by immediate entry into the topic of discussion. If cards are exchanged, it is often at the end of the meeting, almost as an afterthought ("By the way, let me give you a card"). This behavior is disturbing to most Asians, even those who have experienced it before.

The Asian may be concerned about you as a person and is definitely concerned about the business you are proposing. But it is very difficult for him to deal with either until he knows the context in which you and your business belong. Therefore, a first meeting in Asia invariably begins with an exchange of cards. There is also an exchange of bows or handshakes, depending on the country and the individual. As with other customs, you will often encounter a spectrum of behavior, with Japan at one end, Korea in the middle, and China at the other: Japanese bow most frequently, Koreans and Chinese far less, and when dealing with Westerners both the Koreans and the Chinese tend to shake hands. (In group situations, such as acknowledging applause from an audience, the Japanese will bow deeply, the Koreans and the Chinese on Taiwan less so, and the mainland Chinese will return the applause.) Keep in mind, though, that shaking hands is not an Asian custom and that many Asians with little exposure to foreign businesspeople are often uncomfortable with the custom. Since they tend to find it intimidating when a Westerner—who may tower over them—charges at them from behind an outstretched hand, you are well advised to keep your approach restrained. (On the other hand, in Korea—especially when taking leave of a contact with whom you have spent considerable time—you may encounter an extended handshake that may evolve into something very much like hand-holding. Koreans are often quite physical, and as a sign of goodwill a Korean contact may continue to hold your hand for a minute or two after the handshake is over.)

Because of the Asian tendency to categorize individuals (and companies) in a rather precise hierarchical order, it is quite likely that your Asian contact will scrutinize your business card carefully; if he needs clarification, he will ask a couple of questions about your company and your position before going further. And most of the time, he won't just stick your card in his pocket. Rather, he will leave it on the conference table so that he can refresh his memory if need be. At group meetings it is common for each Asian participant to have the business cards of each new acquaintance laid neatly on the conference table in front of him like a seating chart, for reference.

And how should you deal with his card? In the same way. Don't hesitate to ask about things like your contact's last name. Although throughout Asia the family name is given first on business cards, many Asians have "Westernized" the English-language side of their cards by putting the given name first. So, if in doubt, ask—and mark the last name to spare yourself the embarrassment of using the first name by mistake when you write a follow-up letter weeks later. During meetings, follow the Asian custom of putting your contacts' business cards in front of you on the table (in proper order) for ready reference. This can help you avoid the embarrassment suffered by many foreigners who address Asians by the wrong name, or extend invitations or gifts to subordinates instead of the senior representative for whom they were intended.

5. Personal contact first, business second.

At this point, many Americans like to plunge right in and "get down to business." Not yet! Part of the normal Asian business ritual calls for an exchange of pleasantries. Your contact will often ask if you have been in his country before and may make some comment about the weather. On your part, a compliment or two about the country is always a good idea. (If you have been there before under less favorable circumstances—"Yes, I was one of the first members of the Occupation Forces to arrive," "Yes, right after the Inchon landings"—however, it is probably better to keep the details to yourself.)

Your main guideline is simple: Asians, far more than Americans or other Westerners, approach business through the person. They want to feel that there is some sort of personal contact, even if it is strictly a formality. Although an American will enter into a deal if the bottom line looks good enough, the Asian wants to get to know the other party personally, often before even looking at the bottom line. With such a demand for personal contact, you would expect it to be difficult to run a mail-order business in Asia, and in fact statistics indicate that it is. Although direct marketing (mail order) is a $300 billion per year business in the U.S., annual direct marketing sales in Japan (Asia's largest DM market) are only one percent of that figure, or $3 billion.

6. *Use go-betweens to formally introduce you to important contacts.*

Because Asians require a strong element of personal contact in their business dealings, it is advisable to have a formal introduction, even when it would seem superfluous and a waste of time in a Western context. You will find that Asian business leaders, even from large and powerful companies, often ask someone to break the ice for them rather than make the initial approach on their own. Even if it seems unnecessary, follow their lead—that's just the way it is done.

7. *Keep in touch, and participate.*

If you are trying to develop or maintain business in Asia, you can't just go over once or twice a year or stop by for a day on your way to somewhere else. Furthermore, regardless of whether or not your negotiations lead to a successful conclusion, it is very bad form to neglect someone after having been involved in substantive business discussions. A brief note (or, if you are in the country, a phone call) from time to time can do wonders for future business. In this regard, an annual Christmas card is an absolute must in

Korea and Japan. Although some businesses and government offices send cards to virtually everyone with whom they have ever had contact, you are probably safe (and certainly a lot more solvent) if you limit your list to people with whom you have had substantive discussions, people who have helped you (including middlemen and introducers), and people in important positions (even if you merely met and exchanged cards). Asians certainly don't spend the New Year matching the cards they received against the mailing list of those they sent, but they do seem to be aware of whether or not you made the gesture of sending a card.

It is also absolutely essential to attend parties or receptions to which you are invited; in this case it appears that Asian hosts actually do compare the guest list with the list of those who showed up because they will often mention your absence even if the event was attended by a large number of people. If you have employees who are host-country nationals, be sure to make a cash contribution if there is a birth, illness, accident or death in their immediate family. Someone will pass the hat (or envelope) among the local staff; although they may hesitate to bring the matter up to the foreign management, they expect you to contribute as a personal gesture and will resent it if you fail to do so. In addition, someone (usually the top foreign manager) should always go to the funeral if a local staff member has a death in the family. The "family" connection may be pretty tenuous from the Western point of view (an uncle or cousin, for instance, so distant that the staff member doesn't even know the name of the deceased), but it is still a duty. A more pleasant duty, on happier occasions, is to go out drinking and eating with your staff and colleagues. It is part of business, so don't hang back.

8. Do your homework.

Most Asian businesspeople are incredibly well prepared when they sit down for discussions or negotiations, and they expect the same of you. They want to know exactly what your objectives are, and they expect that you have learned enough about local realities to know the principal options and the limitations in the local political and economic context. Probably the most common mistake made by foreign businesspeople is to fly to Asia without a clear-cut plan and no real knowledge of the companies and organizations with whom they hope to deal. This failure to do basic research has sunk many a potential business relationship because the Asian side lost respect or felt that the Westerner's lack of preparation indicated a lack of sincere interest. In addition, society in every Asian country is founded on totally different sets of assumptions (including those governing business-business and business-government relations) than the U.S., Canada or Western Europe. As a result, everything you have learned about marketing, distribution, management and operations needs to be modified, often heavily, to fit Asian business realities. Read up on the subject. Often you will get more out of newspapers and magazines than you will out of books. Subscribe to the *Asian Wall Street Journal* and to one or more English-language newspapers from your target countries, and start a clipping file for each country. This may seem like a lot of work, but your potential business contacts (and competitors) in Asia are doing it religiously, and it is absolutely necessary to emulate them if you want to succeed in the long term.

9. Don't indulge in self-promotion.

The only thing worse than constantly proclaiming that you're just a "good ol' boy" trying to learn about Asia is to keep repeating that you're interested in relationships and you're in the market for the long term. The Asian is perfectly capable of observing whether or not these things are true, and he is liable to get suspicious or irritated if you keep talking about them. It is far better to *demonstrate* your willingness to learn and your commitment to the business relationship and the market. As in other aspects of doing business in Asia, this requires patience since the only way to let the Asian evaluate the strength of your commitment is to put in a consistent effort over time. Your Asian business contacts have seen far too many U.S. company representatives come to Asia once or twice, make promises with the best of intentions, and then gradually let things slip because Asia seems so far away and its peoples and practices so hard to understand and because there are so many things to attend to in their U.S. operations. The cumulative effect of this pattern of thoughtlessness and neglect by so many U.S. businesspeople has been the creation of a strong wait-and-see attitude in the minds of many Asian executives. The only way you will establish credibility is by demonstrating (not touting) your commitment and continuing to follow through beyond the short (one or two years) attention span of less motivated U.S. firms.

10. Don't let language be a barrier.

No matter how good their English, your Asian prospects, contacts and associates will not understand everything you say. Give serious thought to hiring an interpreter for all business meetings. When speaking, avoid jokes, idioms, slang, jargon and references to the latest fads in the U.S. Even Asians who are fluent in English may not be able to follow you.

Although you may have no intention of using a foreign language in business discussions, you will make your business dealings easier if you acquire at least some knowledge of your contacts' native language, thereby giving them more time and energy to devote to business rather than to assisting you. Having to do all the reading, interpreting, and talking for a foreign guest requires an amazing amount of work, and even if you can only learn enough to get a glass of water and find the bathroom by yourself, you are lessening the burden and distraction for your Asian contacts. (For further information on foreign language acquisition, see "Learning the host-country language," pp. 127–29.)

Since most Asians read English much better than they speak it, the printed word is a valuable tool in overcoming communication problems. In discussions you can double the effectiveness of your presentation (whether you are marketing, providing technical information, or negotiating) by having a numbered outline summary of your main points printed in English and the local language. If circumstances make it impossible to obtain a neat, accurate translation, an English summary is far better than nothing. Discuss your points one at a time, by the numbers; when referring to an earlier point, be sure to mention its number. This methodical, visually aided presentation can do a lot to enhance communication.

Because of language barriers (which often reflect different ways of thinking as much as problems of vocabulary or syntax), it is a good idea to summarize in writing the main points of agreement at the end of a discussion or negotiating session and get your Asian contacts' concurrence that the summary does, in fact, describe the present state of the business relationship. This may become an exercise in patience because there is a good chance that the Asians won't have seen and heard things the way you did. Be sure to get a clear statement of agreement (it helps to write something like "we agree that . . ." at the top of your list). Asians will often say something encouraging like "yes" when their real meaning is "I understand what you're saying" or "I can see that you believe what you just said." Therefore, it's a good idea to be persistent (but not overbearing) until you get a clear statement indicating whether or not they actually agree with your interpretation—or until you discover that they decline to agree or disagree.

Failure to get a commitment does not necessarily mean that talks have broken down. In the first place, you may be dealing with a representative selected not for his decision-making ability or even his negotiating skills, but simply because he speaks English; such an individual rarely has much authority to bind his company. In addition, each country has its own limitations on commitment. In Japan, for example, the need for group consensus may keep your contacts from making any sort of definitive comment until they have had a chance to discuss the matter with their colleagues at the office. Moreover, the Japanese will rarely openly reject anything, preferring instead to limit themselves to vaguely encouraging comments like "very interesting" (which may also indicate a genuine interest in your proposal). In Korea, the hierarchical nature of most Korean organizations means that the individual negotiator must get authorization from above on even minor points.

If you find it impossible to get a commitment, try to deduce what your contacts' reluctance means, and devise your strategy accordingly. Until you have a signed contract, be sure to avoid the common mistake of proceeding on the assumption that you are moving in the direction you want to move.

11. Observe correct etiquette.

Asians are considerably more concerned with form, ritual and etiquette than are most Americans, and your business success may depend in large measure on your adherence to their standards during meetings and social events. If you are hosting a meeting (at your hotel, a conference center, or U.S. embassy or trade center facility), plan to serve tea or coffee. If you are meeting in someone else's office, there's a good chance that tea or coffee will be served to you. Wait until your host has taken a sip or asked you to go ahead before drinking. If you have several meetings in one day, you may not want to drain every cup to the last drop—six cups of coffee (or ginseng tea) can wreak havoc on your system.

During meetings there is no need to be stiff or formal, but the lounging or slouching common at American meetings is very offensive to Asians and should be avoided. As in other situations where behavior is important, you can learn correct behavior by simply observing your Asian contacts. They tend to be correct but not stiff: good posture, feet on the floor, no elbows on the table or arms draped over the back of the chair. In small meetings or in situations where you are in a preeminent position (for example, in the speaker's group at the front of the room in a seminar or opening ceremony), it is considered bad form to stretch your legs out in front of you or to cross your legs above the ankle (except when sitting on the floor in a restaurant). It is considered especially rude to spread out with one ankle resting on the other thigh, especially if the sole of your shoe is displayed. Grace and economy of motion are always admired, as is neatness with notebooks, samples and other items. Pay attention to form. You will definitely lose goodwill if you toss things onto a table casually instead of setting them down neatly or if you slide something down the table to someone instead of passing it down or getting up and taking it to him. When you hand something to someone (be it a brochure or a goodwill gift), it is far more polite if you present it with both hands, not just one.

Although there are many differences between Asian countries—and the individuals in those countries—in certain situations Asians show considerably more deference to each other than do

Americans. The Japanese, for example, are often very hesitant to step in front of others in getting on or off an elevator or in going through a doorway; and Koreans will go to great lengths to avoid walking between two people who are talking. However, the degree of attention paid to niceties is inversely proportional to the number of people involved: in small groups or chance face-to-face encounters, polite behavior is expected, but in mass situations (a large group of people waiting for an elevator, a crowded train, a subway at the rush hour) it's strictly "every man for himself." Since there is such a great variety of behavior, the best policy is to observe what others do and use common sense.

12. Remember that the buyer comes first.

In Asian business one of the important principles conditioning behavior is the absolute supremacy of the buyer in any buyer-seller relationship. Because the seller (of goods, services, or investment opportunities) is asking the buyer to do something, he or she owes the buyer a good deal of deference, more than would be normal in a non-Asian setting. When meeting with potential buyers, be sure to thank them for their time and show your appreciation by being well prepared with business cards, brochures, samples, and anything else that is relevant to your presentation. Americans (and many other non-Asians) may be tolerant of sellers who leave materials back in the hotel room (or in the U.S.), but in Asia this sort of lax behavior is considered inconsiderate toward the buyer. It is also important to follow up on promises to send information and samples and to undertake anything else that you have indicated you would do. Some of the few times that I have seen Japanese, for example, get visibly angry was when they mentioned trade missions, companies or individuals who had failed to live up to their word by not sending data and samples as promised. Failure to perform is especially damaging when an action has been requested by the Asian potential buyer because by ignoring his interest in your product, you cause him to lose face.

The relatively higher position of the buyer does tend to create a double standard, and you should be prepared for it. For example, if a seller fails to be on time for a meeting, or cancels at the last minute, it will make a lasting bad impression on the buyer as inexcusably unprofessional behavior; on the other hand, some Asian buyers seem to feel no hesitancy about arriving late (or not at all) to meetings with sellers. Another situation in which this double standard crops up is with proposals. A prospective buyer (who would be extremely irritated if a seller failed to send requested or promised information) may feel perfectly free to utterly ignore proposals submitted by the seller. Of course, many firms will be responsive, but there is a widespread attitude that the buyer is not obligated to respond unless he is interested.

SOCIAL OCCASIONS

Social occasions require a certain amount of ritual, which varies significantly from one East Asian country to another. Although the following suggestions can get you pointed in the right direction it would be impossible to cover all aspects of every situation, so try to acquire the habit of constant observation so that you can quickly learn details on the spot. In Japan I once saw the value of this approach at a small business dinner which included an American businessman who had just arrived in-country. When his pleased hosts asked him where he had learned so much about Japanese etiquette, he answered that he had simply observed what they did and imitated it. He scored two points—one for doing the right thing and one for being sensitive to the local culture.

In Asia the guest at a restaurant is normally given a seat facing the door, so if you are asked to sit in this location, you should not attempt to pay the bill, although of course you should thank your hosts for their hospitality. When going out for informal meals (during an office lunch break, for example) the Japanese often ask for separate checks, but the Koreans look down on such behavior and invariably one of the group will make quite a point of paying the entire bill. If you are treated in this way, then follow Korean custom and reciprocate by paying for coffee at a coffeehouse after lunch; you can do the same if you are hosted by Japanese.

Hosted dinners share one characteristic with those in the

United States: the guests are supposed to relax and enjoy the meal. If invited to a large banquet you should pace yourself, especially in China, where the courses may be endless and where you may be expected to drink innumerable toasts.

As in other aspects of East Asian culture, eating etiquette varies significantly from country to country. The Japanese, whose society was based on Spartan values for centuries, have an abiding respect for self-control: the late Emperor Hirohito always stopped eating when he felt he was eighty percent full, and you will often see businessmen eat only one or two strawberries for dessert, even though they have been served an entire bowl of them. You will make a better impression by not eating a lot. It is considered especially poor form to take the last piece of anything from a serving plate. Although the Chinese tend to serve more dishes and larger portions, many Chinese also believe it is more civilized to leave a bit on serving plates and on your own plate at the end of a meal as well. Koreans, on the other hand, quite sensibly take the attitude that food is there to be eaten and see nothing unusual about finishing every morsel. Side dishes are another important part of Korean meals, and even in restaurants they were served and refilled as often as necessary without additional charge. This was changed in the mid-1980s, when it was decreed by the government that each dish be charged for separately.

If you are invited to someone's home for a meal or coffee, it is customary to bring fruit, cake or pastries rather than wine, as many Americans do. At the meal, you will encounter differences in cooking and service that shed light on interesting aspects of each national psychology. Many Chinese will use copious amounts of oil in cooking for guests because historically oil was scarce and expensive, and to use it sparingly indicated a lack of concern or respect for the guest. You may have to balance your concern for your weight and your cholesterol level with your desire to show your appreciation by enthusiastically eating a rather oily dish. For Koreans, serving rice toward the end of a meal is a similar sign of a good host or hostess; to serve the rice early would encourage the guests to fill themselves with rice rather than the more expensive and tasty main dishes. If you are accustomed to eating in China (where rice normally is served immediately after the soup) or Japan (where rice may be the first thing to reach your table), this custom can be disconcerting.

Drinking rituals vary from country to country, but a useful basic rule of thumb is to keep other people's glasses full. They, in turn, will fill yours. It is considered poor form to pour your own drink—and even worse to ignore your Asian companion's empty glass. If someone offers to fill yours before you have had a chance to drink, rather than decline you are supposed to drink a bit and then extend your glass to accept the offer. In Japan it is impolite to let your glass sit on the bar or table when a friend or associate is pouring; you should lift it an inch or so to show your appreciation and participation. Some Koreans also observe this custom while others do not. In China, you express thanks by tapping your fingertips on the table next to the glass in a sort of scratching motion. (The best way to get this technique down pat is to observe and imitate your Chinese contacts.) Koreans have a rather complicated way of offering you a drink: they will gesture with their glass toward you, drain the glass and then offer it to you. You are supposed to take it, then hold it out toward them so that they can fill it for you. You then drain it and give it back. This ends the ritual although, obviously, you should reciprocate at some point. In Chinese drinking parties there is a different twist. No one drinks without inviting someone else to drink, and since the initiator can't drink unless the invitee does so, no one ever declines. The initiator will get your attention by holding up his glass toward you and saying your name plus the Chinese expression, *wo jing ni* (which, loosely translated, means "I offer to you"). You raise your glass, and both parties drain their drinks, keeping their eyes on each other the whole time.

At times the heavy emphasis on alcohol may seem rather adolescent to some Westerners. The Asians can take their drinking rituals quite seriously, however, so try to be a good sport and go along with them. After all, you don't have to do this every night, and they are your hosts. If you absolutely don't or can't drink, have a good medical excuse handy and be sure to tell your hosts how much you would love to join them if only you could.

GROUP MEETINGS AND COURTESY CALLS

In general, Asians prefer to meet with small groups—not more than three or four visitors. Although many American trade missions want to give all mission delegates a chance to participate in all the meetings, to do so is counterproductive. It is far better to respect the business customs of the host country, especially since, as we've said, in Asia the party in the position of seller (as business, trade and investment missions usually are) is expected to make every effort to accommodate the buyer or potential investor.

If the visiting group is larger than a few people, the Asians may be ill at ease. Because they are very conscious of balance, they will very likely feel compelled to fill up their side of the table with a like number of people, but since the extras won't have any role to play, they are merely wasting their valuable time. Western logic would call for the simple solution of having fewer representatives on the Asian side, but this usually makes the Asians feel uncomfortable, partly because they are outnumbered and partly because they feel they have been made to look like bad hosts or caused you to lose face by assigning a small group to meet with your large one. This feeling is so strong that if a visiting foreign group adds extra participants at the last minute, the Asians may hurriedly send out for a couple of extra players to round out their side. Since this is a waste of resources and goodwill, give everyone a break and keep your group small and predictable.

Be sure to inform your hosts well in advance of the size of the group, the names, company affiliations and titles of each person in the group, and the precise objectives of the meeting. To say that your purpose is "mutually beneficial discussions" isn't very useful; instead, give them something specific. In the case of courtesy calls on organizations like chambers of commerce, it is perfectly acceptable to have the modest goal of making an initial contact to find out about the organization, meet its executives in person, and explain your business objectives.

If the Asian side requests that specific individuals from your group attend the meeting, honor the request if possible, but don't force additions or substitutions. If circumstances require that a member of your group cancel participation in a group meeting, try to contact your Asian host, apologize, and ask if they want to name a substitute. If they don't, then go with a smaller group than originally planned. If it is impossible to make contact in time, go to the meeting with a smaller group rather than make a unilateral substitution. The Asians want to be prepared for the meeting by studying the companies and individuals from your side in advance. If different people show up, they will feel unprepared, off balance and embarrassed. This will cause them to lose face, which will have a negative effect on your business.

Once again, the best policy is to emulate the Asians. Find out exactly who will be at meetings, dinners, receptions and other functions, and know their relative rank and status. Your local agent, the American Chamber of Commerce, or the Foreign Commercial Service or State Department officers and local staff can help you determine which titles are more important than others. This information is valuable not only for seating arrangements (in the case of a dinner) but also for deciding who gets any gifts that are presented.

Identification is especially important because several people on the Asian side may have the same name, and in the case of family-held companies, even a strong physical resemblance. Failure to do this simple, yet vital, bit of homework can lead to the sort of embarrassing situation created by the leader of one U.S. trade delegation who made an elaborate presentation of two gifts at a lavish reception put on by an Asian company—but mistakenly gave the presents to the brother and sister-in-law of the company president who hosted the event. Hardly a professional move.

You will normally meet either in an office or a conference room. If the meeting is in an office, the main figure from the host organization will usually sit in a head chair that presides over two couches or short rows of chairs that face each other. Your group should all sit on one side or the other, with your leader nearest the host's head chair. The seating arrangement in a conference room will be similar; your group should all sit on only one side, with the group leader closest to the host-country group leader and the remaining group members seated in descending order of importance.

This all sounds very undemocratic and antiegalitarian, which of course it is. Nonetheless, you are visitors in a hierarchical society with strong Confucian roots, and your hosts need to know the standing of each member of your group in relation to the others. Since the purpose of the mission is to promote business (and not to convert the natives to Western social values), the wisest course of action is to follow local custom.

In the same vein, foreign missions should decide beforehand who is going to be the group spokesperson for each meeting. In general, Asians feel more comfortable—and more receptive to business proposals—if they perceive a single channel for offering and receiving ideas related to the group's business. Situations in which various group members talk without any sort of order (especially if they interrupt fellow delegates to make observations or ask questions) strike them as disorganized and difficult to deal with. The tendency to have a single point of contact is so strong in Asian societies that even at personal events like weddings there is usually a moderator, complete with microphone, standing off to the side explaining what the priest and bridal couple are doing and saying.

The need for order and a single, identifiable main channel of communication is clearly a factor in the important role of the middleman in Asian business affairs. The middleman—who can often create a relationship that otherwise would be impossible—is also valuable because he allows the principals to save face. A rejection, suggestion or request made to a middleman may be totally acceptable while the same position communicated directly to a principal would be highly offensive. Although the American equivalent of the Asian middleman or go-between is often an attorney, the use of a legal agent (especially in potentially confrontational situations like negotiations and trade disputes) can be detrimental to your business interests in Asia. While "my attorney made me do it" might be accepted by U.S. businesspeople, many Asians bristle inwardly when positions are ascribed to legal advice or when they are contacted by a lawyer. Again, emulate Asian practice and find a go-between of your own from, perhaps, a local chamber of commerce, AmCham, or a U.S. government agency like the Foreign Commercial Service.

As in other situations, it is important at a meeting to identify yourself and your title with a business card, in both English and the local language. Because the numbers of people involved in trade, business and investment missions make it more difficult for host-country contacts to know who's who among the mission members, these groups should be armed with more than just business cards. A mission brochure in the local language giving the company or governmental affiliation and title of each member is a must; the brochure becomes at least twice as effective if it includes a recognizable photograph of each mission member to go with each description. (Not that all foreigners look alike, but. . . .)

To be effective, the brochures should be delivered or mailed to each host-country organization so that they have them in hand with at least two weeks' lead time. In addition, one mission member (not the leader) should bring a supply to the meeting. Ideally, there should be one for each host-country participant; if there are not enough to go around, it is imperative to give one to the leader of the host-country group. There is no hard-and-fast protocol, but it is probably best to give out the brochure before starting the meeting, right after exchanging business cards and pleasantries. This will allow your hosts to be absolutely sure of whom they are dealing with.

GIFT GIVING

At courtesy calls, dinners or similar meetings for the purpose of cementing relationships, a small gift is appropriate. The value may vary, but in general the range should be from about US$10 or $15 for routine courtesy calls to $50 or $80 for gifts at a corporate dinner. As the dollar fluctuates against many foreign currencies, the dollar value of gifts in each Asian country will change. Pick the gift not only in terms of what it would cost in the United States but also with an eye to its value in the country in question. It is important not to give something too expensive; if your gift is significantly more costly than the one given by the Asian side, they will lose face. In the lower ranges, appropriate gifts include tie pins, ties, desk paperweights in the form of state or company seals, small artwork or photo books, and similar items.

At courtesy calls, give the top-ranking Asian participant a slightly better gift than the other two or three Asian executive participants present (there won't usually be more), who should get equal gifts of slightly lesser value. Technical advisers and translators/interpreters normally do not receive anything when participating in a single meeting, but when there are long negotiations or repeated meetings at which they have done a lot of good work, a gift of slightly lesser value than those given the executives is a thoughtful and appropriate gesture. Make it a point to know beforehand exactly who will be at a meeting, and to be safe, bring an extra gift or two in case there are unexpected participants.

Asians appreciate a sense of form and formalism, so when presenting a gift, don't hesitate to be slightly ceremonial. If possible, have the junior member of your party act as custodian of the gifts and hand them to the leader/spokesperson at the appropriate time. To hierarchy- and form-conscious Asians, a smooth presentation is highly preferable to watching as the group leader rummages through a briefcase searching for the gifts in order to make the presentation. In keeping with formalism, don't toss the gift on the table or casually thrust it in the general direction of the intended recipient; instead, face the person and present it with both hands. If circumstances make it more natural to remain seated, then do so. The idea is not to follow a rigid formula but to communicate a sense of sincerity, respect and interest that is often hard for Asians to perceive in a typically casual American style of interaction.

If you intend to give a gift (or written invitation), don't just talk about it, do it. Most Asians do not appreciate it when a mission leader leaves them with a promise to bring a gift tomorrow, or send a personal invitation next week, next month or next year. To do so gives them the impression—usually correct—that the mission was ill prepared and is extemporizing. The easiest way to avoid squandering goodwill is to devote sufficient thought and planning to the matter before you leave the U.S. The next best thing is to do what the Asians would do if they were caught short: before you leave town, and preferably before a full day passes, take the trouble to have the appropriate item prepared and delivered to your Asian contact.

SEMINARS

Foreign business groups putting on trade and investment (or other) seminars should observe the same standards as those that apply to meetings. There should be one obvious leader who serves as the spokesperson for the group. In most cases, it is also advantageous to have a moderator, preferably one who is fluent in the local language.

One of the most common errors made by visiting missions and delegations is to violate the Asians' sense of order and organization by making a haphazard introduction of mission members at seminars and receptions. Asians are nonplussed when members scattered throughout the room are introduced, particularly since some merely nod or give a wave of the hand without standing up, and others may not even be present when their names are called.

All mission delegates present, regardless of whether or not they take part in the seminar presentation, should be at the front of the room prior to the start of the presentation. Those who are not active participants can sit at the side and front (or stand if they plan to leave or move to the back of the room for the presentation). Before starting the seminar, the group leader should introduce each mission member, stating name, company or organizational affiliation, and perhaps one sentence about the individual's purpose. If there are two or more representatives from the same company or organization, they should be located next to each other and introduced in descending order of rank. Each member should fully rise to be introduced and remain standing for at least a second or two. A slight bow (similar to that made by many Western musicians or stage performers at the end of a show or number) is in order, especially in Japan.

In many Asian functions, speakers sit in a row to the front and side of the hall and go one by one to the podium to make their remarks. In Japan it is customary for each speaker to rise, give a slight bow to the other participants with whom he is seated, go to the podium, and bow to the audience before making his remarks. After concluding the speech, the procedure is reversed: the speaker bows to the audience, returns to the speakers' seating area, bows slightly to the other speakers, and sits down. The same actions and sequence apply when getting up from a head table, speakers' table, or other table to take the podium at a luncheon or dinner. As with many other ritualistic actions, the Japanese observe this procedure most closely, the Koreans to a lesser extent, and the Chinese least, if at all. As noted elsewhere, in Japan, Korea and Taiwan it is considered polite to acknowledge applause with a bow while in mainland China the accepted practice is to applaud back.

Many Americans pass all the social events with flying colors but lose their audience in a seminar. This failing is doubly unfortunate because you can avoid it so easily by simply remembering that your goal is communication and that the Asian context creates several obstacles to communication that must be overcome. One of these obstacles is language. Your Asian audience may not have perfect command of the English language—in fact, they almost certainly will not. Perhaps more importantly, they do not have the same thought patterns as Americans. Their logical processes are often different, they tend much more toward rote memory, and they are not accustomed to American humor. Even if they do understand every word and every sentence, they may not understand what you are trying to communicate if you try to impose your ideas in an overly American context.

You can increase your chances of success by making things easy for your audience. For openers, resist the American compulsion to begin a speech or presentation with a joke. Partly because this type of opening is not common in Asia and partly because of the language barrier, your audience may well think that the joke is not a joke but that it is somehow supposed to be an integral part of your presentation. If they do understand that it is a joke, they may be distracted or irritated because to them a joke is inappropriate in this context. Pay special attention to language. Use simple vocabulary (not "Dick and Jane," but avoid elegant variation, idioms, sports jargon, slang and rare or unusual words), well-structured sentences, and a measured delivery. If you are using an interpreter, be sure that he or she has had at least several hours (and preferably several days) to become familiar with the material. To ensure a smooth and complete translation, remember to pause after every sentence or two to avoid overloading the interpreter. The best way to ensure a coordinated presentation is for the speaker and the interpreter to have identical copies of the presentation or speech with hash marks indicating pauses.

Help your audience by using slides or printed material as much as possible. Since any meeting place will have some sort of large clipboard and stand available, it is easy to bring (or mail in advance) flip-chart sheets rolled up in a tube. Materials should be in both English and the local language and should cover, in outline form, all the main points to be included in the presentation. As a backup, have the same points (if not the entire text of the presentation) available in printed or photocopied handout sheets, so that the audience can follow your discussion. These materials may be in English; if they are numbered to correspond to the outline on the flip chart, your audience can follow easily. Of course, the ideal is to have all materials available in the local language. If you are giving each local attendee a copy of the entire text, one easy compromise is to leave the text in English but print the main points, in the form of numbered section titles, in both English and the local language. This makes what you are talking about crystal clear and keeps costs down. Whatever you do, be sure to have an accurate and linguistically acceptable translation. Many business and trade groups have suffered severe loss of face by handing out speeches, brochures and other literature translated by native speakers (including college professors) who lacked technical or business knowledge and vocabulary or who had been out of their native country for so long that their rendition of the material sounded like a slightly addled comic trying to revive the idiom of the Roaring Twenties. To avoid this, have the translation checked by at least one additional expert who has no connection with the translator. Host-country natives will often hesitate to tell you if the translation is substandard, so try to get another professional source.

Many Asian audiences are hesitant to participate in question-

and-answer sessions. There are a number of reasons for this, including an educational system that concentrates on rote memorization at the expense of questioning or an exchange of ideas. Since their reticence is increased by the language barrier, it is doubly important to have an interpreter or other qualified native speaker to field questions in the host-country language. As with many other things in Asia, patience is your best ally. Don't be afraid of a little silence before the first question. Use the time to mentally review your presentation and identify points that may need clarification. If need be, you can then use these points to elicit questions from the floor.

RECEPTIONS

Many of the same criteria that apply to seminars should be observed at receptions as well. If possible, have a native speaker serve as a moderator. His or her role is to announce what is happening, to introduce one of the principals (who in turn will introduce others), and to interpret. At the start of the reception, it is considerate to introduce all the U.S. mission or company members present. They, and anyone else to be introduced, should be together at the head of the room, not scattered about among the guests. The reception is not a purely social function and the host group is expected to show a sense of organization.

In most cases, the host-country guests will not eat until the spokesperson for the hosts has given a few words of welcome and instructed them to eat and enjoy themselves. It is customary to have a "bottoms up" toast to get the ball rolling after the welcoming remarks. Your host-country contacts will be pleased if you give the final words of the toast, literally meaning "dry cup"—in Japanese (kampai), Chinese (ganbei) or Korean (konbeh).

Mission leaders should have interpreters and a local contact who knows which attendees are main players in the local business community. The leaders should approach all of these key people during the evening, thank them for coming, and exchange a few words. All too often, U.S. mission members congregate among themselves when they should be out working the room like politicians the night before an election. It is helpful to brief your mission members on the need for extensive interaction and to work out a game plan for the reception. You may want to go over the guest list with your local contact and assign specific invitees to each mission member. You are neither required nor expected to engage guests in lengthy conversations. The idea is to thank them for coming, find out a little about their business and let them know that you are ready, willing and able to assist them. As in all other situations, have an ample supply of business cards ready. To get the best results, be somewhat less hearty and energetic than you might normally be in a similar situation at home. Asians often don't mix well with strangers, especially foreigners, so don't rush up to your targets with an outstretched hand or "double team" them—it will probably make them nervous.

End the event promptly at the scheduled time. A couple of minutes before the end of the function, the mission leader should take the floor again to thank everyone for attending. (This also lets them know it is time to go.) It is customary to have a bag or folder with brochures and perhaps a small souvenir prepared for each departing guest. These should be presented just outside the door; several locally-hired assistants should be on hand to give them to the attendees.

LEARNING THE HOST-COUNTRY LANGUAGE

You can enhance both your Asian business dealings and your after-hours activities by learning something of the language in the countries where you are the most active. This doesn't mean that you need to become fluent or spend a lot of time, energy and money taking classes. By following a well-designed self-study program and making good use of your spare time, you can easily (yes, easily) learn enough to accomplish the following:

1. Let your hosts and business contacts (be they Japanese, Chinese or Korean) see that you respect them enough to make

an effort to meet them part way. This will in turn earn a lot of respect and goodwill for you.

2. Smooth your initial contacts by breaking the ice.

3. Give you a feeling for what is being discussed and which way the discussion is going. This gives you valuable time to think even before your interpreter explains what has been said. Eventually, you may even evolve to the point where you can tell whether or not the interpreter is giving an accurate account.

4. Enable you to participate far more fully in the after-hours events that are so important to doing business in Asia.

5. Make all aspects of your Asian business travel more enjoyable and productive by letting you use the local language to get things done.

Although some people believe that it's smart or crafty to hide their knowledge of the host-country language in the hope that they will pick up careless remarks by their unsuspecting hosts, this tactic has a very low ratio of return and forces the user to forego the benefits derived from acquisition and open use of the language.

One of the great advantages of learning at least a little of the major East Asian languages (Chinese, Korean, Japanese) is that much of the knowledge gained in one is transferable to the others. This is perhaps especially true of Korean and Japanese, which until a few hundred years ago were essentially variants of the same language. In addition, both of these languages draw a high percentage of vocabulary (and some important sentence patterns as well) directly from Chinese, which means that most of the key words for business and trade are identical in all three languages, the only difference being pronunciation. For some words, the pronunciation differs significantly, but in many cases it is very close or even identical.

Reading will involve a more sustained effort, but it is nothing like the horrendous obstacle it is often made out to be. In the first place, both Japanese and Korean have their own alphabets, which can be learned in a few days. The Korean alphabet (*hangul*), which is the simplest, has about the same number of letters as English and is so sensibly developed that it can be learned fairly well during the course of a couple of rainy weekends and a transpacific flight. The Japanese alphabet (*kana*), consisting of forty-eight syllables in two forms (*katakana* and *hiragana*) that differ much as capital and lower-case letters differ in English, takes a bit longer but offers no complications.

Chinese characters, if approached in a logical way, are only slightly more time-consuming. All Chinese characters are made using some two hundred basic components, most of which are characters in their own right, each with its own meaning. Fewer than one hundred of these components are very common, and these basic "building blocks" of the written language can be mastered in a matter of months. This mastery enables business travelers to identify documents, offices and places of business and eventually to get a good start on learning the compound characters most commonly used in business and other relevant contexts.

Even if you learn enough of a foreign language to express yourself, you will always have occasion to use English in situations involving foreign contacts. You can make these situations more productive by speaking slowly, enunciating clearly and using a fairly basic vocabulary. Make an effort to observe and remember what English words are commonly used in the host country; by using these words wherever appropriate, you will communicate more meaning and put your foreign associates at ease. This same effort will also lighten the burden of learning the local language since you can insert English loan words (pronounced with a local accent) when you try to speak the local language. This approach will get you the farthest in Japan because the Japanese have borrowed more English words than either the Koreans, who rank second, or the Chinese, who have the fewest English-language borrowings.

SMALL TALK

A big part of doing business in Asia is socializing after hours. There are many settings, ranging from a Japanese or Korean businessman's favorite watering hole to the cavernous banquet halls encountered in China. In all these situations, you will need to talk about something besides business with your hosts. Since Asians place a great deal more value on the human, personal side of business than do Western businesspeople, the impression you make in after-hours get-togethers can do much to help or hurt your business over the long haul. Since most Americans still know far too little about the social, linguistic and historical context of the Asian countries in which they are trying to do business, you can give your hosts a pleasant surprise by showing even the most elementary knowledge. In addition, you can gain an extra edge and add a little more life to the relationship by knowing something of the interesting and revealing lore that is part of every Asian's store of common knowledge. The measurement of time, for example, gives some unexpected insights into Asian thinking.

TIME AND THE ASIAN WORLD

In much of East Asia, the Western calendar and Western notions of time have imposed themselves upon local cultures. But as in so many other facets of East-West relations, the Western element is merely a convenient overlay, beneath which ancient traditions still hold sway. The traditional Asian calendar is based not on the position of the sun but on the movements and phases of the moon. As a result, the month and day of annual events (including birthdays, many official holidays and the Lunar New Year) change from year to year with variations in the lunar calendar. Since institutions like schools and official records now follow the Western calendar, one often encounters interesting (and sometimes perplexing) situations in which a person's birthday falls on a different date each year, or a business trip undertaken at exactly the same time as the preceding year suddenly coincides with a national holiday.

In addition, in some parts of East Asia (most noticeably Japan), the base year for determining the date is not a single fixed event but the date of accession of the most recent regime. In Japan the death of each emperor quite literally marks the end of an era, and as soon as a suitable name is chosen for the new emperor's reign, all documents (including receipts, calendars and government forms) begin marking the new era with the year one and the new name. In Taiwan, the starting date for the present era (*Minguo,* or "Republic") is the Chinese revolution of 1911 under the ideological guidance of Dr. Sun Yatsen (who, it should be noted in passing, is equally revered on Taiwan and on the mainland).

For Westerners, mentally converting such Japanese dates as *Shoowa* 15 (1941) or *Heisei* 2 (1990) or instantly recognizing that in Taiwan the year *Minguo* 89 will be the year 2000 is a confusing chore, but the Asians who use such systems keep the dual count with no apparent effort, just as they juggle solar and lunar dates or plan their business around a bewildering array of fixed and movable holidays.

The Asian tradition of counting years by dynasties or emperors, restarting the count with each new ruling family, may account for the rather high degree of attention paid to the Asian zodiac among even educated people. The zodiac, which continues in its perpetual round regardless of political system, is Asia's only stable, non-Western method of counting years.

The Asian zodiac is a thread that runs throughout the complex cultural fabric of East Asia. It is calculated on an annual, rather than a monthly, basis, and the symbols (with one exception) are not taken from mythology as in the Western world but are humble inhabitants of the Asian world. Within the repeating twelve-year cycle, each year is represented by a different animal, each of which supposedly heeded Buddha's call centuries ago.

In order, they are: Rat (1936, -48, -60, -72); Ox or Bull (1937, -49, -61, -73); Tiger (1938, -50, -62, -74); Rabbit (1939, -51, -63, -75); Dragon (1940, -52, -64, -76); Snake (1941, -53, -65, -77); Horse (1942, -54, -66, -78); Sheep or Ram (1943, -55, -67, -79); Monkey (1944, -56, -68, -80); Rooster (1945, -57, -69, -81); Dog (1946, -58, -70, -82); Boar (1947, -59, -71, -83).

(The numbers in parentheses indicate birth years falling in each animal's sign; to go beyond the range of the years given above, simply subtract or add by twelves until you reach the desired date. For example, 1990 is the Year of the Horse, followed by Sheep (1991), Monkey (1992), Rooster (1993) and so on.)

The presence of the dragon amidst such lowly creatures as the rat, the rabbit and the snake suggests another aspect of Asian culture: the acceptance of the marvelous in the context of the normal and the constant presence of symbolic elements in otherwise pragmatic and utilitarian contexts. Unlike Westerners, who tend to feel more comfortable when things are black or white, right or wrong, real or fanciful, Asians are completely at ease with the ambiguity of seemingly incongruous components functioning in harmonious coexistence. This attitude applies to business dealings as well.

Because of Western influence, there are different ways of determining your Asian zodiac year. Originally, all of Asia followed the lunar calendar, and the zodiac year changed on the Lunar ("Chinese") New Year. Many people in Asia still follow this custom, and some still figure their birthdays on the lunar calendar, which means that by the Western calendar, these birthdays fall on a different date each year (just like the Christian Easter, which is also a lunar-based event).

Another interesting fact about birthdays is that many Asians consider a child to have gained a year on New Year's Day (either Western or lunar). This means that a child born on December 31 is one year old on the following day although by Western calculations it is only one day old. As if this weren't enough, many Asians consider prenatal time to be one year (a good example of the Asian tendency to dispense with strict fact and rigorous logic to make reality easier to deal with) and add it to the age. This means that our December 31 baby is one year old at birth and attains the age of two on the following day!

CHAPTER THREE

Conducting Business

TRADE SHOWS

There are several ways to participate in trade shows in Asia. Shows are organized by the U.S. Department of Commerce (USDOC), by U.S. trade centers and U.S. embassy and consulate commercial sections, by host-country agencies (both public and private), and by international trade show organizers. American companies considering participation in a show should get as much information as possible—and a candid opinion on the value of participation—from U.S. trade and commercial officials in the host country and from any U.S. companies that may have exhibited in previous shows. American industry associations and USDOC officials in Washington are less reliable sources of assessment since their job performance is judged partly on a purely quantitative measure of activity (including the number of events that they helped promote), with effectiveness often taking a back seat to numbers. Even when they want to give you an accurate assessment, they may be handicapped by overly optimistic information received from Foreign Commercial Service (FCS) officers in the field, who are also rated partly on volume and who would like to attract you to their next show.

Whether you are exhibiting in a show in Asia or hoping to attract Asian buyers to a show in the U.S., there are several important points to keep in mind. The majority of Asian buyers have no complaints about the quality of much American merchandise (although many Japanese chide U.S. manufacturers for not designing products to suit the Japanese market), and even when the dollar is relatively high, they are willing to pay more than they would for more cheaply made products. Still, when you are exhibiting overseas, it is essential to have an export catalogue showing export prices only. No domestic prices should be in evidence since the presence of a dual pricing structure creates a negative impression (irrational though it may be) even on many experienced international buyers who are fully aware of the extra costs involved in filling export orders. At any show where Asian buyers are expected, all catalogues should include the appropriate Asian languages, including the language of the country where the show is held. It is at best unprofessional to use, say, Chinese brochures in Japan; and because of historical relations and present-day issues between Japan and Korea, it is downright offensive to use only Japanese-language brochures in Korea (and vice versa). If both languages are used, there is no problem.

Asian buyers consistently voice a number of complaints about American exhibitors in shows in the U.S. In keeping with the Asian view that the seller is obliged to make an extra effort, the biggest complaint is that the American representatives in their booths in U.S. shows are not eager to sell, and especially not eager to sell to Asians because of the extra effort involved. Many Asians also complain about the lack of international awareness—ranging from no foreign-language skills to ignorance of the location of major Asian countries like Japan and China—shown by U.S. exhibitors. Other common complaints include a lack of authority to negotiate, insufficient knowledge of the product, and insufficient product literature (apart from promotional fluff with no technical content).

Amazingly, many of these same complaints surface when U.S. companies exhibit in Asia. American firms that have spent thousands of dollars on travel and shipping expenses, staff time and participation fees fail to take basic, low-cost steps to ensure their success.

The first common-sense rule of participation in foreign trade shows—one that is broken far too often—is to have a responsible U.S. company employee, with full power to negotiate, at the booth at all times. No matter how much they like the product, few Asian buyers will come back to a booth if they find it empty or staffed by an unqualified person the first time around. It is equally important for the company representatives present to maintain what could best be described as a respectful attitude toward potential buyers. Asians are quickly turned off by the sight—common in American sales situations—of a bored-looking sales rep lounging in a chair and drinking coffee or leaning against the wall, talking to another foreign exhibitor. The extra effort it takes to look alert and be on your feet the whole time pays off in the end. Don't swarm all over visitors, but do give some indication that you are aware of their presence. Since Asians are always pleased and surprised to be greeted in their own language by foreigners, learn how to say at least a few words, even if only "welcome" and "thank you."

The booth, and everyone staffing it, should have an ample supply of business cards and brochures in the local language. If circumstances (which, if looked at honestly, usually boil down to a lack of preparation or commitment) have precluded translation of entire brochures, there should be copies of a sheet with highlights and key items described in the local language. This elementary courtesy can do wonders for sales in Asia.

Asian business is often slow to develop, and trade show business is no exception. Since it is expensive to fly to Asia, plan on staying at least a couple of days after the show to follow up on contacts you have made. Even if there is interest, however, it is unwise to expect immediate sales, especially for new-to-market companies selling expensive items. Asians want to be sure that you are in the market to stay, so you should commit yourself to participating in a show for at least three successive years, the time many non-Asian companies report that it takes to generate significant orders. This commitment should be coupled with continuous follow-up with companies contacted at previous shows. All these firms should not only be invited to each show, but they should also be contacted by your company during each visit.

This kind of patient persistence and attention to personal contact can yield big dividends by showing the Asians that you are willing to do business their way. One U.S. industrial supplier learned this by sending its Asian marketing manager to three successive shows even though not one penny in sales resulted. The company was uneasy, of course, so much so that the vice president for marketing went with the Asia representative for the third show to find out what he was doing wrong. His performance was a flawless demonstration of salesmanship, so he was given one more year to produce. Failure would mean withdrawal from the Asian market.

When the fourth show closed, not one order had been placed. The marketing manager had to conceal his disappointment as he paid calls on the prospects he had developed at earlier shows. Calls in the capital city where the show was held yielded nothing more than polite expressions of interest, but he persisted and traveled as planned to a major industrial center several hours away to meet with his last prospects. This effort paid off. On one of these final calls he garnered an order for several hundred thousand dollars worth of products. This order not only led to follow-up orders but also created a presence in the market that helped land new customers. Clearly, not every case will be as dramatic as this one, but it shows how important persistence and personal contact can be.

DEALING WITH THE ASIAN BUREAUCRACY

In Asia, with its hierarchical and authoritarian value system, the citizens, including businesses, are supposed to be responsive to the government rather than the government being responsive to the citizens as in the U.S. and most other Western countries. Because of this attitude, governmental authority is regarded as a given, and the procedures and regulations of the bureaucracy, which are created by the government for its own use, are not transparent and are subject to change whenever it suits the government's purposes. This philosophy and practice is a constant and frustrating problem for Western companies operating in Asia. Activities are permitted or restricted, licenses issued or denied, and regulations interpreted and applied in what often seems to be a highly arbitrary manner. Explanations, when forthcoming, are often vague and based on "internal guidelines" that are not available to the businesses affected by them. The host-country bureaucracy may tell a company that there are no rules yet cite unidentified regulations to justify a negative decision. In such situations, it is very difficult to determine whether or not there actually is some sort of internal instruction or guideline or whether the bureaucrats or functionaries involved are avoiding action because there is no precedent for them to follow.

In this type of situation, avoid confrontation. Instead, call on as many different host-country officials as possible to try to find one who will help your project or proposal move forward. At each stop, ask who else might be involved. If you have a local agent or partner, get what information you can from him, but do not regard him as the sole source of truth. Always do your own investigating. The American Chamber of Commerce and the U.S. embassy or consulate can provide valuable information and advice; contact them early on. If you become convinced that you won't get anywhere on your own, enlist the help of the embassy (consulate) commercial section. If your proposed business has enough potential, you may be able to get a commercial officer to accompany you on your first visit to host-country officials to break the ice and show them that the U.S. government sees merit in your plans. Often a verbal representation on your behalf can be a tremendous boost for your case; if such a representation produces no results, the U.S. embassy or consulate may send a written note. You should be aware, though, that written notes are used very sparingly because under the rules of diplomacy they require a response from the host-country government agency involved. Embassy and consulate officials hesitate to make this kind of demand unless all other possibilities have been exhausted and unless the issue is of considerable significance.

If an official note from the embassy gets you nowhere, you may want to reconsider your plans. In consultation with embassy officials, your host-country agent or partner, and other host-country contacts (including government officials), try to identify modifications that might make your proposal more acceptable to the host-country government. If you believe that your proposal will be turned down, it is often advisable to withdraw your application before it is rejected, make the modifications, and resubmit the amended application. Once a proposal has been rejected, it can be extremely difficult to get a favorable ruling in spite of modifications. For this reason, pay close attention to unexplained delays in processing, for they can be a warning that your proposal will not be approved and that the bureaucracy is giving you a chance to withdraw, modify, and resubmit.

Within each Asian bureaucracy there are different constituencies and interests that, depending on the situation, are anxious to either keep foreign businesses out or to allow them in. Since in most situations Asian governments allow virtually all ministries and similar high-level agencies to take a shot at foreign proposals, a foreign business can end up running quite a gauntlet. It is usually quite difficult to find out which government agencies had a say in the final decision and what their inputs were; but one case from Taiwan—when the Ministry of Economic Affairs invited representatives from various ministries and departments to comment on possible restrictions on foreign investment—revealed how various ministries were allowed to rule on the exclusion of foreign investors in different industrial sectors:

Interior Ministry and Council for Agricultural Development: agriculture, forestry, fisheries, animal husbandry, salt mining.

Communications Ministry: life insurance, postal services, telecommunications, transportation services.

Finance Ministry: banking, finance and trust companies, cooperatives, short-term bill exchange business.

Government Information Office: broadcasting, motion picture industry (including enforcing restrictions that keep Japan and communist countries out of this industry).

Defense Ministry: weapons, chemical warfare.

National Health Administration: certain chemical products.

Industrial Development Bureau: energy-consuming products, products with environmental consequences, products on which the investor's home country has import quotas.

It is worth noting that the original intent of the Ministry of Economic Affairs, which precipitated this particular discussion, was to consider just four sectors: agriculture, forestry, fisheries and animal husbandry. The ease with which widely divergent products were added to the discussion by various agencies is a good example of how quickly Asian governments can generate trade protection and how foreign businesses can face unforeseen challenges from almost any quarter.

RESOURCES AND MULTIPLIERS

Many American businesspeople argue that doing business in Asia is intrinsically more difficult than in other parts of the world, certainly more so than in Canada or Western Europe. Luckily, there are several inexpensive and effective sources of assistance.

In noncommunist Asia, industry associations have a tremendous amount of influence on government policy. For example, in many product and service sectors, host-country industry associations determine—through official and unofficial channels— whether or not foreign companies can participate in trade shows, import certain products, or invest in a given sector. Although many Americans take a confrontational approach to these associations because they view them as intrinsically hostile, there is nothing to be lost by contacting them to learn their position and consider ways to enter the Asian market without arousing their opposition. The same holds true for specific projects in which host-country industry associations or lobbies have an important voice.

A good example of how this approach works—and how American companies and the U.S. bureaucracy fail to use it—is the Kansai International Airport, a multibillion dollar project in Osaka, Japan. Spurred on by the ill-considered advice of ambitious U.S. consular officials on the spot, the U.S. government took a head-on, confrontational approach and badgered the Japanese agency in charge of the project with demands for in-depth participation by American companies. Meanwhile, Korean contractors, who had followed the Asian custom of quietly making personal contacts and creating a cooperative atmosphere, were able to get into the action while the Americans still blustered in Washington and in the press. The same contrast between effective Asian technique and the all-too-common American approach is also evident in Korea, where the Japanese—still resented both as past colonialists and as richer and more powerful competitors—do more business through the careful building of low-profile relations than the U.S. is able to generate through pressure.

A careful investigation of industry associations often reveals natural allies whose support can be enlisted to overcome objections by associations with different or competing interests. For example, although host-country manufacturers of weaving machines might be opposed to the import of rival machines, the spinners and weavers association is likely to favor opening the market to any product that will help them be more competitive in textile production.

The same approach is also valuable when dealing with host-country government agencies and ministries. In many cases where one or more ministries are opposed to a foreign company's proposal, there are others whose interests are furthered by the same proposal. If, for example, a trade and industry ministry opposes an investment project because it competes with a host-country industry, an economic planning ministry may support it because it will contribute to the economic development of a given region or the country as a whole. For the same reason, regional political and economic interests should also be taken into consideration and officials representing those interests sounded out. To many U.S. companies, this sort of groundwork is almost second nature at home, but for some reason they fail to do—or even consider—it when trying to do business in Asia, even though it often works equally well in both settings.

In the host-country private sector, import and export associations can provide valuable support and advice to foreign companies whose plans further the business interests of their members. Likewise, host-country chambers of commerce are often among the most helpful organizations to foreign missions and individual companies since in their broad membership base there is bound to be a significant number of companies that can benefit from trading or entering into joint ventures with foreign firms.

U.S. RESOURCES

The American Chamber of Commerce

One of the best sources of practical information can be the local chapter of the American Chamber of Commerce. AmCham members, who experience on a daily basis the business realities that new-to-market companies want to learn about, know that combined, private-sector efforts are essential in promoting the cause of foreign business in Asia.

Although AmCham and its members can provide useful information on starting business activity in a given country, their long suit is usually the day-to-day problems and issues facing foreign businesses already in operation in the country. In addition to valuable data contained in AmCham monthly bulletins, each AmCham chapter produces detailed reports and position papers that contain a wealth of information on the operating problems of specific industries. If you are planning on doing business in a country, a good first step is to take out a nonresident membership so that you can receive the AmCham bulletin, and then to make contact with the executive director and appropriate committee chairs to find out about existing or planned reports on topics of special interest to your business.

AmCham branches compile and distribute a great deal of information, but for some types of information (including macroeconomic reports, trade and investment opportunities, lists of potential agents, distributors and partners, and laws and regulations), U.S. companies should use U.S. government sources.

Foreign Commercial Service

From the 1930s until 1980, the U.S. Department of State was responsible for most overseas trade and business facilitation for U.S. firms and individuals. During that period the U.S. Department of Commerce was essentially limited to running U.S. trade centers for the display of American products. This arrangement, which worked very well during the Second World War and the subsequent era of American international preeminence, began to show signs of weakness as the U.S. encountered increasingly stiff business and trade competition from a resurgent Europe and a postwar Japan that had retooled for the production and export of consumer goods. The State Department officers at U.S. embassies and consulates were competent, but their mission—to focus on political issues and macroeconomic trends—was only marginally compatible with the increasing need to provide close support for U.S. exporters and multinationals abroad.

As a result, in 1980 the Foreign Commercial Service was formed. An arm of the Commerce Department, the FCS was charged with providing active assistance to all types of U.S. business activity overseas. To accomplish this goal, FCS began to place commercial officers in U.S. embassies and consulates in virtually every country with significant U.S. business or trade activity. Knowledgeable in international trade matters and supported by locally recruited commercial specialists, these officers (now numbering about 170) work with country specialists in Washington, D.C., and with USDOC district offices throughout the U.S. in a comprehensive, international consulting service network.

What sort of services does FCS provide? The following list will give you a general idea.

Trade Promotion

U.S. trade centers (also called "export development offices" or "EDOs" in USDOC jargon) have been incorporated into FCS. They put on U.S. product exhibitions and, in conjunction with overseas FCS offices and USDOC in Washington, promote U.S. pavilions at major trade shows in their respective countries. They also provide support (appointments, translators and interpreters, publicity) for U.S. trade and investment missions (although in the case of Tokyo, the EDO is located far from the main business center of town, so the FCS office in the embassy normally handles this function). Other EDOs or trade centers are located in Seoul, Tokyo, Hong Kong, Singapore and Taipei. (Be aware that in Taipei the U.S. Trade Center is not well known and that unless you point it out on a map, taxi drivers will tend to take you to the mammoth Taipei World Trade Center, several miles away).

In the late 1980s USDOC reduced fiscal support for trade center activity and there is some doubt about the long-term survival of many trade centers. Their elimination would be a loss to American exporters because they provide valuable market presence to many small and medium-sized U.S. companies that would have considerable difficulty establishing themselves in foreign markets without trade center services.

Here are some cases in which you may wish to use the services of a trade center or EDO (note that in all these cases, your request may be handled by FCS as circumstances dictate):

1. You have a local distributor, and you want greater exposure in the market. For a fee, EDO may provide a site and assistance in putting on a solo product exhibition or a technical seminar.
2. You want to participate in a local (overseas) trade show. EDO can help you get information on the show and assist with logistic support and business appointments.
3. You are part of a trade mission to East Asia. For a fee, EDO can provide a venue for seminars and meetings, arrange appointments, contract for translation and printing of brochures, hire interpreters, and handle publicity and catering.
4. You are part of an inward investment ("reverse investment") mission to East Asia. EDO can provide the same services as for trade missions.

In many cases, FCS (working out of the U.S. embassy or U.S. consulate in the Asian city) will provide (for a fee) some or all of the above services in cooperation with the EDO. In addition, local chambers of commerce and other business groups may handle some or most of the arrangements, depending on the country and city and the type of function.

Business Contacts

The Foreign Commercial Service has a number of services to help you make Asian business contacts. To obtain these and other services, contact the nearest USDOC district office well in advance of your trip. In some cases it is advisable to also make direct contact with the FCS or EDO in each foreign city you plan to visit, both to confirm your plans and objectives and to verify that they have been properly notified by the district office in the U.S. The Foreign Commercial Service can help you with the following business contacts:

1. You want to find an agent or distributor for your products. Before going overseas, it is worth your while to pay the price (currently $125) for using USDOC's Agent Distributor Service (ADS). This service, which you get through the nearest stateside USDOC district office, puts the FCS to work for you on-site to identify interested potential agents or distributors.

2. You want to find a joint-venture partner. The Agent Distributor Service can also be used for this purpose.

3. You need a background check (financial strength, credit history, general business reputation) on a foreign company. USDOC offers another service called World Traders' Data Report (WTDR), currently priced at $100. The quality of these reports is often quite high. In some countries where there is adequate, reliable private sector expertise, USDOC has abandoned this activity and will recommend private credit reference and research firms instead.

4. You are going to Asia and want to meet with potential agents or distributors. The FCS office or EDO where you are going can set up appointments and provide an interpreter for a fee. This service is sometimes referred to as "Repfind." Allow plenty of lead time (at least four to six weeks between your

initial contact and your arrival in the country), and be prepared to send the FCS office or EDO a half-dozen or more brochures and other information on your company and your objectives in the target market.

5. You are going to East Asia and want to meet with potential joint-venture partners. The FCS or EDO will provide the same service outlined immediately above.

Business and Trade Problems

The FCS (backed, if necessary, by the ambassador) is able to help solve a wide range of business and trade problems, including market access, intellectual property rights infringements, changes in host-country investment regulations, and others. Avoid the common mistake of trying to contact the ambassador first, which actually takes longer to get results. His or her office will routinely refer your case to the commercial section of the embassy and he or she will probably not be informed of your request for assistance, even if it concerns important business. An approach to the top also starts you off on the wrong foot with the embassy staff by marking you as a greenhorn who doesn't understand the system. Even though it may seem cumbersome to work a problem up through successive levels of the embassy or consulate, there is a good reason for doing so: the U.S. Embassy quickly loses credibility if the top people go to the host-country government on every single issue; therefore, the ambassador is used only as a last resort in high-priority cases. Try to resolve each problem at the lowest possible level. In most cases, this will yield results without bucking the matter to higher-ups.

USING U.S. GOVERNMENT RESOURCES EFFECTIVELY

Going to the top can also be a mistake when dealing with any U.S. government office (whether in the U.S. or overseas). Because of the way the government bureaucracy works, people at or near the top of their sections are often far better at in-house politics than at practical business matters. One longtime Asia office head in Washington, for example, speaks no Asian language, has no significant academic background on Asia, and has never worked or done business there—but has done a good job of playing the bureaucracy to get and hang on to the top slot in the section. The same is often true at embassies as well. To get the highest level of effective support, you are often better off with younger, lower-level staffers, who are more likely to know the language and the thought processes of local businessmen (rather than host-country diplomats and politicians) and who are more inclined to take an interest in everyday business problems.

Another reason to make contacts at lower levels in the government is that many higher-level officials are looking for high visibility and/or the possibility of an offer of employment in the private sector. Unless you are well placed in a large company, they may not be interested in talking to you because the types of problems you need help with won't advance their own agenda to any significant degree. At lower levels, you will usually find far more dedication to the job of helping all American businesses—not just the large and the glamorous ones—succeed overseas.

To become active in a new market, or to solve problems in an existing market, a three-pronged approach usually works best. Contact (1) the commercial section in the appropriate U.S. embassy or consulate, (2) the nearest Department of Commerce district office in the U.S., and (3) the appropriate "country desk" (i.e., Japan desk, Korea desk, China desk, etc.) at the Department of Commerce in Washington, D.C. Explain your objectives, and ask for advice and information that will help you attain them. The quality of the answers you receive and the speed with which you receive them will help you identify which individuals are effective. Concentrate on developing contacts and relationships with these people, and try to get their opinion on other good contacts in the government. In larger offices, job responsibilities are often allocated along product or service sector lines, which means that you may be stuck with someone who is less than effective. You can get around this problem by turning to the private sector: the Chamber of Commerce of the United States (COCUSA), more commonly known overseas as the American Chamber of Commerce.

As mentioned earlier, in Asia the local AmCham chapters are

among the most useful and productive sources of information on doing business in their respective countries. Since their primary function is to serve their in-country membership (mostly branches and subsidiaries of U.S. manufacturers), you should, as previously noted, be prepared to join as a nonresident member. Do not, however, expect AmCham to help you find trading partners or answer questions related to import and export. It exists to help American business in-country, not to engage in trade promotion. If you are uncertain whether it is appropriate for you to contact an AmCham chapter, get clarification from COCUSA's main office in Washington, D.C.

At the same time you make contact with U.S. government offices, write to the appropriate AmCham chapter with essentially the same message. In addition, ask them for tips on embassy personnel who are effective in providing assistance to business. Although the embassy and USDOC in Washington will usually have more in the way of statistical information and reference sources, AmCham may have excellent information on specific problems and issues faced by foreign business. AmCham members (some of whom are non-U.S. foreign businesspeople) are dealing with these issues every day. Ask for a list of AmCham committees, and contact the head of any committee that deals with your main areas of concern. Also obtain an AmCham membership directory, and get in touch with people in your line of business. Although you could call their U.S. office, you will get much better information, and a clearer picture of conditions in the field, if you take the trouble to write to their man on the spot overseas. Finally, if you are planning a trip to Asia, find out the schedule of the local AmCham's general monthly meeting and of any committee meetings that may be of interest to you. If you coordinate your travel with these meetings, you can add immensely to the value of your trip.

PART II

COUNTRY

BRIEFINGS

China: Background

The political evolution of China after the Second World War created a thicket of ethnic and political terminology through which Westerners dealing with China must learn to thread their way. Many well-meaning Western visitors unwittingly offend their hosts and business contacts by applying terms which, while vague and interchangeable in their minds, have specific and weighty implications to the Chinese.

On Taiwan, one such term is the word *China* itself. Since most Chinese on Taiwan (like those on the mainland) consider Taiwan to be part of China, they tend to bristle when a foreign visitor who has travelled to the mainland casually mentions that he or she has been "to China." As far as residents of Taiwan are concerned, the visitor is *in* China (specifically, in Taiwan Province) and the visitor's wording implies that Taiwan is excluded or that the People's Republic of China is the sole legitimate government of China. On the mainland, it would be equally offensive and even more peculiar to refer to Taiwan as "China." The best solution is to do as many Chinese do: refer to the mainland as the mainland and call the island Taiwan.

This solves much of the problem of political terminology but leaves unsolved the questions of ethnicity and language.

On Taiwan, the term *Taiwanese* applied to persons normally means ethnic Taiwanese or native Taiwanese, people whose ancestors inhabited the island prior to the sixteenth century. Some mainland Chinese whose forebears arrived from the mainland after that time, but before the arrival of large numbers of mainland

Chinese between 1945 and 1949, also refer to themselves as Taiwanese; those arriving after the Second World War call themselves Chinese. Thus, to refer to someone from Taiwan as "Taiwanese" implies not only political but ethnic differences with residents of the mainland. To avoid offending anyone, it is best to use expressions like "from Taiwan" unless you are absolutely sure that the person being discussed is, or considers him- or herself to be, native Taiwanese.

Finally, there is the question of language. The official language on both Taiwan (Republic of China) and the mainland (People's Republic of China) is what Westerners call "Mandarin." On Taiwan it is referred to as *gwoyu* (national language); on the mainland it is called *putonghua* (common speech). In addition to Mandarin there are several major dialects of Chinese, most of which are so dissimilar that speakers of different dialects are unable to understand each other in normal conversation (although they can communicate in writing since all dialects may be written using the same set of Chinese characters). One of the Chinese dialects spoken on Taiwan is called *taiwanhua* "Taiwanese"; although it is used by significant numbers of people, many residents of Taiwan who arrived after the Second World War or who were born after that time speak it little or not at all. Since everyone on Taiwan (and on the mainland) studies Mandarin Chinese in school, it is the only dialect you need to learn to communicate.

People's Republic of China (PRC)

T he PRC has undergone many dramatic changes over the last few years, not the least of which has been an opening both to Western businesses and to selected Western business and management practices. Nevertheless, it would be a serious mistake to believe that the PRC is going to westernize either its economy or its culture. The liberal tendencies that led to large-scale foreign business involvement in the PRC from the early 1980s are still suspect in some Chinese political, military and even intellectual circles. Periodic bouts of inflation, coupled with financial scandals and widely publicized cases of profiteering, have confirmed existing fears of an excessive opening of the economy. Successive waves of student demonstrations in the late 1980s surprised and shocked the mainland leadership and allowed conservative elements to assert themselves more aggressively than before. As a result, both social and economic liberalization have been, and will probably continue to be, erratic.

Even conservatives understand that if the PRC is to develop, it needs a more flexible economy, but no one has yet discovered a way to create the needed flexibility as long as the country is run by a ponderous and often rigid political bureaucracy. In addition, the PRC runs the risk of creating serious regional imbalances as the select coastal cities and special economic zones develop under different rules than the rest of the country. Another constant danger (which simmered throughout the 1980s and exploded into violence in the spring of 1989) is that the contradictions between social conservatism and economic evolution will create tensions that could disrupt national harmony or even destabilize the country.

This phenomenon of imbalance and resulting upheaval has occurred repeatedly in Asia. Examples include the Meiji restoration in Japan (which, among other things, gave the business and merchant class political influence more in keeping with their economic power), periodic outbursts on Taiwan (where the Taiwanese majority has been allowed business success but until recently was denied effective political participation), and the massive, violent street demonstrations in Korea in the spring of 1987, when for the first time significant numbers of middle-class citizens joined traditionally rebellious students in opposing a politically conservative government in spite of consistent economic and business success. The business risk created by this type of social tension is increased if, as often happens, host-country authorities yield to the temptation to turn public ire away from themselves and onto foreigners, always a relatively easy scapegoat in Asia. In the PRC the complicating factor of communist ideology has the potential to vastly increase the obstacles and risks to foreign business.

Another complication could arise from the PRC's continued determination to assert control over Hong Kong (1997), Macao (1999), and Taiwan. The mechanics of administering Hong Kong may well trigger intense bureaucratic and political rivalries and ideological conflicts within the maze of the PRC's power structure which could spill over into areas of vital interest to the foreign business community in both Hong Kong and the rest of the PRC. Furthermore, if the PRC is unable to absorb Hong Kong without destroying Hong Kong's vibrant economy, Taiwan's resistance to any eventual merger will increase, adding to general political tensions in the region. These tensions, in turn, can have adverse effects on the overall business climate. Although the late 1980s was a period of detente in Asia, it is wise to remember that the underlying political problems of the region are far from solved. The PRC may be doing business with Taiwan and South Korea, but the resulting optimism does not alter the fact that the PRC remains determined to become the sole and undisputed political reality for all the Chinese people. Not surprisingly, the Chinese on Taiwan (like those in Singapore) are equally determined that this shall not happen.

Although the PRC government has pledged peaceful reunification with Taiwan (a "peace offensive" was begun in 1981) and promises "one country, two systems," with capitalism for Taiwan, Hong Kong and Macao, PRC leaders have made several veiled references to the possible use of force in case persuasion fails. On the other hand, in the summer of 1986 a rumored Taiwan reunification proposal supposedly contained a number of specific points (including Kuomintang administration of six provinces in eastern China) that would be totally unacceptable to the mainland government, indicating how far apart the two sides are. Although budding trade and other unofficial relations between the PRC and Taiwan make the situation far more encouraging than the stalemate between North and South Korea, the bottom line of any reunification in the foreseeable future would be the same: total subordination and absorption of the weaker side by the stronger. It is worth noting that the Chinese dilemma, like the Korean problem, is not comparable to the situation in Germany, where a large, economically powerful West Germany absorbed its small, tottering eastern counterpart. In the case of China, economic strength is concentrated on one side while manpower and military might remain on the other. (The division in Korea is in some respects more similar to the one that existed in Germany, but the North Koreans, having made self-reliance a cornerstone of state policy, would seem more capable of independent existence than was East Germany.)

The PRC, which is dealing from a position of military strength vis-à-vis Taiwan, has made numerous overtures, including a proposal for unification under which Taiwan would retain its own administrative system and some defensive capability. However, the PRC's strong negative reactions to the sale of Dutch submarines and U.S. military equipment to Taiwan indicate that absolute military superiority remains a primary goal. On the civilian side, the PRC encourages "three links" (trade, travel, mail) with Taiwan, and fishermen from both sides frequently take shelter from storms in the other side's ports. (This sort of impromptu citizen exchange has led to some bizarre situations, including the case of a dozen PRC

fishermen who for obscure reasons came ashore in southern Taiwan, bought train tickets to Taipei, and would have arrived there
undetected if one of the group had not gotten off halfway by mistake and attracted attention by asking directions in a thick, mainland accent.)

Chinese attitudes on liberalization are affected by several external political factors. On the international front, the PRC is effectively ringed by the Soviets and their allies (Afghanistan, India,
Vietnam-Laos, and Outer Mongolia); China's historical suspicion
of Russia and friction with Vietnam are not likely to be quickly
overcome by *glasnost* and *perestroika,* or by the Vietnamese withdrawal from Cambodia. In this regard, it is interesting to note that
even a noncommunist Taiwan, strategically located and under the
U.S. defense umbrella, constitutes a virtually unassailable Chinese
bastion, and in fact military forces from Taiwan are rumored to
have assisted the PRC in skirmishes with Vietnam over a disputed
chain of small islands (the Spratleys) in the South China Sea. The
PRC, which in 1986 sent the first high-level official to the People's
Republic of Mongolia (Outer Mongolia) since the 1960s, is trying
to use diplomacy to diminish the shadow of Russian domination
there, an effort that should be aided by U.S. recognition, in 1987,
of Mongolia (Soviet Russia's oldest ally and the second oldest communist state in the world). The Russians, meanwhile, have taken
advantage of ancient rivalries and hostilities between the Mongols
(who invaded China in 1211 and ruled it until 1368) and the
Chinese to create a strong diplomatic and military presence in
Mongolia.

In the late 1980s the PRC responded with guarded optimism
to Russian diplomatic overtures that formed part of Soviet leader
Mikhail Gorbachev's Asian diplomacy drive, but the PRC leadership steadfastly refused normalization of relations with the Soviets
until the "Three Obstacles" were eliminated: Soviet troop and
weapon concentrations on the Chinese border (including those in
Mongolia), Soviet support for Vietnam in Cambodia, and Soviet
intervention in Afghanistan. Even though all these conditions may
have been substantially met, China's historical experience with the
major powers (including the Russians) will tend to keep it from

embracing the Russian bear too warmly in spite of changes in Soviet posture. After all, the Russians are a land power in Asia, and the West is not only less threatening (Mao Zedong once dismissed the possibility of any conflict between the PRC and the U.S. by asking how an elephant could fight with a whale), it has more to offer in technological and commercial terms.

The Russians are also a major factor in the PRC's Korean policy. Since the PRC fears driving North Korea into the Soviet camp (thus putting still another Russian client on its borders), it has been very cautious about engaging in commercial contact with South Korea even though the ROK's size and level of economic and industrial development make it an ideal partner for trade, investment and technology transfer. The ROK has much to offer the PRC, and the PRC could team up with Korean business interests without running the risk of economic domination that is inherent in dealing with Japan or the U.S. Because of political circumstances, however, the PRC relies heavily on Japanese technology for the development of natural resources and has experienced heavy Japanese trade penetration that led to student demonstrations in the second half of the 1980s. As a result, the Japanese wisely lowered their commercial profile, and Japanese billboards in the PRC were quietly removed. Since China suffered intermittent Japanese domination in the military, political and economic spheres for about one hundred years, the Chinese are leery of allowing history to repeat itself; Japanese businessmen complain that their natural advantages of geographic proximity, a similar written language, and many common cultural and social traditions are often not enough to gain them equal treatment with U.S. and other foreign business competitors. Asian politics do indeed influence business in many ways.

On the other hand, the PRC (like the dynasty that preceded it) still has trouble inspiring respect in either Japan or the ROK (DPRK opinions are unknown). Although mainland China is recognized as the source of virtually all Japanese and Korean culture, it is often compared to a disorganized older brother who has failed to live up to the Confucian role of setting an example for the others to follow. Both the Japanese and the South Koreans are eager to show the Chinese what they can accomplish in business, however, and if the South Koreans manage to gain more open access to the PRC, all competitors—including Japanese and American—should be ready for some very tough going. The Korean people have a long history of cooperation with the Chinese, they are conveniently located, their language is more similar to Chinese than is Japanese, and the ROK can deliver the kind of low-cost, medium-tech, functional goods and technology that the PRC needs.

MAJOR TRADE AND BUSINESS OBJECTIVES

As is true of many lesser developed countries (LDCs) and newly industrialized countries (NICs), one of the overriding concerns of the PRC is the conservation of foreign exchange. As recently as the early 1980s, the PRC had apparently ample foreign exchange reserves, but these soon dwindled in the face of massive (and often speculative) buying triggered by market-opening measures adopted in 1981 and 1984. These measures, which loosened restraints on foreign trade by allowing the formation of trading corporations and other trading entities outside the traditional ministries and state-run trading apparatus, led to freewheeling entrepreneurial practices which, although proving that the capitalist spirit was alive and well in the PRC, created serious price and cash-flow problems.

A combination of scarcity and pent-up demand (both consumer and commercial/industrial) created by centralized control caused imports to command wildly inflated prices. As a result, new companies—many of them, called "suitcase" companies by the Chinese, operating with little capital and equally scanty long-term objectives—rushed to make quick profits on imported goods. At the same time, PRC producers eagerly exported their products at loss-leader prices in order to acquire the foreign exchange needed to finance purchases of foreign goods, which they, like the suitcase companies, imported and sold at hefty markups that more than made up for the losses on their exports. In the ensuing misallocation of resources, internal shortages of domestic goods—the result of overexporting—could be found side by side with depressed prices for domestic products. This unusual sitution was caused both by overproduction motivated by the hope of export and by competition from the flood of high-priced but sought-after imports. Most damaging, the country's foreign exchange reserves melted away like ice cream at a Fourth of July picnic.

To stem the flow, on April 1, 1985, the PRC put into effect a number of steps designed to control foreign exchange, exports and imports. The reaction toward tighter controls, while fully justifiable from the PRC's point of view, has caused severe difficulties for U.S. traders and businesspeople. Perhaps the most prominent case is that of AMC's Jeep project, which deserves a few words because it illustrates so well the problems that can spring up in a nonmarket economy with free-market ambitions.

From the American point of view, the Jeep project, a twenty-year joint venture formed in 1983 between AMC and the PRC, seemed relatively straightforward. American Motors would set up a plant in the PRC and build Cherokee Jeeps, using kits imported from Ontario. (The original intent was to design and produce a new jeep-type vehicle, but further study showed that this was beyond the capability of the Chinese industry.) Most of the vehicles would be bought by the PRC government, which would pay partly in foreign exchange; in the short term the foreign exchange would be used to pay for the kits, and over the long term it would fund retooling that would meet the final goal of having Cherokee parts (70 percent by 1991) made in the PRC.

Almost immediately after beginning production in September 1985, however, the operation ran into serious problems. Because of new foreign exchange restrictions on state-run enterprises, the government claimed it was unable to come up with the hard currency to pay for the imported kits. It also appears that the PRC hoped to funnel most of what foreign exchange was available into retooling to speed up the import substitution process and to somehow force the acceleration of exportation of the Chinese-made Jeeps—hardly a practical objective in view of their high price created by imported kits and an inexperienced and inefficient labor force. For whatever reason, beginning in October the Chinese failed to make payment for kits received. After that date, just one payment was made: in January, 1986, for the October shipment. The plant's modest target of thirteen vehicles per day fell to about seven per day, and by the summer of 1986 production had ceased altogether. Only eight hundred Cherokees had been built by the spring of 1986, and about three hundred of those remained unsold. It took a two-month shutdown, rounds of meetings between AMC and PRC officials, and U.S. government intervention to produce an agreement to resume payments and restart production.

American Motors invested eight years of complicated negotiations and about US$8 million in the project. What was the company looking for in the PRC, and what did it find? And what expectations did the Chinese have?

American Motors objectives:

1. To obtain low labor costs (80¢ per hour, versus $24 per hour in the U.S.)
2. To bypass other Asian manufacturing centers, including Korea, which appeared likely to become prohibitively expensive within a relatively short time
3. To create a new vehicle with a new image and a new market in Asia

What AMC encountered:

1. An inefficient labor force (eighty-eight man-hours per vehicle versus thirty-two hours in the U.S.) and no near-term parts manufacturing capability
2. Unrealistic official expectations as to the exportability of the product and the ability to retool and create an indigenous vehicle, which helped create unexpected foreign exchange problems
3. An inability to create the new vehicle and to tap any significant market.

American Motors might have avoided many problems if it had been more acutely aware of the PRC's objectives, which were considerably different from AMC's.

China's objectives:

1. To create new technological and automotive manufacturing capability and skilled employment
2. To gain foreign exchange through the export of automobiles
3. To diversify automotive production

Variations on the AMC experience are not at all uncommon in Asia. The reasons are almost always the same: as the Asian saying puts it, "one bed, two dreams." To be successful, foreign businesses must put a priority on thoroughly understanding the objectives of the Chinese (or other Asian) partner. In the case of the PRC, the very different business philosophies and objectives of Western and Asian business are separated even further by the great disparity in levels of development and in their political and economic systems.

In contrast to AMC's experience, Volkswagen's success story in China is an illuminating example of how foreign business can succeed in China. Established as a joint venture between the German automaker and three Chinese partners in the fall of 1985 (about the same time as the AMC joint venture), Shanghai Volkswagen Ltd. began production of the "Santana" model on September 1 of that year and cranked smoothly up to its monthly production target in May 1986.

The Germans were more successful with their start-up than were the Americans even though many of the problems faced by AMC also cropped up in Shanghai. Local officials, concerned over loss of turf, were less than cooperative, and the labor force was woefully inefficient. Volkswagen management overcame these difficulties—and the currency problems that hamstrung AMC—in several ways.

Problems:

1. Foreign exchange
2. Poorly qualified and unmotivated labor force
3. Limited technological capability

Solutions:

1. Sales of the Santana (US$17,000) to foreigners in the PRC for hard currency. This sharply reduced net foreign exchange outflow.
2. Limited use of Chinese products (tires and radios) until other Chinese-made parts and components became available. This further reduced hard currency needs.
3. Long-term plans to manufacture 100,000 engines a year by 1992 for export, mainly to West Germany. The export of engines was more easily realized than the more ambitious goal of exporting entire vehicles and took advantage of VW's established manufacturing, repair and service networks in Germany.
4. A bonus system under which everyone received the same productivity bonus according to the output of finished vehicles. This caused peer-group pressure for performance since good workers lost their bonus if lazy or incompetent workers slowed things up. It is noteworthy that production schedules were met for the first time in the month that this system was adopted.
5. Ongoing training in such basic concepts as responsibility, cooperation, teamwork and the need for product quality.
6. A timetable for localization (90 percent by 1992) and distribution of locally made parts between the joint venture (35 percent) and contractors. By giving PRC officials a fixed target, the timetable reduced the likelihood that they would try to manipulate time schedules; the contracting of parts met their goals of diversification and allowed VW to take advantage of specialized manufacturing capabilities in different plants and different areas, rather than trying to put everything together under one roof.

Finally, VW had the benefit of AMC's unfortunate experience: the PRC, which could hardly afford two such unsightly situations at the same time, undoubtedly tried harder to keep VW on track.

On October 11, 1986, the PRC announced new regulations governing foreign investment in the PRC. This document (portions of which appear to have been written with an eye to the problems and misunderstandings endemic to the AMC project) is useful not only because it sets forth the ground rules for foreign investment but also because it makes a clear statement about the PRC's objectives where foreign investment is concerned. Furthermore, by reading between the lines foreign businesspeople can learn much about Chinese (and other Asian) attitudes toward business.

Perhaps the most instructive portion of the law is Article 3: "Contracts should be made in conformity with the principles of equality and mutual benefit, and of achieving unanimity through consultations." With these few, well-chosen words, Article 3 says a lot about Chinese sensitivities regarding a long history of "unequal treaties" imposed by various foreign powers, most of them Western. It also gives an indication of the Asian attitude that business is conducted for the benefit of society. Keep in mind that "mutual benefit" is not the mutual benefit of two private enterprises but of a foreign private enterprise and the Chinese state, which exists—at least in theory—to serve the Chinese people. Finally, the goal of "unanimity through consultations"—so different from the Western norm of compromise through adversarial negotiations—reflects the widespread Asian insistence on harmony in all human endeavor, including business. The PRC may espouse Marxist socialism, but the bedrock beneath the socialist topsoil is almost pure Confucianism.

Foreign companies seeking business relationships in China can use their corporate legal staffs to research the application of the law; executives would do well to keep the law's stated objectives in mind so that they can structure proposals in such a way that the proposals' relevance to PRC objectives is clear to the Chinese. In this regard, a portion of Article 1 is worth repeating here verbatim. The purpose of the law is to " ... introduce advanced technology, improve product quality, [and] expand exports in order to generate foreign exchange and develop the national economy."

Other sections of the law are noteworthy because they hint at problems that foreign investors have encountered or might encounter when doing business in the PRC. For example, Article 15 orders that government agencies and officials " ... shall guarantee the right of autonomy of enterprises with foreign investment and shall support enterprises with foreign investment in managing themselves in accordance with international advanced scientific methods." The implication seems to be that some bureaucrats have obstructed, blocked or frustrated the efforts of foreign concerns to operate rationally and have meddled in management practices by attempting to impose political rather than business standards on some parts of the operation. And in fact, such problems do present themselves in the PRC. Article 16 likewise calls attention to a problem by referring to the "indiscriminate levy of charges on enterprises" and "unreasonable charges," while Article 17 takes a direct swipe at unproductive bureaucrats by calling on them to "strengthen the coordination of their work, improve efficiency in handling matters and ... promptly examine and approve matters ... that require response and resolution."

Article 15, which might be termed a mini bill of rights for foreign enterprises in the PRC, also gives foreign enterprises full control (within the parameters of their approved contracts) over personnel matters. If effectively implemented, this provision will do much to solve one of the major obstacles to productivity and efficiency in foreign factories in the PRC.

The doctrine that there is only one China and that Taiwan belongs to it is reflected in Article 20, which lumps Taiwan in with Hong Kong and Macao, both of which will revert to the PRC before the year 2000.

THE SEVENTH FIVE-YEAR PLAN (1986–1990)

During this period, the main international economic goals of the PRC have been (1) to increase two-way foreign trade (exports plus imports) by up to 50 percent and (2) to modernize the PRC's industrial structure through infusions of foreign investment and foreign technology.

To obtain the needed foreign exchange to pay for technology

and allow for repatriation of profits from foreign-invested companies, PRC planners recognized the need to generate significantly increased amounts of export earnings. This was to be accomplished through strategies involving changes in the mix of export products. The overall strategy was to substitute finished goods for primary products (raw materials) and upgrade manufactured exports to more finely processed products. At the same time, however, the plan called for increased exports of petroleum, coal, nonferrous metals, agricultural products, and indigenous articles. In keeping with the earlier emphasis on light industrial development, the export of textiles and other light industrial products was to be promoted more vigorously. The food processing industry, still in a phase of rapid expansion, was also expected to contribute significantly to export earnings. Finally, the PRC aimed to create strong exports of machine tools and electrical equipment and machinery by developing a line of world-class products.

Like all bureaucratic plans and strategies, this one ran into serious snags, many of which were created by the bureaucracy itself. PRC planners, wrestling with the issues of modernization and development, kept tinkering with the economy. Shifting official stances on individual enterprise, existing and new enterprise zones, acceptance of foreign investment, market access and other business-related issues are inextricably intertwined with the problems of recurring inflation and uneven development that in turn have led to more tinkering.

Nevertheless, the Chinese need new export products, and their drive to produce them should spell opportunities for U.S. manufacturers, investors and owners of technology as the Chinese look for new industrial processes and upgrade their existing manufacturing facilities. However, as the AMC experience illustrates, it is absolutely necessary to be aware of the built-in limitations created by the present state of economic and political development of the PRC. To succeed, one must set very modest initial goals and expand incrementally in the time-honored Oriental tradition. The PRC is not the U.S., and the investment philosophy followed by the Chinese for generations still holds true: never invest more than you can afford to lose, and keep expenses low enough to at least break even from the start. This is very different from common American strategy, but sound advice in the environment of the PRC.

The primacy of exports (including the export of technology) should create new market opportunities for U.S. suppliers. In order to increase the quantity and upgrade the quality and value of exports, the PRC intends to give priority to the importation of computer software, advanced production and other technology, and key equipment. At the same time, PRC planners are intent on extensive import substitution in consumer goods to avoid any repetition of the rush to consumer imports that disrupted the economy in the early 1980s. As did the Koreans from the late 1970s onward, the PRC also intends to follow a policy of reducing reliance on imported parts and components and to create plans ensuring that imported technology contributes to domestic capabilities by complementing domestic research and development.

To stimulate the development of infrastructure (including energy, transport and telecommunications), foreign development loans on preferential terms will be channeled into those areas, while foreign commercial loans will be directed toward sectors that can attain the highest levels of foreign exchange earnings and import substitution. Foreign investment (both in joint ventures and 100 percent foreign-owned operations) is welcomed, but preference will be given to investors in technologically advanced sectors and those which will generate foreign exchange through exports. In the area of engineering and technical services, a major implied objective is to engage in headhunting to acquire hired expertise in product development, technological design and project construction.

In spite of the perennial problems encountered in the PRC whenever the central government gives local authorities and managers free rein, current thinking calls for letting lower-level managers have more power in the handling of foreign trade. The import and export of staple commodities, however, is to remain under "unified management," that is, centralized control, as is the management of foreign exchange. In a continuation of existing trends, various enterprises may enter directly into foreign trade agreements. Of potential interest to U.S. traders is the intent to allow foreign trade corporations to act as agents or purchasers.

PRIVATE ENTERPRISE

Ever since Deng Xiaoping revealed his pragmatic plans for Chinese economic growth, there has been considerable ballyhoo in the Western press about private enterprise in the PRC, with some commentators predicting (or even claiming to see) a capitalist mainland regime. At this stage of the game, such analyses are just wishful thinking. The mainland regime is pragmatic, but it is decidedly Marxist (although it has learned from experience that Marxism-Leninism, a mishmash of theory that was developed under very different circumstances of time, place, and economic and social reality, can not possibly have all the answers for the PRC). In addition, there are still traditionalists who would love to put the PRC back on an orthodox road. Although Western logic indicates that the mainland Chinese have gone too far to turn back, that is merely Western logic. The PRC's track record is full of policies and movements—including the disastrous Great Leap Forward and the equally disastrous Cultural Revolution—that make no sense at all in Western logical terms. And sudden reversals can occur quickly in the PRC. After Mao's death, for example, who would have predicted that things in the PRC would develop as they have, and with such speed?

In addition, a look at the numbers indicates that today's PRC, although light-years away from the dark days of the Cultural Revolution, is still only tangentially engaged in free enterprise and only on a minuscule scale. In the mid-1980s there were under twelve million registered private enterprises in the PRC, employing less than eighteen million people—or about 1.5 percent of the PRC's population of over one billion. This works out to just over one and one-half persons per registered business, not even enough to keep both Mom and Pop together in the store (or behind the pushcart), and certainly a far cry from an aggressively capitalist society.

A better reading of the emergence of private enterprise in the

PRC confirms what Chinese leaders keep repeating: it is strictly a practical move to help the country develop. In addition to increasing productivity, it bypasses the horribly inefficient and corruption-ridden state production and distribution system—which today still includes such features as bribery and so-called "linked sales," whereby a purchaser has to agree to accept a certain percentage of defective items in order to be able to buy anything at all from a given factory.

Perhaps most important, controlled private enterprise functions as a safety valve. Even under the terrorism of the Cultural Revolution, people persisted in trying to escape from the countryside (which was being starved to feed the cities); more recently, the PRC has experienced all the problems that can accompany large-scale migration to urban areas, including unemployment and underemployment, prostitution, black marketeering, and a variety of other crimes both petty and serious. Permitting the establishment of private enterprise gives the most creative and ambitious among the unemployed a productive outlet and generally makes work for idle hands that otherwise might be engaged in some sort of antisocial—or antisocialist—mischief.

As happened in the Soviet Union at the end of the 1980s, large numbers of people in the PRC (accustomed as they were to a life of low expectations that required no diligence) resisted the reappearance of private sector economic activity on even a small scale. The depth of this resistance was indicated by the propaganda campaign undertaken by the PRC government to tout the benefits of free enterprise; in the mid-1980s the media were full of accounts of successful entrepreneurs, who were portrayed as the new socialist heroes of the Chinese revolution. If their activities had been accepted by a majority of people, presumably the media blitz would have been unnecessary. What the media didn't mention were incidents in which jealous neighbors threatened or physically attacked successful entrepreneurs and destroyed their products and businesses to eliminate the threat of an ambitious individual in their midst. This dark side of the picture was revealed only in generally worded exhortations to work hard and resist envy.

THE PERSON ACROSS THE TABLE

Just as a knowledge of the national and regional history of Asian countries can help you do business there, an awareness of the history experienced by the person with whom you are negotiating or doing business can give you a big advantage by helping you understand some of that individual's motives and underlying psychology. The following section, organized by approximate date of birth, provides an overview of the general background and experience of a person you might face across the negotiating table in the PRC.

* * *

1925: Childhood and youth under Japanese occupation or attack, with resulting starvation and misery. Lost many family members to war and related causes. May have served in the KMT Army or the Red Army of the Chinese Communist party. Attained workforce age during the chaotic period at the end of World War II (1945) and communist victory (1949). May have seen service in the Korean War (1950–1953) at the age of twenty-five or so. In middle age, may have been victimized by the Red Guards or sent to reeducation camp and forced labor during the Cultural Revolution (1966–1976). Saw China go from a backward, prostrate victim of warlords and invaders to a self-absorbed and dogmatic state and then to an emerging world power with a pragmatic government.

1935: Childhood under Japanese invasion and occupation, youth under struggles between the KMT and the Red Army, with attendant liquidations and purges. May have served in Korean War (1950–1953) in late teens. Saw what happened to critics of the regime during "Hundred Flowers Campaign" (1956). Attained work force age during the disastrous Great Leap Forward (1958) and resulting famine (1959–1961). At about age twenty-five, saw the PRC break with Russia. Experienced the Cultural Revolution (1966–1976) in early thirties, and may have carried—and quoted—Chairman Mao's "Little Red Book."

1945: Early childhood under KMT-communist struggles and the confusion and misery following the Second World War. Grew up under communism and the Great Leap Forward (mid-1950s). Reached work-force age (twenty-one) at the time of the Cultural Revolution (1966–1976) and anti-U.S. feelings caused in part by the Vietnam War. May have been in the Red Guards, or may have been forcibly sent to the countryside to work. Younger brothers and sisters unable to finish school because of closures during the Cultural Revolution. In his mid-twenties, may have seen action in border clashes with Russia (late 1960s-early 1970s); saw Nixon visit the PRC (1972).

1955: Fully Marxist upbringing. As a beginning middle school student, had education interrupted by the Cultural Revolution. As a young man in his twenties, witnessed the biggest political changes in China since 1949: dissenters who expressed themselves through posters on the "Democracy Wall" and soon paid for their daring (1978), U.S. recognition of the PRC (1979), and the PRC's transition from an ally to an enemy of Vietnam. May have seen service against Vietnam in border clashes (late 1970s-early 1980s). Well positioned to be part of the first generation of the PRC's new international traders and technocrats.

DEALING WITH THE CHINESE

The legacy of recent history—including the many twists and turns of official PRC policy, which has embraced such opposite extremes as the Cultural Revolution and Beijing's Democracy Wall—has had a profound effect on the people that foreign businesses deal with in the PRC. At higher levels of government and industry, many talented and knowledgeable individuals were eliminated at various times following the communist victory in 1949. Middle bureaucrats and managers sometimes seem to have lost any spirit of initiative or innovation, and the working class can appear listless and dispirited at times.

Nevertheless, the business and trading instincts that have characterized the Chinese for centuries never seem to be too far beneath the surface. Even during the anticapitalist, antitraditionalist waves that were allowed to sweep over the country, the authorities kept track of the holdings that had been confiscated from leading Chinese industrialists and even dutifully calculated interest on them as if planning to hand them back when the proper moment arrived (which, in fact, is what happened in many cases). Although it is doubtful that Mao's government had a master plan calling for the rehabilitation and restoration of key capitalists, whenever it came time to use them in China's postrevolutionary industrial development, the foresight and pragmatism behind the decision to segregate and conserve their assets says a lot about the Chinese as a group. It also demonstrates that in China, dramatic reversals can never be ruled out.

Because the PRC's political and economic system can lead to arbitrary, capricious and uneven application of regulations, it tends to create a wide gap between ambitious risk takers and more cautious, conformist or lazy individuals. For the same reason, the PRC today probably has greater extremes of work attitudes, flexibility of thought, and willingness to learn than any other Asian country. Some U.S. companies have been pushed beyond their frustration threshold by incompetence, inconsistency and stubborn inflexibility. Others have encountered human resources—including factory managers who, without formal training, used sheer native intuition and business sense to create vertically integrated networks that enabled them to run manufacturing operations several cuts above the surrounding technical and managerial environment—that would be a major asset to any business anywhere in the world. The important thing is to be prepared to look harder for good people and to spend longer training them. The results will be worth it.

THE CHALLENGE OF DOING BUSINESS

A blend of economic, social, political and geographic factors lends a special challenge to doing business in the PRC, as Western companies have been finding out ever since the PRC announced an "open door policy" on foreign investment in 1979.

Many potential foreign investors are put off from the start by a nagging lack of detail from the Chinese side. It is often difficult to get definite answers to questions on costs, operating conditions and requirements. Many factors, including the PRC's inexperience in business, a sprawling bureaucracy where efforts at decentralization often end up creating additional administrative layers, and the generic inability of many bureaucrats to understand the importance of all the considerations that go into making business decisions, contribute to the problem. The solution involves patience and the willingness to pound the pavement among a variety of authoritative sources (including local officials, relevant ministries and the People's Bank of China) until a clear picture and clear commitments are obtained from the proper authorities.

Commitments, however, are no guarantee since the PRC (like the ROK) reserves the right to change its mind. Projects may be cancelled for economic or other reasons. Foreign investors engaged in manufacturing may be informed that minimum export ratios or local content ratios have been raised. Even projects approved at the highest levels of government have run into sudden snags when the Chinese bureaucracy made operations or profitability impossible by reversing earlier positions. In 1985, for example, a Japanese-Hong Kong joint venture suffered a rude shock when the PRC informed them that key provisions of the financing of their nearly completed, HK$200 million (US$25.6 million) project would not be permitted after all. After lengthy negotiations, by late 1986 the developers had only a vague agreement that at some point they would be able to recover their capital and some sort of "appropriate" return on their investment. On a more routine level, many foreign companies find that the Chinese authorities are highly unpredictable when assessing customs duties and taxes. In view of this inconsistency and ambiguity on the part of the authorities, foreign companies venturing into the PRC are well advised to start small, develop experience and good working relationships with the Chinese, and expand incrementally as new opportunities present themselves.

A major problem for foreign investors is foreign exchange limitations. Foreign companies find themselves hampered by restrictions on the repatriation of profits. PRC officials, who seem to have unrealistic expectations about the ability of foreign manufacturing operations to generate foreign exchange, usually require that these operations rely totally on export earnings for necessary foreign currency. One way to get around this problem is to borrow the necessary foreign exchange from PRC government agencies. Local government, for example, may be persuaded to temporarily put up foreign exchange as an inducement to the establishment of an economically attractive foreign joint venture that can create positive foreign exchange flows within a year or two.

Many foreign companies seeking to do business in the PRC resist the Chinese tendency to force them into joint ventures. One reason is that the Chinese partner—backed by PRC government pressure on the foreign partner—will often insist on handling matters beyond its competence in order to gain experience. Although it is true that an inexperienced local partner can be a brake on business, the local partner also contributes a valuable knowledge of Chinese priorities and the workings of the system. However (as in Korea), beware of potential partners who try to sway you by trotting out a list of their important contacts in high places. There is virtually no case in which a word to one or two key people is going to swing a deal or get a needed approval. The Chinese bureaucracy is far too complex for that.

When you get down to manufacturing, the problems become more mundane but just as wearing. Because of China's vast size, underdeveloped infrastructure, and surging pace of change, the sourcing and transportation of raw materials, ingredients, parts and components are often difficult and time-consuming. If items are sourced within the PRC, it may take a long time to find anything that meets your required standards of purity, quality and reliability, and even after locating a supplier, quality may change. Also, you may of necessity end up with suppliers scattered all over the country, which means long lead times for delivery and at best an unpredictable flow, with shipments of different items arriving at varying times in relation to each other. Sourcing outside of China can be even more trying since in addition to possible foreign exchange headaches, there can be long and often inexplicable delays in clearing customs, and items may be assessed at different tariff rates on different days. Learn to expect the unexpected.

Another important consideration is the labor force. Decades of centralized planning, production that aimed exclusively at quantity without regard for quality, and a near total disregard for the needs of end users (whether commercial, industrial or individual) have resulted in a lack of concern for productivity, quality, or efficiency among a significant percentage of the work force. If you are intending to have articles manufactured under contract or under license, be prepared to spend a lot of time educating both management and labor on the need for these things. Remember, a high percentage of the people you will be dealing with are willing, even eager, to change their work philosophy and habits, but they are starting from scratch. One successful U.S. importer of Chinese products made to specifications began its efforts with repeated seminars on consumer choice and demand as a factor in design, price and quality; company executives spent two years making a series of month-long visits to the Chinese factory to patiently guide the Chinese through every conceptual and physical step of the design and manufacturing process. As a result, they report that they now have a product comparable to anything made outside of the PRC—and at a fraction of the unit cost.

If you are investing in manufacturing, by all means get as much control as possible over personnel operations, including salaries, hiring, firing, bonuses and general work rules. Even though the authorities have traditionally kept full control over hiring and firing, some persistent foreign companies have succeeded in getting the right to choose their employees. Since the mid-1980s, foreign companies have legally had broad authority over personnel decisions, and even before that, creative foreign executives were able to get a say in personnel matters. Consider hiring totally inexperienced workers, since they won't have picked up bad habits from previous jobs. You have no control over your suppliers' work force, of course, but to keep quality up you may want to consider educating them about quality and consistency, just as some foreign buyers do when they have products manufactured in the PRC to their specifications.

Foreign businesses operating in the PRC face a special set of challenges with their expatriate employees as well. Living conditions can range from reasonable to rough. In the absence of houses, apartments or compounds, foreign staff may be confined to living in hotels at outrageous rates. Some people report problems with food and health. Families with school-age children may have to find educational facilities outside the PRC, probably either in the U.S. or Japan. People with active lives may find resources to meet recreation and leisure needs limited, and the chance to make local personal contacts is restricted by language and by social and political barriers. Single foreigners should be very discreet about contact with local residents of the opposite sex; the alternative may be to become another international incident of the type that pops up periodically when foreigners mingle too obtrusively with PRC citizens. It is advisable to budget extra time—and money—for cross-cultural orientation training for executives and dependents, and for staff home leave.

When Western businesspeople travel to the PRC for negotiations, they immediately notice how expensive hotels and food are, particularly in terms of value received. As negotiations drag on at an excessively leisurely pace, they realize that whether by accident or by design the combination of expense and time creates considerable pressure to close the deal on Chinese terms. There are not many ways to get around this, but some companies have tried and been successful. Negotiating teams can work in relays, allowing key members to be back in the U.S. when needed. On occasion the Chinese have agreed to hold negotiations alternately in the PRC and at another site (either the U.S. or a convenient middle ground elsewhere in Asia). In any case, be mentally and logistically prepared to spend more time and money than would be necessary elsewhere in the world.

In spite of the unique difficulties of doing business in the PRC, companies who have made a commitment to do so are often completely satisfied with the results. Things should improve as the PRC government, which has perhaps overreacted to several situations in which foreign business interests took advantage of its naiveté, moves toward a more balanced and realistic view of international trade and business relations. The future should bring more flexibility on foreign exchange requirements, more consistency, and a greater willingness to allow joint ventures and licensing agreements a long enough life to ensure a fair return on the time and money invested by foreign partners or licensors.

TRADE AND TRADE REGULATIONS

Since the early 1980s, business and trading procedures in the PRC have undergone massive and often bewildering changes. In spite of some ups and downs, the general trend has clearly been toward a more open system, with more opportunities for U.S. businesses. The following guidelines should prove helpful.

Most of the PRC's foreign trade is carried out by Foreign Trading Corporations (FTCs), which are state entities under the control of the Ministry of Foreign Economic Relations and Trade (MOFERT). The FTCs are organized according to commodity or product sectors. In addition to the FTCs, there are import and export corporations established by the PRC's industrial ministries; these entities are also empowered to deal directly with foreign firms in both commercial and technology licensing matters. Some industrial plants and factories also have the authority to negotiate sales contracts—but rarely technology licensing agreements—with foreigners. Finally, individual municipalities and provinces have the power to conclude agreements with foreign interests. Only corporations granted export licenses by MOFERT, however, are allowed to export certain commodities, generally metals, minerals, textiles and some light industrial products which are import-sensitive in foreign markets.

Trading in about thirty strategic items is controlled by the PRC's national foreign trade organizations, and only negotiations with central government authorities are valid for these commodities, which include silk, cotton, crude petroleum and petroleum products, and coal. Since ambitious local or provincial authorities have been known to overstep the limits of their authority and conclude agreements—invalid, of course—for trade in strategic products, check with the appropriate central PRC government agency before entering into any serious discussions. In addition, large contracts may require approval from the central authorities in Beijing. Because there is considerable difference of opinion on the exact size and type of contract that is subject to central approval, prudence dictates thorough investigation, including contact with the appropriate central government agency in case of doubt.

Trade and business negotiations are further complicated by the Chinese tendency to regard discussions and negotiations as a two-stage process. In the first, or *technical,* stage, the main objective of the Chinese side is to assess the technical features of the products or services offered by the U.S. firm and the technical skill and depth of the U.S. company itself. In addition, the Chinese side wants to learn about overall technology in the sector in question. To be successful in the PRC, U.S. firms must realize that their first discussions should probably be seen as a fact-finding exercise for both sides, with the U.S. company investigating the technical competence and technical requirements of the Chinese while at the same time educating the Chinese side on the products or services it is marketing. The main difference between this approach and the type of technical seminar and demonstration commonly used in international (or domestic) marketing is duration: the Chinese will often question every possible detail over a period of days or weeks before moving on to the second, or *commercial,* phase, that is, the actual negotiations leading to the placing of an order.

In simpler times, most initial trade contacts could be made through the appropriate FTC or industrial ministry, or through the China Council for the Promotion of International Trade (CCPIT). Decentralization, which has created far more channels, has complicated things in many ways. Most municipalities and provinces have established their own business entities, including Foreign Trade Bureaus (FTBs), local FTCs, and investment and trust corporations.

The FTBs serve as a point of contact for foreign business interests and also handle trade activities where local FTCs have not yet been formed. Where available, FTCs act as local coordination centers for the branches of locally active national FTCs. Local investment and trust corporations have two main roles (which may also be played by the trust divisions of a dozen branches of the People's Bank of China including Tianjin, Dalian and Nanjing): (1) to attract foreign investors and find appropriate joint-venture partners for Chinese entities (local enterprises, government organizations and industrial firms) and (2) to arrange financing for joint ventures and compensation trade agreements. These activities of the local investment and trust corporations parallel those of the China International Trust and Investment Corporation (CITIC). They are not subordinate to CITIC but are limited to local investment and trade projects.

Trade Categories

There are two broad categories of trade with the PRC: trade under agreements and trade without a signed agreement.

Trade under Agreements

Trade (both import and export) carried out under agreements between the government of the PRC and foreign governments includes agreements entered into by PRC trading corporations and similar nongovernmental organizations; it falls into three main types:

1. *Specified barter.* Types, amounts and values of products to be bartered are spelled out in detail, and contracts place both parties under strict performance requirements. Usually, this type of transaction involves the transfer of credit (redeemable either for currency or for goods) in addition to the barter of goods. As in normal international trade, the currency of account and settlement is specified, and trade accounts (similar to letters of credit) are opened to cover payment for goods, freight, insurance, service charges or commissions, and other fees and expenses. It is possible to obtain account terms under which the seller accepts deferred payment in return for interest paid by the buyer.

2. Countertrade. There are several types of countertrade, but they fall under two main categories: the purchase of PRC products as a condition of exporting to the PRC and the use of PRC products as payment for foreign goods or services. Specific agreements take many forms; in some sectors (notably textiles and other light industry) the foreign firm exports materials or components to the PRC, and a Chinese factory, using the imported materials or components in whole or in part, manufactures to the foreign firm's specifications the items to be received as countertrade. Another arrangement is "compensation trade," whereby a foreign company selling equipment and technology to a factory in the PRC is repaid with a specified share of the production—either free or at a discount—over a specified period of time (usually five years or less).

No Chinese income tax is levied on compensation trade, which makes it attractive to the Chinese or joint-venture producer in the PRC and provides an incentive to foreign licensors of technology, who would otherwise have to pay Chinese income tax (withholding tax) on the royalties received. The PRC favors this type of agreement because it requires no foreign exchange, but the risks to the foreign party are obvious: possible damage to materials, components or equipment supplied by the foreign firm; quality control problems that affect the value of the goods received in exchange; and, since the passage of the PRC's bankruptcy law in 1986, possible failure of the Chinese company. Perhaps for these reasons, most compensation trade agreements have been for under US$500,000.

Transactions come under two lists, one composed of detailed products and quotas and a second list which is nonbinding. The payment agreements are of the same type used for specified barter transactions.

3. "Open" transaction. Although there may be a suggested product list, no specified product list is used. In theory this arrangement gives both parties the greatest leeway by letting them barter or trade any combination of products from the suggested list, but in practice there may be severe constraints caused by foreign exchange and other considerations.

Trade without Agreement

Trade without agreement is less highly regulated and is done on a cash basis. Products, quantities, prices, terms of delivery and payment, and other details are left more to market forces. Transactions are developed in a normal way, through mutual agreement of the parties, and formalized by a written contract. In some cases, PRC commercial offices overseas may be authorized to sign contracts for PRC trading corporations. There are also off-the-floor sales and import agreements made at the Chinese Export Commodities Fair that is held twice a year (spring and fall) in Guangzhou.

Trade Agencies and Trade Promotion Vehicles

Although the PRC has yet to acquire (or reacquire) the sophistication found in the major trading nations of the world, most of the usual mechanisms for trade promotion and facilitation are in place. They include the following:

- PRC commercial offices outside the PRC.
- PRC trading corporation offices and trade centers, both in the PRC and overseas. The offices in Macao and Hong Kong have an important role.
- Representative offices of foreign (and Hong Kong and Macao) companies in the PRC.
- Trade fairs in the PRC, most notably the Chinese Export Commodities Fair in Guangzhou. There are also smaller fairs, including vertical fairs restricted to a single well-defined product or industrial sector, which are held in various cities in the PRC. The organizers and sponsors of these fairs are PRC import and export corporations. Fairs in the PRC may be designed to promote the export of PRC products or may include foreign products.
- Trade fairs outside the PRC, organized either by PRC agencies or by foreign sponsors.
- Joint ventures in Hong Kong, Macao, and other areas outside the PRC proper, involving both import and export products.

- Distributorships granted by PRC trading corporations to their foreign agencies. These distributorships are subject to performance (i.e., minimum volume of transactions) and reporting requirements.
- Agency agreements between PRC trading corporations and overseas agencies. The activity of the overseas agent, which is usually closely controlled, is restricted to certain products in certain regions and does not include the right to sign trade agreements on behalf of the granting PRC trading corporation.
- Tender, auction and consignment arrangements. These may be widely used in the future but are not as yet.

It should be kept in mind that the PRC still has a shortage of world-class expertise in international trade and commercial matters. As in the business and investment sectors, this has led to a wide variation in behavior among PRC officials. Inexperience causes some of them to enter into disadvantageous business agreements; it conversely leads others to overprice exports, undervalue imports and set unreasonable terms and conditions on trade. As a result, many of the mechanisms to facilitate trade tend to be ponderous and unreliable when put in motion, and the U.S. purchaser or supplier must be prepared for the unexpected at all stages of a trade transaction.

One of the main difficulties in trading with the PRC is that the activities of the PRC trading corporations are severely circumscribed by the government. The products handled by PRC trading corporations are usually limited to a single sector, and the relevant government department for that sector must approve the business lines and activities of each company under its bureaucratic wing. The result is a bewildering hodgepodge of specialized import corporations, export corporations, corporations engaging in both manufacturing and trade, consolidated or unified export corporations that handle several manufacturers from the same industrial sector, and local trading corporations. As if this weren't enough, there is often a division of responsibility and authority between the head office of a given trading corporation and its branch offices. It requires a real commitment to track down the proper type of trading corporation and identify the right points of contact in order to start talking business.

The good news is that PRC trading corporations may engage in a number of activities besides simple export, import and distribution. They will also undertake a wide variety of manufacturing, processing, packing and other manipulative activities.

Contracts, Price and Payment

PRC trading corporations use two types of written sales agreements when dealing with foreign trading partners. Formal contracts are preferred for transactions involving staple commodities, capital equipment and other large purchases, especially with relatively new or unknown foreign firms. For smaller transactions, or transactions with established suppliers or customers, a letter of sales confirmation will often suffice.

When importing staple commodities or large (shipload) quantities, PRC trading corporations prefer FOB terms so that they can use Chinese ships. However, it is also possible to sell under C&F or CIF quotations. When exporting, particularly in small quantities, the PRC trading corporations favor CIF pricing because it allows them greater leeway in arranging for transportation. Again, they will also provide FOB and C&F quotes.

For payments, letters of credit (L/Cs) are the mechanism most often used, with irrevocable sight L/Cs being the most common. However, the PRC generally does not issue confirmed L/Cs. In some cases, of course (particularly those involving favorable transactions or customers of long standing), usance L/Cs of 30, 60, 90, or 120 days may also be used. As in the capitalist world, interest—added to the purchase price—is charged for the extension of credit. When exports of staple commodities are involved, the PRC side may wish to load the same commodity at different ports to take advantage of production and shipping patterns. In such cases, the PRC trading corporation will ask the buyer to open a transferable L/C or an L/C providing for shipment by installments. Letters of credit are handled by the People's Bank of China.

For countries having trade and payment agreements with the

PRC, settlement on account may also be used. This involves making payment against shipping documents through a designated bank by crediting the account of the seller.

Bank collections, rarely used in trade with the PRC, are almost totally limited to documents against payment (D/Ps), sight and after sight. Payment on a documents against acceptance (D/As) basis is uncommon.

In the case of products and equipment requiring long production times (including manufacturing plants, heavy industrial machinery and ships), installment and deferred payment terms are used, with time frames, interest rates and payment periods established by agreement of the parties.

The PRC trading corporations prefer that payment and settlement be made in convertible and relatively stable currencies. If deemed necessary, they will protect themselves against currency fluctuations by inserting appropriate language in the contract.

When drawing up and executing a contract with the PRC, it is very important to pay close attention to all details, to spell out everything, including definitions and terms that are commonplace in international trade and business, and to leave nothing to chance. The PRC's forty years of communism have not eliminated the effects of over two thousand years of Confucian legalism, which may explain why the Chinese interpret contracts very literally and strictly. In addition, the Chinese, like other Asians, are very skillful at leaving conditions vague when it suits them and generally structuring agreements in such a way that most of the burden is on the other party.

PRC entities like to use their own standardized sales and purchase contracts, and you may have to be very firm and persistent to make any changes or additions to those contracts. However, it is worth the effort in the long run. For example, since much of the PRC's trade with the West is motivated by a desire to acquire technology, many contracts call for the foreign side to supply "current" or "up-to-date" technology. Unless the meaning of these terms is carefully defined, however, a foreign supplier may have problems, especially in the case of delivery schedules extending over a long period of time or when dealing with industrial sectors in which the rate of technological change is extremely rapid. Unless everything is clearly spelled out in the contract, the PRC side may refuse the goods shipped, demand discounts, or insist on constant upgrades to match the latest technological developments.

For major purchases, including plants and capital equipment, standard PRC contracts call for guarantee periods of one or two years and the partial (up to about 5 percent) withholding of payment until the end of the guarantee period. Often, foreign suppliers face prolonged haggling over whether or not all the terms of delivery and guarantee have been satisfactorily met.

Under PRC law, the China National Import and Export Commodities Inspection Bureau must inspect specified imports and exports. Foreign purchasers are also allowed to make their own inspections although, in some areas, outside inspections are resisted. Some foreign buyers have also contracted with the China National Import and Export Commodities Inspection Corporation (CHINSPECT) for inspection services, with satisfactory results. For imports, standard PRC contracts specify CHINSPECT as the inspecting agency. Although foreign suppliers may—and in some cases are required to—furnish certificates of testing and inspection, these are rarely accepted as evidence in case of damage claims by the PRC buyer.

Normally, the PRC purchase contract is more detailed and has more rigid requirements than a PRC sales contract. In other words, under a standard PRC contract, a foreign seller is bound to a much higher standard of performance than a Chinese seller. For example, standard export contracts often leave shipping dates poorly defined and fail to include penalties for delays, which saddles U.S. importers with considerable risk, especially in the case of time-sensitive merchandise, and removes all incentive for the Chinese party to ship promptly. In the case of import contracts, however, both delivery dates and penalties are clearly defined, and the Chinese side usually has the right of cancellation if delivery is delayed beyond a given date. The problems inherent in this imbalance are magnified by the Chinese tendency to purchase on an FOB basis, but ship on a CIF basis. By purchasing FOB, they take control of import shipping arrangements—and possible shipping delays—from the hands of the foreign supplier.

U.S. Trade Controls

Although continuing rapprochement between the U.S. and the PRC has led to considerable relaxation of U.S. government controls on trade with the PRC, the Commerce Department still maintains restrictions on products and technology related to national security, and restrictions are sometimes tightened to show the U.S. government's displeasure with PRC government actions.

The Commerce Department's Office of Export Administration (OEA) maintains a list of controlled commodities and information (contained in the "Export Administration Regulations") on which of these commodities requires a validated export license for export to the PRC. For any commodity requiring a license, the exporter must make a specific application to OEA. With the exception of information generally available to the public, any technical data to be exported requires an export license, but the OEA will make efforts to provide expeditious licensing for many types of technology. Unfortunately, the OEA will not make any official determination on licensing until a formal application has been filed, but OEA staff will often give an advisory opinion on the prospects for approval of a proposed application. Approval or denial depends mainly on (1) the technology involved, (2) the proposed end use, and (3) the end user in the PRC.

For further information and application forms, contact any USDOC district office or write to Exporter Services Staff, Office of Export Administration, U.S. Department of Commerce, Washington, DC 20230. The OEA will not discuss any aspect of a specific application with any party other than the applicant.

Traders wishing to import from the PRC should be aware that in the past some PRC products have failed to conform to U.S. laws and standards. Possible problem areas (relevant U.S. regulatory agencies are given in parentheses) include pharmaceuticals and Chinese medicines (FDA), foodstuffs (FDA), ivory products (U.S.

Customs), and ceramic ware (FDA). Some PRC products have also been the subject of dumping investigations, and others are subject to quotas (textiles, clothespins) and countervailing duties. Still other products, which are subject to international quotas, may require special licenses. For information, contact the Office of Investigations, Import Administration, International Trade Administration, U.S. Department of Commerce, Washington, DC 20230. Importers should also be aware that some types of marketing and other business agreements (for example, those that call for extensive representation of PRC corporations in the U.S.) may make the U.S. party liable for registration under the Foreign Agents Registration Act (FARA). If in doubt, contact the Registration Unit, Criminal Division, U.S. Department of Justice, Washington, DC 20530.

JOINT VENTURES

Although the PRC's objective in establishing joint ventures is to process or produce goods for export, a significant percentage of production may be destined for the Chinese market, and a few joint ventures have been allowed to aim exclusively at the internal market. The best joint venture opportunities in the in-country market are in the foreign travel and tourism sector, including catering and hotel services. Since regulations governing joint ventures are constantly changing, it is imperative to research the latest laws and regulations before getting deeply involved in the formation of a joint venture in the PRC.

There are two types of joint ventures possible under the PRC Joint Venture Law: equity joint ventures and contractual joint ventures. Equity joint ventures comprise only about 15 percent of all foreign joint ventures in the PRC. In an equity joint venture, the head of the corporation must be a Chinese official, and the foreign equity investment must be at least 25 percent of total equity. The contributions of the parties are regulated: the Chinese partner may provide land; improvements, including factory and infrastructure; labor; and some materials and machinery. The foreign partner may supply technology, capital equipment and machinery, management, external marketing expertise, and capital. The foreign partner's profits may be repatriated.

The PRC aims to keep foreign partners in joint ventures involved until the operation is well established. Therefore, the parties usually must commit to working together for five to twenty years.

Income from joint ventures is subject to taxation at a central government rate of 30 percent, plus a local surcharge of 10 percent of the central government tax—a total tax rate of 33 percent. An additional 10 percent income tax is levied on profits remitted outside the PRC. There is a 20 percent withholding tax on income from royalties and technology or "know-how" fees, which may be reduced to 10 percent by agreement of the Chinese partner in some cases. If the technology involved is considered vital to the PRC, the Ministry of Finance can waive the remaining 10 percent.

Joint ventures with an intended life of over ten years may be granted a two-year tax holiday and pay taxes at a reduced rate in the third through fifth years. In addition, investments in forestry and farming and other types of investments in selected geographic areas in the PRC receive favorable tax treatment, as do profits that are reinvested in the PRC.

Contractual joint ventures, which allow additional flexibility, have been more popular with foreign investors. Under a contractual joint venture, the capital contribution may be something other than money, and the profits of the contractual joint venture may be distributed in any proportion agreed upon by the partners, rather than being proportional to the partners' respective equity shares.

LICENSING

A few years ago, the PRC still tended to purchase technology as part of a package including complete, turnkey plants and equipment. Increasingly, however, advances in the PRC's capability and the need to conserve foreign exchange have limited acquisitions of technology and equipment to items that cannot be locally produced, with a strong emphasis on the purchase of bare technology and the use of technology to upgrade existing manufacturing facilities.

It is vital to define all terms when licensing technology to the PRC. The Chinese often expect far more in the way of "complete" documentation than Western firms are accustomed to providing, and in the absence of stipulations to the contrary, they have been known to require documentation that was nonexistent, irrelevant, subject to extensive ongoing revision, and/or requiring considerable investment of human resources to compile. Foreign owners of technology should also exercise extreme care in establishing the limits of the technology to be provided and in protecting all relevant intellectual and industrial property rights.

INTELLECTUAL PROPERTY RIGHTS

Like other Asian countries, the PRC has been slow to grant intellectual property rights protection. The common Asian propensity to regard ideas and the advances resulting from them as part of the public domain was intensified by communist theory, which regarded intellectual property rights as a manifestation of bourgeois cupidity.

Copyrights

The PRC has made a commitment to give U.S. authors equivalent protection to that extended by the U.S. However, there is no PRC copyright law and none appears to be forthcoming in the near future. This situation has led to a surprisingly low level of piracy. And in many cases PRC interests request permission to translate and publish foreign works, resulting in agreements that provide contractual protection in individual cases.

Trademarks

The PRC has had trademark legislation since 1983, and in this area the situation is fairly close to the rest of Asia. Trademark protection is granted not to the first user, but to the first applicant, which allows for the possibility—frequently realized elsewhere in the region—of foreign marks being registered with the primary intent of selling them to the original international owner at a later date. A registered trademark is valid for ten years and may be renewed for successive ten-year periods. Failure to use the mark for three years results in termination of all rights to the mark; publication, advertising and exhibition of products bearing the mark all constitute use. Trademark-related decisions may be appealed within fifteen days of the decision to the Trademark Appeals Board, and the fifteen-day period may be extended twice, thirty days each time (for a total sixty-day extension).

The owner of the mark has exclusive rights to the mark in the PRC and retains primary responsibility for the quality of all goods bearing the mark, even if the mark is subsequently assigned to another party. Penalties for consumer deception involving the mark include warnings, fines and cancellation of the mark. The PRC trademark law prohibits the use of certain words and designs in trademarks, including national flags or emblems, any insignia that discriminates against national minorities, and any description that is "exaggerated and deceptive," "harms social morality," or has "other harmful effects."

Penalties for infringement and consumer deception include damages equivalent to the infringer's profit or the trademark holder's losses resulting from the infringement, destruction of infringing goods, mandatory rectification of the quality of inferior goods, cancellation of trademark rights, and fines not to exceed 5,000 yuan.

A foreign party may apply for trademark registration in the PRC, provided that the mark in question is already registered by the applicant in his own country and that there is a reciprocal agreement on trademark registration between that country and the PRC. For U.S. applicants, the latter requirement is met by the fact that Chinese FTCs have the right to register trademarks in the U.S. Subsidiaries of U.S. firms established in countries that have bilateral trademark agreements with the PRC may also register marks in the PRC and may subsequently transfer any such mark back to

the parent company in the U.S. by following the assignment procedures contained in the PRC legislation.

The registration process for all foreign applicants is handled
by the China Council for the Promotion of International Trade, and
all applications must be accompanied by a power of attorney em-
powering CCPIT to undertake all actions necessary to obtain registration. The power of attorney and all supporting documents must
be notarized and must be written in Chinese or accompanied by
a Chinese translation. The application must also be accompanied
by ten sample copies of the trademark being applied for.

Patents

Even after the normalization of relations between the U.S. and
the PRC in 1979, it took PRC officialdom until 1982 to arrive at the
realization that the transfer of necessary technology would be impossible until some system of patent protection was created. Until
the resulting patent law took effect in 1985, the only patent protection available in the PRC was contractual. Foreign businesses using
proprietary technology, processes or products in the PRC were in
a high-risk situation. Because the patent law is relatively recent, it
is difficult to assess its effects.

The purpose of the law, as stated in Article 1 ("... for meeting
the needs of the construction of socialist modernization"), leaves
no doubt that the intent of the PRC is to strengthen its technological
base, not to protect the profitability of foreign companies who will
be involved in much of the research and development in China for
some years to come. This attitude, which is shared throughout
Asia, can cause problems for unwary Westerners who presume
that the law exists to protect their interests. Chapter VI (Articles 51
through 58), which provides for compulsory licensing after three
years, allows insufficient time for most industrial patent holders to
recover the costs associated with the research and development
of a new product. Clearly the Chinese government places a lower
priority on foreign investors' profits than it does on assuring that
they contribute to China's economic and technological progress.
Like many Asians, the Chinese lawmakers appear not to com-

pletely understand the fact that if Western businesses do not see an acceptable return, they will not invest in research or allow the Chinese to have access to their latest products and technology.

From the U.S. business point of view, one of the most serious defects in the law is the lack of protection for the items listed in Article 25, including scientific discoveries; methods for the diagnosis or treatment of diseases; food, beverages and flavorings; pharmaceutical products; and substances obtained by means of a chemical process. Both this article and Article 62, which protects from infringement proceedings the use of a patent "for the purposes of scientific research and experimentation," are examples of the common and troublesome (to Western business) Asian mindset that fails to recognize the value of creativity and that views ideas, concepts and inventions as part of the public domain. If broadly interpreted, the exemptions for "scientific discoveries" (Article 25) and "scientific research and experimentation" could permit Chinese or other competitors to engage in most forms of reverse engineering and unauthorized use of proprietary information.

Hong Kong

H ong Kong is an integral part of China, leased to the British until 1997. The current leadership of the People's Republic of China has repeatedly asserted that under a "one country-two systems" arrangement, Hong Kong will be allowed to retain something resembling its present capitalistic system for fifty years after 1997 (when, by mutual agreement reached with England in 1984, full territorial rights and administrative authority will revert to the PRC). However, PRC policies are notoriously fickle, and there is no way to know what direction will be taken after the transfer of control is effected. Since the PRC's treatment of Hong Kong will have great influence on future relations between the PRC and Taiwan and since Hong Kong is valuable to the PRC as a conduit for trade, investment and technology transfer, the most logical course—from a Western point of view—would be to adhere scrupulously to the promised formula. Unfortunately, Western logic has often failed to predict the course of events in Asia.

Even if the mainland regime wants to keep Hong Kong capitalist for fifty years and more, there are at least two major difficulties that make this scenario unlikely. The first is perhaps the more obvious of the two. Even with a well-controlled and guarded border between Hong Kong and the PRC, the freewheeling colony has acted as a magnet, attracting large numbers of mainland Chinese, some of whom have braved considerable hardship and risk to reach Hong Kong in search of greater economic opportunity. Once the border is eliminated, it will be even harder to prevent this kind of flow. At the same time, the presence of a free-enterprise enclave in a controlled socialist economy will arouse widespread resentment and calls for similar arrangements in other places. It is unlikely that the PRC will discover a formula that will allow free enterprise to survive in Hong Kong, much less be reproduced elsewhere. The inevitable solution will be to socialize Hong Kong.

The second problem is related to the problem of centralization and bureaucracy. Hong Kong cannot be run by means of any sort of centralized planning system, and yet it must be administered from Beijing if it is to be a part of the PRC. At the same time, bureaucrats (whether on site or in the capital) are not entrepreneurs, nor do they understand anything resembling a bottom line. The bureaucratic administrative structure of the PRC, as much as the Marxist premises upon which it rests, will prevent it from maintaining the business environment on which Hong Kong's vitality depends. Bureaucrats simply don't know how. This is good news for Taiwan and Singapore, which can pick up the business and financial activity that will move out of Hong Kong in search of more favorable conditions.

The PRC has long used Hong Kong as a trade and foreign exchange window and undoubtedly wishes to keep doing so. PRC finance, trade and investment entities operate offices in Hong Kong, and most foreign traders and investors planning business in the PRC establish some sort of presence in Hong Kong as a prelude to full-scale entry into the PRC. By the late 1980s, there were about six hundred U.S. trading companies in Hong Kong, most of them dealing extensively with the PRC.

A high percentage of Hong Kong's export trade is in the form of reexports (items assembled in Hong Kong from imported parts and components). Another large chunk of export volume consists of semifinished goods that cross the border to Shenzhen, undergo low value-added, labor-intensive processing, and return to the Colony. Fluctuations in this flow give an indication of how changing PRC policies may work to the detriment of Hong Kong businesses after 1997. Following a record volume year in 1984, the PRC, which is the Colony's largest market for reexports, cut back drastically on buying in 1985, causing Hong Kong's trade balance to fall into the red. After the transfer to PRC control, it is likely that national priorities will continue to take precedence over Hong Kong's economic health and vitality.

In fact, as early as the period 1981–1983, uncertainty about the territory's political future caused a deep depression and a substantial flight of local capital. At the same time, foreign investors (farther from local reality) were giving Hong Kong a vote of confidence by pouring money into manufacturing, assembly and other facilities, including trading company offices. In 1981–1982, there was a net outflow of capital, but by 1984–1985 the situation had reversed to a net capital inflow of about US$4 billion. At the same time, however, 1985 was the worst year in two decades in terms of exports (which fell 6 percent by value) and the worst in a decade for growth in GDP (0.8 percent). By the late 1980s there was a steady stream of outbound Hong Kong Chinese seeking overseas havens. Since a quirk in U.S. immigration law (which skeptics attribute to a confidential agreement reached between the U.S. and British governments to keep the flight from turning into an exodus) kept Hong Kong business investors from gaining entry into the U.S. under the investor status available to other Asians, Hong Kong money and the people who controlled it poured into Canada and Australia to such an extent that the economies of cities like Vancouver and Calgary were transformed from slack to boom.

In recent years, about half the new foreign capital investment in Hong Kong has been from the U.S., with Japan a distant second at about one-fifth of the total. There has also been significant investment from Australia, Singapore, the Philippines and Western Europe. Most of the foreign capital has gone into electronics (about one-third of the total) or textiles and apparel (one-tenth). Although direct U.S. investment is something under US$1 billion, total U.S. investment is about US$3 billion. A significant percentage of U.S. investment is in offices for buying and production control of goods manufactured in Hong Kong for export. Foreign-invested businesses and related activities account for about 10 percent of Hong Kong employment and about 12 percent of the Colony's exports. Hong Kong is also a small but major importer of U.S. goods, several hundred U.S. dollars per capita each year. Because this figure is far higher than U.S. imports of Hong Kong goods, and since Hong Kong has virtually no restrictions on the import of U.S. products into the Colony, there is considerable bitterness over U.S. trade restrictions (supposedly intended to create a "level playing field") that restrain Hong Kong's exports to the U.S.

As Asian countries go, Hong Kong is wide open to foreign business, including services. Foreign banks, insurance companies, law firms, and others operate freely. In manufacturing (which accounts for some 45 percent of total economic output and about 34 percent of total employment), foreign investors receive essentially the same deal as everyone else. Local manufacturing companies tend to be very small (often about ten employees) and highly adaptable. This makes it possible for foreign companies to create "captive factory" arrangements that guarantee steady work for the Hong Kong manufacturer and a reliable source of supply for the foreign buyer. Larger companies frequently enter into joint ventures, including joint ventures with PRC agencies. Under competition from LDCs with lower labor costs, Hong Kong manufacturing, like that in other Asian countries, is continually moving toward higher technology and greater value-added production.

Although the U.S. made the lion's share of new investment in the mid-1980s, overall Japanese investment may well be equal (exact figures are difficult to come by). American investment is concentrated in electronics and chemical products while Japanese concentration on investment in the manufacture of watches and clocks has helped make Hong Kong the world's largest exporter in terms of volume. The rapid rise of the yen in the latter half of the 1980s, however, forced additional Japanese firms offshore in search of lower manufacturing costs and is resulting in new patterns of Japanese investment, including greater emphasis on electronics.

In recent years, electronics has received far greater foreign investment than any other industrial sector (over one-third of total foreign investment by value), with textiles and garments a distant second at about 10 percent. When compared by employment, electronics outweighs the textile and garment industries three to two.

In financial sectors, doing business in Hong Kong can be risky for those who are swayed by the glamor of supposed political connections or who are taken in by the sound of large numbers. During the early and mid-1980s several Hong Kong companies (including banks, shipping firms, and others) were able to fool investors, U.S. bankers, and their own directors with a combination of kited checks, juggled books and self-serving stories that covered up both their activities and their losses. One particularly gullible U.S. banker, for example, was taken in by a fanciful tale of intrigue that included the supposed concealment of vast sums of Nationalist Chinese wealth from the communist (PRC) government. The result was losses of vast sums from the bank's assets.

The PRC is very active in Hong Kong's business, trade and financial sectors. PRC entities have provided major infusions of capital to financially troubled Hong Kong companies, a tactic that has enabled them to cheaply acquire expertise, participation in going concerns and, in some cases, greater access to trade and business with Taiwan and South Korea. About US$1.1 billion in Taiwan-PRC trade flowed through Hong Kong in 1985; in 1986 the PRC's Hong Kong connection resulted in US$646 million in trade with the ROK. PRC organizations and individuals active in Hong Kong (including the People's Bank of China, with a BOC branch and twelve affiliated banks) still have a lot to learn about doing business in the Colony's freewheeling, volatile environment, however. Their inexperience has led to serious lapses in investment judgment (one of which, in 1984, caused a major slide in the Hong Kong stock market) and generally low rates of return on shareholders' equity.

MAJOR TRADE AND BUSINESS OBJECTIVES

Since the present Hong Kong government is in a caretaker position, its objectives are generally limited to the short term. For Hong Kong businesses, the major long-term preoccupation is to establish and maintain close commercial, industrial and financial relations with appropriate entities in the PRC as a form of insurance against future events. Meanwhile, many of them must also engage in a delicate balancing act to protect existing lucrative business with Taiwan, which accounts for over one-fifth of the value of the Colony's publicly recognized imports and an undetermined but substantial amount of behind-the-scenes trade between Taiwan and the PRC.

At present (and probably for at least a few years after 1997, when the PRC takes over) the main goals of the Hong Kong government are stability and credibility. The former has been threatened by uncertainty over the future, which has contributed to dramatic and harmful fluctuations in the Colony's property markets. The latter has been damaged by several multimillion dollar financial fiascos, which have stemmed from the freewheeling character of Hong Kong business and which have also affected the Colony's stability.

Somewhat belatedly, the authorities have recognized that many of these problems are the result of overly laissez-faire financial disclosure laws, which make it extremely difficult for lenders and investors to get accurate financial analyses or a clear picture of business ownership and activity. As one step toward correcting the situation, the Legislative Council in 1986 passed a banking bill that tightened ownership rules and reserve requirements at financial institutions. Unfortunately, nothing has been done to address the damaging tendency of family-owned business groups to commingle public and private funds, which has led to several major bankruptcies.

INTELLECTUAL PROPERTY RIGHTS

The Colony has also had an image problem caused by the counterfeiting of U.S. and other Western products. Although the counterfeiting was probably no worse than the misappropriation of intellectual property in other Asian nations, it was potentially more damaging to Hong Kong's smaller, narrower and more volatile economy, which is heavily dependent for survival on the goodwill and patronage of foreign buyers and foreign manufacturing orders. In response to the problem, Hong Kong has enacted—and vigorously enforced—one of the strongest intellectual and industrial property rights laws in Asia.

Hong Kong authorities have attacked the counterfeit problem head-on, both legally and through public relations campaigns. The Hong Kong government has acceded to the Paris Convention for the Protection of Industrial Property, the Berne International Copyright Convention, and the Geneva and Paris Universal Copyright Conventions. Hong Kong law specifically makes the following provisions on intellectual property rights.

Trademarks

Full protection is offered to holders of trademarks registered with the Hong Kong government. Fraudulent use of a trademark or possession of equipment for the purpose of fraudulent use is a criminal offense punishable by a maximum fine of HK$500,000 and imprisonment of up to five years.

Copyrights

Copyrights, if registered in accordance with the U.K. Copyright Act and the Hong Kong Copyright Ordinance, are protected, and violators are liable for both civil and criminal penalties (maximum fine, HK$50,000; maximum prison sentence, two years).

Patents

Patents may be registered in Hong Kong only if previously registered in the U.K. (This provision covers European patents registered in the U.K.) Protection is through civil courts only.

Registered Designs

Designs registered in the U.K. in accordance with the Registered Designs Act are generally protected by that act, and it may be possible to initiate civil action against violators even if the design in question has not been registered in Hong Kong.

Trade Descriptions

The application of a false trade description to any goods, or the possession of goods bearing a false trade description for the purposes of sale, trade or manufacture is a criminal offense punishable by a fine of not more than HK$500,000 and imprisonment of up to five years.

The investigation of infringement complaints and related enforcement action is the responsibility of the Customs and Excise Department of Hong Kong. This department, which has a special task force set up for the purpose, has powers of search, seizure and forfeiture. The Hong Kong government has set up a "one-stop" unit in the Industry Department to field all types of inquiries regarding industrial and intellectual property rights.

Having said all this, it is still important to note that Hong Kong is far from squeaky clean. One of the main areas of concern is computer hardware and software. American and other foreign owners of intellectual property in this sector claim that Hong Kong authorities are not doing enough to dissuade infringers and that penalties imposed are little more than slaps on the wrist. Whatever the reason, it is still easy to find—and buy—very cheap and functionally satisfactory counterfeit personal computers and a wide variety of pirated software programs to go with them. In fact, to boost sales in the face of vigorous competition, some computer dealers will cheerfully give a buyer as many programs as he or she requests, for just the cost of the blank diskettes.

ESTABLISHING A BUSINESS

As you might expect, Hong Kong is a relatively easy place to set up shop. Foreign-invested businesses face no special obstacles and receive no special favors. Because of the preponderance of light industry in Hong Kong, the vast majority of the Colony's 47,000 manufacturers have fewer than a dozen employees, are privately financed, and only rarely enter into joint ventures with foreign firms. Among larger Hong Kong companies joint ventures, in keeping with the overall business environment, tend to be flexible and amorphous, changing form and function in order to keep up with changing patterns of production and trade. As entities from the PRC increase their business activity in the Colony, joint ventures with PRC firms are becoming more important.

There are three basic options for opening a business in Hong Kong:

1. A company with unlimited liability.

This involves the simplest and quickest procedure. All that is necessary is to file an application for a Business Registration Certificate (together with an annual registration fee) with the Business Registration Office, wait two or three days for the Business Registration Office to process the application, and you are ready to set up shop.

2. A branch office of a foreign company with limited liability.

This procedure is also simple and takes little time (about three weeks to process a correctly completed application). The foreign parent company registers with the Company Registry of the Registrar General's Department by filing a certified copy (in English) of the parent company charter and/or articles of incorporation, together with a list of the directors of the company and the name and address of at least one person resident in Hong Kong who is authorized to accept service on the company's behalf. There is a filing fee. The name of the Hong Kong branch office must be the same as the name of the parent company; this name must be registered with the Business Registration Office. The parent company must also apply for a Business Registration Certificate with the Business Registration Office.

3. Incorporating a company with limited liability.

This process, while slightly more complicated and time-consuming, is still quite simple in comparison with elsewhere in Asia. The first step is to request advice from the Registrar General's Department on whether the proposed company name may be registered. This step, which involves a modest fee, requires about four weeks for processing. After affirmative advice is received, the applicant has three months to file an application for a certificate of incorporation. Once all required documents have been filed and fees paid, the processing time is seven to ten days. The application is made to the Company Registry of the Registrar General's Department.

Taiwan, Republic of China (ROC)

Taiwan's ruling party, the Kuomintang (KMT), shares with the PRC the belief that there is only one China, but in spite of periodic upheaval and repression on the mainland it is clearly behind in the international battle for recognition as the legitimate government of that one China. It calls itself the Republic of China and publicly and steadfastly refuses to deal with the PRC, frequently invoking its policy of the "Three No's": no negotiation, no compromise, no contact. In practice, however, the KMT has accepted (and appears to welcome) the burgeoning trade and tourism with the mainland. Since the ROC government decided in 1987 to allow private citizens to visit relatives on the mainland, there has been a massive flow of Chinese traveling to the PRC for this purpose. (Even before the travel ban was lifted, thousands of Taiwan Chinese violated it every year, entering the PRC via Hong Kong or Japan). At the same time, businesses based on Taiwan have been using their mainland travel to set up manufacturing operations there. Using cheap mainland labor and their own manufacturing and marketing expertise, they have been able to gain significant cost advantages as the yen has soared and the new Taiwan dollar has risen sharply against the U.S. dollar.

To the ROC government, a bigger worry than the observance of the symbolic three no's is the ongoing battle for international status, where the ROC's position is being steadily eroded as Taiwan is displaced or joined by the PRC on international bodies (among the most recent: the Asian Development Bank), where the PRC usually gets to use the name China while the ROC, usually under protest, is forced to accept *Taiwan*. While over 130 nations now recognize the PRC, the ROC is recognized by only twenty-three countries, none of them populous or (with the exception of the Republic of Korea) economically significant. The U.S., which withdrew recognition from Taiwan at the end of 1979, maintains relations through an ostensibly private organization, the American Institute in Taiwan (AIT), which is supposedly staffed by private citizens who take a leave of absence from their government jobs during their tours of duty with AIT. Interestingly, the U.S. used a similar device to deal with the PRC prior to recognition by President Carter in 1979. The National Council for U.S.-China Trade, set up to handle ostensibly unofficial relations with the PRC when that country had not been recognized by the United States, still plays a major role in trade and business matters.

After 1949, Taiwan was under martial law for thirty-eight years, a world record. Although martial law was lifted in the early summer of 1987, other, equally restrictive security legislation allowed the ruling KMT to continue to stifle dissent if the need arose. Taiwan has come a long way since the days when the native Taiwanese (some 80 percent of the population) had virtually no voice in the government or in the KMT, which is dominated by a small percentage of the roughly two million mainlanders (and their descendants) who fled to Taiwan after the communist victory in 1949. Following the influx, the mainlanders controlled politics and the military while the native Taiwanese were allowed to predominate in business. However, in 1986 late President Chiang Chingkuo (son of Chiang Kaishek) declared an end to the Chiang dynasty and announced that the political opposition could open offices—a step toward eventual political party status.

Following Chiang Chingkuo's death in 1988, the accession of the ROC's first native Taiwanese president, Lee Tenghwei, was symbolic of the increasingly participatory nature of Taiwan politics. Equally important was the 1987 legalization of opposition parties (a move made after at least one such party had already been formed). Nevertheless, the rules governing politics in the ROC (including the fact that the KMT legislators who occupy a majority of seats in the legislature do not have to stand for reelection unless and until the KMT returns to the mainland to hold elections there) still limit the role of the opposition.

Because of its size and level of economic development, Taiwan competes head to head with Hong Kong and Korea in many business areas. Decades after shedding Japanese colonial status, the island still has a special relationship with Japan (for example, some Japanese trade shows are open only to Japanese and Taiwanese exhibitors, and Japan accounts for the lion's share of foreign direct investment in Taiwan).

MAJOR TRADE AND BUSINESS OBJECTIVES

Like other countries in the region, Taiwan is worried about the danger of protectionist legislation in the U.S. In Taiwan's case, such legislation might be triggered by any of several factors, including tariff barriers, restricted market access, and massive exports to the U.S. (particularly textiles). Taiwan, which even more than Japan is embarrassingly rich (an expanding economy, large foreign exchange reserves, and a healthy annual trade surplus running well over US$10 billion a year in the late 1980s), is the source of America's fourth largest trade deficit (after Japan, the European Economic Community, and Canada). Furthermore, the U.S. is Taiwan's largest export market, so the threat of any action to restrict Taiwan's access to the U.S. market is taken very seriously indeed. Partly for this reason, Taiwan has been in the forefront in attacking the problem of intellectual property rights violations, an issue which is clouding U.S.-Asian relations in many sectors.

Taiwan is also concerned that a nagging surplus in trade with the U.S. may cause American protectionists to call for restrictions on products from Taiwan. However, it appears to be difficult for Taiwan to reduce the imbalance, in part because the relative size of the two economies places a greater burden on Taiwan. Although trade volume is in Taiwan's favor, Taiwan imports far more from the U.S., on a relative percentage basis, than the U.S. imports from Taiwan. The U.S. does absorb a significant percentage of Taiwan's total output, but these imports only amount to about 4 percent of total U.S. imports, and U.S. per capita purchases of Taiwan products are only about US$60 or US$70 annually. On the other hand, over 23 percent of Taiwan's total imports are of U.S. origin, and Taiwan's average annual per capita consumption of U.S. goods is a healthy US$200 (perhaps 2 or 3 percent of annual per capita income). It may be difficult for the ROC economy to consume many more American imports without suffering indigestion.

An especially touchy trade issue between the U.S. and Taiwan is textiles. While American textile manufacturers clamor for protection from relatively inexpensive imports from Taiwan, Taiwan (which depends heavily on the U.S. market for survival) is struggling to stay ahead of other Asian textile manufacturers with even lower production costs. Taiwan understands the Americans' problem, but (as in Korea) textiles are still such an important source of employment and foreign exchange earnings that to significantly reduce exports to the U.S. could be disastrous for Taiwan's economy.

As is the case with the PRC and Korea, many trade and business issues in Taiwan are heavily conditioned by political considerations. Because of the competition with the PRC, in which both political entities claim to be the sole legitimate ruler of China's one billion-plus people, the government of Taiwan actively fosters trade and business ties (including preferential trading and financing terms) with Third-World countries as a means of maintaining the friendship and moral support of the handful of countries that still recognize Taiwan as the Republic of China.

Ironically, trade relations closer to home are making it increasingly difficult for Taiwan to maintain its avoidance relationship (based on the "three no's") with the PRC. The same industrious, entrepreneurial spirit that motivates the citizens of the PRC to engage in private enterprise drives the residents of Taiwan to do business with the PRC. Trade with the PRC, although theoretically frowned upon, has increased steadily over the years and had exceeded US$2 billion per year by the late 1980s. Although most of this trade is still via Hong Kong (and thus easier to officially ignore), Taiwanese fishermen and others have long carried on a thriving direct business by sea with mainland coastal areas directly across from Taiwan, and in the late 1980s the ROC government even allowed a freighter or two to make an overt direct shipment because of "exceptional circumstances."

With the three no's having become, in practice, the three maybe's, in 1987 the ROC began allowing residents of Taiwan to travel to the mainland to visit relatives. Flights out of Taiwan were overbooked for months as hundreds of thousands of people attempted to make a temporary return to their home provinces. A significant side effect of the easing of travel restrictions was to give businesspeople from Taiwan an easy way to take advantage of the mainland's cheap labor. By making frequent trips under the guise of family visits, they could effectively establish and run manufacturing operations in the PRC.

Certainly, the profits to Taiwan from full trade relations with the PRC could be enormous and, as many Taiwanese businesspeople are quick to point out, open trade channels with the mainland would take much of the sting out of any protectionist moves against Taiwan by the U.S. In addition, formal legalization of investment by residents of Taiwan would provide limitless access to the PRC's vast supplies of cheap raw materials and labor and fully free Taiwan from the present squeeze between low-wage competition from developing countries and high-tech, automated producers of more sophisticated goods. A marriage of Taiwan's technical, managerial and production know-how with the PRC's materials and manpower would lead to the economical, high-quality manufacture of labor-intensive items that would benefit both parties economically. At the same time, it would help the ROC politically by injecting a large dose of entrepreneurial capitalist spirit into the areas on the mainland where Taiwan business is active. Unfortunately, progress in this direction was severely impeded by the PRC's heavy-handed crackdown following the violent repression of student demonstrations in Tiananmen Square in May 1989 (over a year later, the PRC announced the group execution of twenty dissidents to ensure harmony at the Asian Games). In spite of the cloud cast over the immediate future of business relations, the continued development of a de facto commercial rapprochement, which could inject moderation into mainland politics, appears to be in the best interests of all concerned parties.

Although Taiwan maintains significant restrictions on foreign entry into the Taiwan market and participation in the Taiwan economy, the situation is fluid and generally moving in the direction of an increasingly open economy. However, mere participation by foreign firms in local markets may not suffice to overcome ROC resistance to penetration; although foreign banks, for example, outnumber local banks in Taiwan, they have only about 20 percent of the local financial market.

More significant progress may occur in the area of direct investment, including overseas investment by Taiwanese citizens. In the early summer of 1987, the KMT announced an easing of foreign exchange curbs as a way to stimulate new areas of economic development and reverse (or at least slow) the rising tide of surplus foreign exchange. Earlier, in the late spring of 1986, the Legislative Yuan revised the laws governing investments by overseas Chinese and foreign nationals. The changes opened the service sector to foreign investment; in addition, the new regulations allow foreign-invested firms to remit capital gains (excluding profits from the sale or reappraisal of land) abroad after one year. (Such remittances were formerly restricted to originally invested capital.) Foreign-invested firms are also exempted from Article 267 of the Company Law, which requires that any company increasing paid-in capital must reserve 10 to 15 percent of new shares for purchase by employees.

These moves, coming at a time when a dramatic rise in the value of the Japanese yen put heavy pressure on the exporting competitiveness of Japanese manufacturers, undoubtedly helped stimulate a flood of new Japanese investment beginning in 1986.

Unlike Korea, which developed its economy through heavy industry and huge industrial conglomerates on the Japanese model (plus heavy doses of central planning and government intervention), Taiwan's economy is based on small and medium light industry and responsiveness to market forces (although under strict currency controls). So far, this strategy has been resoundingly successful: Taiwan, with roughly half the population of the ROK, enjoys a per capita income which is one and one-half times as large and far more equitably distributed. In addition, Taiwan's high savings rate (estimated in 1988 at an incredible 36 percent, the highest in the world) and export successes have propelled the small island to a position of world leadership in foreign exchange reserves: over US$70 billion and growing at a dizzying rate.

Traditionally, Taiwan's industry concentrated on labor-intensive items like footwear and textiles, now under heavy protectionist pressures from importing countries, including the U.S. In recent years, however, the island has developed a considerable capability in the manufacture and assembly of electronic parts and components, which will contribute to a planned shift to higher technology industries. In addition, the continuing migration of U.S. and European investment seeking lower production costs is accelerating the pace of industrial diversification, as is the recent influx of Japanese investment that was stimulated by the rise of the yen in 1985–1986. As a further precaution, Taiwan is making efforts to reduce its dependency on the U.S. as a market for exports, although diversification of trade patterns (the U.S. currently buys almost half of Taiwan's exports, with Japan and Europe taking about 11 percent each) is necessarily a slow process. Taiwan is also examining ways to encourage offshore manufacturing investment as a way of using excess foreign exchange and protecting access to the U.S. and other markets.

THE PERSON ACROSS THE TABLE

Just as a knowledge of the national and regional history of Asian countries can help you do business there, an awareness of the history experienced by the person with whom you are negotiating or doing business can give you a big advantage by helping you understand some of that individual's motives and underlying psychology. The following section, organized by approximate date of birth, provides an overview of the general background and experience of a person you might face across the negotiating table in the ROC.

* * *

1925: Saw the end of Japanese rule in 1945 (age about 20). If from mainland China, probably came in mass exodus following 1949 defeat of KMT forces by the Red Army. Experienced deprivation and unemployment as hundreds of thousands of refugees were forced to create new lives on the small island. If born on Taiwan, was brought up speaking Japanese in a heavily Japanese culture; was probably resentful of the dislocations caused by the overwhelming influx from the mainland. May have seen friends and associates lose rights, privileges and perhaps property as the KMT minority took control of the island and imposed martial law. Entered the labor force when Taiwan's economy was based almost totally on agriculture (Japan's breadbasket). Well qualified to do business with Japan. May have sent son to school in Japan to learn language and business.

1935: If born on Taiwan, had to switch from Japanese to Chinese language around middle school years. May have served in KMT Army during invasion scares and the PRC's shelling of Quemoy and Matsu (1950s). Was in a good position to get in on the ground floor of Taiwan's transformation from agricultural backwater to dynamic manufacturing center.

1945: Remembers little of life on the mainland. Entered the labor force when manufacturing economy was becoming well established, although on a low level. At the same time, large numbers of U.S. military from Vietnam used Taiwan as an R&R stop, causing mixed feelings about Americans. In his late twenties, his attitudes about the U.S. were further jolted by Nixon's visit to the PRC (1972).

1955: Grew up in an expanding economy, entered the labor force when Taiwan was evolving into a small but sophisticated manufacturing center and supplier of electronic components. Good timing for a career in export or electronics manufacture. In middle twenties most likely felt betrayed by U.S. recognition of the PRC (1979). If Taiwanese, may have sympathized with demonstrators demanding democratic rights (demonstrators were allegedly dispersed with extreme violence by KMT forces in Kaohsiung incident in 1979).

INTELLECTUAL PROPERTY RIGHTS

The ROC, once a notorious pirate lair, has moved farther and faster than many of its Asian neighbors to clean up its act and, beginning in the early 1980s, has made a number of moves to reduce violations of foreign copyrights, trademarks and patents. In the area of computers, for example, in 1984 an overly zealous Taiwanese judge sentenced a computer counterfeiter to a prison term even before the regulation under which sentence was passed had gone into effect. There is still much room for improvement, however, and purchasers have little difficulty buying counterfeit items ranging from music cassettes and designer watches to computer hardware and software.

In the more traditional realm of books and other printed matter, considerable progess has also been made. Although Taiwan is not a signatory to any international copyright convention, the threat of U.S. retaliation against Taiwanese products and the ever-present desire to gain political points with members of the U.S. Congress and others who might otherwise favor the PRC in trade and military matters induced the ROC government to extend protection to American authors. (The motives for the decision are indicated by the fact that writers from other countries are still fair game.) Effective January 8, 1986, the ROC government extended "national treatment" to American writers, meaning that U.S. authors now enjoy the same rights—including automatic de facto copyright protection upon completion of a work—previously enjoyed only by local writers.

Like the mainland Chinese (and other Asians), however, the Taiwanese government and business community do not give away anything unless they have to. Although the agreement covering American authors was good public relations, the concession was not much of a sacrifice since pirated books are the least important pirate/counterfeit sector in economic terms. Furthermore, Taiwan refused to extend protection to translations, which means that locals can still legally print and sell unauthorized Chinese-language translations of foreign works.

Although the ROC is not a signatory to the International Convention for the Protection of Industrial Property, foreign inventors or manufacturers may obtain patent and trademark protection by registering industrial property with the National Bureau of Standards, Ministry of Economic Affairs. Protection is limited to nationals of countries that give reciprocal treatment to nationals of Taiwan. Counterfeiting violations are handled by the Anti-Counterfeiting Committee of the Ministry of Economic Affairs, and any individual or entity with a complaint is encouraged to contact the committee. In all cases of counterfeiting, it is also advisable to contact the commercial section of AIT.

An inventor may file for a patent personally or use an assignee or successor or an authorized agent in Taiwan. Foreign inventors must apply through a local attorney. The length of patent protection is variable and runs from the date of proclamation as follows: invention—fifteen years; product—ten years; design—five years.

Penalties for patent infringement can be stiff. For counterfeiting items covered by one or more patents of invention, the maximum penalty is three years' imprisonment and/or a fine of NT$120,000. In addition, the patentee or licensee may be awarded damages through civil action. For utility patent violations, penalties range as high as two years' imprisonment and a fine of NT$30,000. Design patent violations can bring up to one year of imprisonment and a fine of up to NT$15,000.

As in much of Asia, trademark rights are granted to the first registrant, not the first user. After filing, there is a three-month waiting period to allow for any opposition to petition for denial of registration; after that time a ten-year trademark license, renewable for another ten years, is issued. The granting of rights to the first registrant often means that anyone can register any mark not already registered in the ROC, and force the established international owner of the mark to ransom it in order to use it in the ROC. There is, however, a provision in the law making it illegal for anyone, with intent to deceive others, to use a trademark which is identical with or similar to a well-known foreign trademark not registered with the Trademark Authority in connection with the same goods or goods of the same class, provided that the owner of the foreign mark in question is from a country providing reciprocal protection to nationals of the ROC. The penalty for violators under this provision is imprisonment not to exceed three years, and/or a fine of NT$90,000.

Penalties for registered trademark infringment range up to five years' imprisonment and/or a fine not to exceed NT$150,000. The following acts are considered violations:

1. Using the device of a trademark identical with or similar to a registered trademark on the same goods, or on goods in the same class;
2. Using the device of a trademark identical with or similar to a registered trademark on advertisements, labels, descriptions, quotations, or any other documents concerning the same goods, or on goods in the same class, and displaying or circulating the advertising materials.

Further, any person who knowingly sells, displays, exports or imports goods covered under the provisions discussed above is subject to not more than one year of imprisonment and/or a fine of up to NT$30,000, and the goods in question are subject to confiscation.

As noted above, American authors of printed matter enjoy copyright protection upon completion of the work. For Taiwan nationals, since 1985 all works including books, movies, records, photographs, videotapes, and computer programs enjoy this protection, which lasts for 30 years. Foreign nationals, however, are protected only if they meet the following criteria: the work is initially issued in Taiwan, *or* their home country recognizes ROC copyrights; *and* they follow all ROC procedures for copyright registration. Application for registration is made with the Copyright Committee, Ministry of the Interior. The ROC government advises foreigners seeking copyright protection to appoint an agent domiciled or with a place of business in the ROC.

TRADE AND TRADE REGULATIONS

Government trade policy of the ROC is evolving rapidly and trade regulations are subject to change. Traders are advised to contact the China External Trade Development Council (CETDC) and the Coordination Council for North American Affairs (CCNAA), which functions like a diplomatic and commercial corps for the ROC in the U.S., to get specific, detailed instructions and information regarding specific products.

Imports

The ROC divides import products and commodities into three categories: import permissible, import controlled, and prohibited. Over 97 percent of all listed import items (totaling 26,755 items) are in the "permissible" category, with under 2.5 percent in the "controlled" category and only fourteen items (mainly narcotics and some toxic chemical compounds) on the "prohibited" list.

In general, any registered trader may import items on the permissible list. However, certain raw materials and semifinished products may only be imported by manufacturers.

Controlled items, including military supplies, defense and communications equipment, explosives, radioactive substances, toxic chemicals, alcoholic beverages and cigarettes, may be imported by public trading agencies or by private sector manufacturers and end users for their own use. However, applications must be submitted to the Board of Foreign Trade (BOFT) of the Ministry of Economic Affairs for review on a case-by-case basis.

At present, 41 percent of the items on the permissible list require no import license, and a qualified importer merely needs to file an application for a letter of credit with an authorized foreign exchange bank. For other permissible imports, importers must apply for an import license issued on a case-by-case basis by the Board of Foreign Trade. Application may be made through any authorized foreign exchange bank. After obtaining the BOFT import license, which is normally valid for six months, the importer can get foreign exchange from the Central Bank and open an import L/C. There are also special licenses for importers who can provide their own foreign exchange.

Settlement for imports may be made in any of several ways: letters of credit in foreign currency, documents against payment, documents against acceptance, consignment, installment, or open account.

Customs duties on imports are assessed according to tariff schedules of the ROC, which are based on Customs Cooperation Council Nomenclature (CCCN). The range of duty rates is wide— from zero to 75 percent—and rate changes are frequent. The ROC also imposes a commodity tax ranging from 2 to 120 percent ad valorem on nineteen different types of commodities. Importers also have to pay a harbor construction fee, which is assessed at a variable rate of from zero to 4 percent of the dutiable value of imported goods. Items that enter the ROC via air freight or parcel post are exempt from this fee, however.

Samples without commercial value are duty-free, but the decision to place them in this category is made by the customs officials at the port of entry. Most advertising materials and catalogues also enter duty-free, but those deemed to have commercial value (including calendars, cigarette lighters, pens and similar items) are subject to duty at the normal tariff rate for the product in question.

In principle, customs duties are calculated on the CIF price of imported goods, and items lacking a "true" CIF price or bearing an incorrect or falsified price are valued at the wholesale market value at the port of importation. During the summer of 1986, Taiwan began to value all imports according to an arbitrary government price schedule, which in some cases had little relation to the actual price or value of the goods. But under U.S. pressure, the ROC government abolished the practice within a few months. This incident—and the frequent changes in ROC duty rates—illustrates the readiness of Asian governments to intervene vigorously and aggressively in the marketplace in order to maintain trade advantages.

Exports

Export goods are also divided into three categories: export permissible, export controlled, and prohibited. For most export permissible goods, export licenses are granted automatically by authorized foreign exchange banks, but it is still necessary to file an export application form with the bank in question. Export licenses are normally valid for thirty days, and complications can ensue if shipment is not made while the license is valid. For a number of goods, BOFT has waived the export license requirement. For these goods, if payment is made by an L/C, a qualified exporter may file an application ("Application for the Export of Chinese Goods") and supporting documentation directly with ROC Customs.

In the case of export controlled goods, the export license application is first filed for approval with the Board of Foreign Trade of the Ministry of Economic Affairs for approval and then filed with an authorized foreign exchange bank for issuance of the license. The criteria for approval are that the export of the items has no adverse affect on the ROC economy or the livelihood of ROC citizens and that no strategic goods will be transshipped or supplied to the PRC. Prohibited goods may not be exported under any circumstances.

Overseas remittance of export sales commissions is regulated by law.

ESTABLISHING A BUSINESS

Under the Civil Code and the Company Law (the two laws governing the formation and operation of business enterprises in the ROC) there are eight possible types of business entities: sole proprietorship, partnership, unlimited company, unlimited company with limited liability shareholders, company limited by shares, limited company, branch office of a foreign company, and representative office of a foreign company. According to the ROC government, the last two forms are "the most suitable" for foreign firms.

Branch Office (Purchasing Office)

It is important to note that under ROC law, a branch of a foreign company is treated as an extension of the home company overseas. This means that the home company is subject to the jurisdiction of ROC courts and is liable for any and all actions of the branch. In the event of litigation or tax disputes, liability will be extended to the total assets of the entire company. Once a branch has been established, any and all income derived by the home company from sources in the ROC is subject to both business tax and income tax under ROC regulations.

The first step in forming a branch office is to file an application for admission (under Articles 434 and 437 of the Company Law) and supporting documents with the Commerce Department, Ministry of Foreign Affairs (MOFA).

Once approval has been obtained, the foreign company may engage in business in the ROC, and is subject to all the same taxes and regulations as local companies.

Representative Office (Liaison Office)

A representative office (liaison office) or liaison representative is used by foreign companies who wish to set up a purchasing office in some form other than a branch or subsidiary. In the case of a liaison representative, any business transacted by the representative is subject to ROC tax laws. Any foreign company is advised to issue a letter of appointment spelling out the functions and scope of activity of the representative and to place a copy of this letter on file with the authorities as protection against tax liability for other business conducted by the representative.

To establish a representative office (under Article 386 of the Company Law) the interested party must file a report with the Commerce Department, Ministry of Foreign Affairs.

Commercial Agents

Rather than incur the trouble and expense of opening an office in Taiwan, foreign firms may use registered ROC companies or foreign companies or branches in Taiwan as commercial agents. The former requirement that commercial agents register with the Board of Foreign Trade, Ministry of Economic Affairs, has been abolished.

FOREIGN INVESTMENT

Foreign investment is regulated by the Company Law, by the Statute for Investment by Foreign Nationals, and by the Statute for Investment by Overseas Chinese. The existence of a special statute for overseas Chinese is yet another confirmation of the notion that Asia may be viewed as a number of ethnic clubs with special rules and treatment for members. Both the ROC and the PRC regard ethnic Chinese, regardless of current formal citizenship, as citizens of China and, as such, subject to different treatment than that extended to nonethnic Chinese.

The ROC allows four types of capital investment:

1. Cash in the form of foreign exchange, either remitted or brought into the ROC
2. Imports, against foreign exchange provided by the enterprise, of necessary machinery, equipment, raw materials for use of the enterprise, or commodities for sale (permissible imports category) to raise funds for working capital or plant construction
3. Technical know-how or patent rights
4. Any portion of principal, net profit, interest or any other income from investment that has been approved for exchange settlement

Foreign firms may make capital investment to establish new enterprises or expand existing enterprises. Such investment may be made individually, with other foreign nationals, or with ROC nationals. Foreign investors may also extend loans of cash, machinery, equipment or raw materials to the invested company. Detailed investment information is available from the Industrial Development and Investment Center (IDIC).

The ROC government provides a number of investment incentives, including the following:

1. New productive enterprises in the "encouraged" category may receive either a five-year income tax holiday, or accelerated depreciation of fixed assets. Within two years after start-up, specified capital-intensive or technology-intensive enterprises may choose to defer the application of the tax holiday by one to four years.

2. Productive enterprises in the "encouraged" category that increase capital to take measures that increase production are entitled to a four-year income tax holiday or accelerated depreciation and deferment of tax holiday benefits equal to those permitted for the original investment.

3. Enterprises that explore, exploit and process natural resources abroad and ship the products back to the ROC are eligible for a five-year income tax holiday and deferred application of tax holiday benefits.

4. Productive enterprises and large trading companies that conform to ROC criteria enjoy a cap on business income tax and surtaxes: maximum 25 percent of taxable income, reduced to 22 percent for specified capital-intensive or technology-intensive enterprises.

5. Research and development costs may be charged to the current year's operating expenses.

6. Machinery and equipment purchased specifically for energy conservation, waste treatment or pollution prevention are eligible for accelerated depreciation.

7. New replacement equipment is eligible for accelerated depreciation.

8. Payments to a foreign company for technical services related to plant construction for an "important productive enterprise" in the ROC are tax-exempt.

9. An approved overseas investor who is a director, supervisor or manager of his or her enterprise and who resides in the ROC for more than 183 days in any tax year need file no

income tax return on dividends received. Instead, dividends received are subject to withholding tax at the source.

10. Executives and technical personnel of a foreign enterprise with ROC approval for investment in Taiwan who reside in Taiwan on enterprise business for 183 days or less in any tax year are not taxed on salaries or other remuneration paid outside of Taiwan.

11. If a productive enterprise reinvests undistributed earnings for new or replacement equipment, machinery, or transportation facilities, the new issue of registered stock to shareholders is tax exempt in the current year. Subsequent sales or transfers of such stock are liable for tax assessment.

12. For productive enterprises, retained earnings may not exceed paid-up capital. For strategic industries, retained earnings may not exceed twice paid-up capital.

The first step in obtaining approval for investment is to file an investment proposal with the Investment Commission.

EXPORT PROCESSING ZONES (EPZs)

To expand local industrial capacity and diversify the economy, the ROC government has created three export processing zones (EPZs): Kaohsiung, Nantze and Taichung. Exports from these three EPZs, which employ about 85,000 workers, are over US$2 billion annually; yearly imports to the zones total over US$1 billion. The establishment of an export enterprise in an EPZ requires a minimum capitalization of US$150,000.

The EPZs offer foreign investors several advantages. Raw materials, parts and machinery may be imported into the zones duty-free, and finished products exported from the zones are also free of duty. If products manufactured in the EPZs meet standards set by the ROC ("Criteria and Standards for Encouragement"), and if the firms producing them are operating with new, locally purchased machinery and equipment, the firms pay no sales tax or commodity tax, and are granted a five-year tax holiday on corporate income tax or accelerated depreciation on fixed assets. Financing is available in the form of factory-building loans (ten-year loans of up to 70 percent of purchase price on standard factory buildings), factory-construction loans (for factories built to specifications) and export loans against L/Cs. All profits, in the form of distributed dividends, may be 100 percent repatriated after payment of any taxes due. Starting from the third year of production, invested capital may be repatriated at the rate of 15 percent per year.

To simplify procedures for foreign investors, the EPZ Administration and related agencies are empowered to handle all aspects of operations in the zones, including investment application processing and approval, company registration, construction licensing and approval, import/export licensing, customs clearance, and foreign exchange settlement.

Japan

For over a hundred years, Japan has owed much of its success to its ability to adapt and assimilate without compromising its identity. In much the same way that ancient China was able to survive invasion and ultimately defeat her conquerors by absorbing them, modern Japan has been able to integrate her commercial and industrial development with that of the West in a way that has enabled her to compete and win on Western terms. During the period of expanding contact and interaction with the West, this ability has also enabled the Japanese to rise above their neighbors in industrial and economic terms. At the same time, Japan has avoided the wrenching divisions that have shaken other societies attempting to achieve a necessary balance between modernization, development and tradition. While maintaining close contact with their roots and preserving the core of their cultural and social traditions perhaps more completely than other Asian nations, the Japanese have at the same time managed to utilize Western technology and methods with great success, as bricks held together by the mortar of Japanese tradition and social cohesion. Japan's freedom from the type of political division that hampers Korea and China is undoubtedly due in large measure to this accomplishment.

In addition, the forced demilitarization and democratization of Japan after the Second World War was the best thing that could have happened, in economic terms. The postwar political structure (totally dominated by the Liberal Democratic party for decades) has kept politics and ideology, which have been a serious handi-

cap in much of Asia, secondary to business and economic development. Demilitarization (since 1976, Japan has maintained a de
facto 1 percent ceiling on defense spending) has freed up enormous amounts of capital, technology and manpower for productive economic pursuits.

Because of language, culture, business practices, experience,
and proximity, the Japanese are more successful than any other
country at doing business with Korea and the PRC. However, the
Koreans are now giving the Japanese a run for their money in
several industrial sectors, and it is likely that they will be formi-
dable competitors in the PRC as political changes in the region
(less anticommunist militancy in the ROK and more pragmatism
in both the PRC and the DPRK) continue to make direct Korean-
Chinese business less politically sensitive.

Japan faces several potential handicaps in future competition
with Korea. Korean business with China will be helped by the close
interaction and cultural affinities between the two countries, by
their historical tendency to cooperate against the Japanese, and
by their resentment of Japan's recent military and economic dominance in the region. Official, high-level contacts between the ROK
and the Soviet Union (which came into the open when Korean
president Roh Dae Woo met with Mikhail Gorbachev in the
United States in June 1990) should give the resource-starved Koreans access to the abundant raw materials in the eastern part of the
Soviet Union. In addition, if detente between the ROK and the
Soviets leads to similar rapprochement between the United States
and North Korea, the ROK may be able to devote fewer national
resources to defense and more to trade and development.

At times the Japanese, normally astute international diplomats,
make ill-considered moves that could have a negative impact on
their commercial position in East Asia. As noted before, both China
and Korea were predictably outraged when, in the early 1980s, the
Japanese government ordered changes in history texts to eliminate
reference to the Japanese invasion of China and Korea. Other new
history texts favored by Japanese nationalist groups kept the dispute going through the middle of the decade. In 1985 the Japanese
prime minister's visit to a shrine honoring Japanese war dead cre-

ated another storm of protest in China, where some twenty million people lost their lives during the Japanese invasion of the 1930s and 1940s. In spite of Korean and Chinese sentiment, the Japanese still have the lion's share of Korea's foreign trade and investment penetration and have a very strong trade and investment position in the PRC. Nevertheless, in 1990 the Japanese emperor saw fit to break 2,600 years of tradition by formally apologizing to the Korean people for the damage and suffering inflicted on their country by Japan—the first outright apology (as opposed to vague expressions of regret for unfortunate events) ever uttered by an emperor of Japan.

For their part, many Japanese believe that their accomplishments in developing an economic infrastructure and expanding the educational base in Manchuria and Korea were unappreciated. They argue, with considerable accuracy, that the Korean ruling dynasty and its appointees were medieval autocrats who cared little for the welfare of their people or the progress of their countries. (In fact, the first Japanese move leading to the annexation of Korea came as a result of a popular uprising against the Korean king.) The Japanese also feel, with some justification, that the criticism they endure for their trade surpluses with China, Korea and the West is mostly a rationalization masking other countries' failure to organize effectively, modernize their industries, and manufacture superior products at competitive prices.

MAJOR TRADE AND BUSINESS OBJECTIVES

From 1945 until the 1980s, Japan had a very simple and clear-cut set of objectives: develop industry (always moving "upstream" into higher tech areas), export, and increase market share overseas. A corollary objective, one that has been shared by many Asian countries, was to protect the home market.

This aggressive "Japan first" strategy worked well for decades. After the shattering defeat of World War II, Japan's recovery (aided by demand generated by the Korean War) was nothing short of phenomenal. And the Japanese invasion of U.S. and other foreign markets was so swift and so complete that entire foreign industries were wiped out or put at risk by their Japanese competitors.

Beginning with the late 1970s, however, overseas businesspeople and politicians began to take note of Japan's economic expansionism, and by the early 1980s Japan was faced with a firm and growing opposition to its growth. The Japanese, ever quick to react to international change, responded by giving JETRO (the Japan External Trade Organization, a branch of Japan's Ministry of Trade and Industry charged with promoting Japanese exports) the task of helping balance Japan's trade position by providing guidance to Americans and other foreigners trying to penetrate the Japanese market. Not surprisingly, the JETRO fox was not the best guard for the chicken coop full of foreign competitors. The Japanese market remained a risky place for foreign business, and Japanese exporters, who were JETRO's original clients, continued predatory practices in a number of sectors.

By the mid-1980s it was clear to everyone that something had to change. An aroused U.S. Congress, backed by labor unions, manufacturers, and a significant portion of the American public, began to prepare severe countermeasures, and the U.S. Department of Commerce took a new, tough line on the issue of dumping by Japanese (and other Asian) companies. In response, the Japanese moved to protect their share of the U.S. market (and defuse criticism and retaliatory action) by setting up manufacturing in the U.S. At the same time, numbers of Japanese firms entered into manufacturing in other Asian countries, with the goal of exporting the finished product to the U.S. with the essentially Japanese origin camouflaged by the non-Japanese point of manufacture.

The steep rise in the value of the yen relative to the dollar from the fall of 1985 to the spring of 1987 added a new factor to the equation. Although the Japanese economy enjoyed some windfall benefits because of the extra de facto discount on dollar-priced petroleum imports (the price of petroleum had already fallen drastically on world markets because of the collapse of OPEC's ability to control the market), Japanese exporters were unable to show a profit without raising prices on shipments to the U.S. In some cases (most notably automobiles, where American manufacturers foolishly raised their own prices instead of going after a bigger piece of the market), the price increases had little effect on market share. In others, however, Japanese exports became uncompetitive, resulting in a spate of bankruptcies.

Ironically, exporters of American products to Japan were also caught in this squeeze. Since many Japanese trading firms were involved in both import and export, some Japanese companies hit by losses on the export side found themselves so strapped financially that they were unable to place new orders for U.S. goods, even at lower yen prices, while others were unable to pay for U.S. merchandise ordered before the yen's meteoric rise.

Another result of the yen's rise was to make imports from the rest of Asia far more competitive in Japan's quality-conscious internal market. (Other Asian currencies have also risen against the dollar, but by smaller percentages.) Thus, Japanese manufacturers found themselves competing both at home and abroad with other Asian goods that were steadily improving in quality and had become relatively cheap. Survival-oriented Japanese firms responded by taking more manufacturing offshore, not only to export to the U.S. but also to sell back in their home market. At the same time, many Japanese manufacturers were able to cut operating costs in Japan to the point where they regained or even improved on earlier profit margins. There is no way to tell, at this point, what the net result of the changes in the 1980s will be. Historically, the Japanese have shown an impressive resilience and adaptability as well as a sense of realism in trade matters the United States would do well to emulate. The odds are that Japan will continue to grow as the world's premier exporter of manufactured goods, often by aiming at and cornering the top end of a given market or sector.

THE PERSON ACROSS THE TABLE

Just as a knowledge of the national and regional history of Asian countries can help you do business there, an awareness of the history experienced by the person with whom you are negotiating or doing business can give you a big advantage by helping you understand some of that individual's motives and underlying psychology. The following section, organized by approximate date of birth, provides an overview of the general background and experience of a person you might face across the negotiating table in Japan.

*　*　*

1925: Childhood in an expanding, militarized, imperial Japan. May have served in armed forces during World War II. During and after high school, lived through near starvation, saw saturation bombing of cities and widespread poverty after the war. Entered the labor force under the U.S. Occupation (1945–1952). Has seen Japan expand and rise, fall to the bottom, then rise again to the top.

1935: As a child, experienced bombing and deprivation. During the Occupation, saw total social change, including radical revision of educational system (even including the writing system) and new constitution. Was seventeen years old when the Occupation ended in 1952. May have been part of massive student demonstrations against the Japan-U.S. Security Treaty (1960). Entered the work force when the Korean War (1950–1953) had given the Japanese economy and industry a shot in the arm—perfect timing for an entrepreneur.

1945: Grew up in constantly expanding economy, but experienced the scarcity and the gritty, shabby atmosphere of the postwar years. Whole life has been spent under a democratic system. Entered the labor force just as Japan was becoming established in technology (world's first high-speed train line, 1964) and world events (Tokyo Olympics, 1964). Right age and experience for a career in Japan's first generation of international managers.

1955: Grew up in a modest but increasingly prosperous era. Entered the work force at the start of Japan's major expansion in the manufacture and export of top-quality durables, optics, consumer electronics. Has seen Japan transform itself into the world's premier manufacturing and economic power. Still has the famous work ethic and may be disturbed by younger colleagues who seem less dedicated. More superficially cosmopolitan than his older colleagues, but often less aware than they of the reality of international politics and economics. Also more accustomed to foreigners—and more adept at tuning them out.

DEALING WITH THE JAPANESE

The Japanese behave quite differently from the Chinese or Koreans, and the difference is often one of kind, not just degree.

Many foreign businesspeople and negotiators are nonplussed at the lack of feedback they receive when dealing with the Japanese. In technical seminars or trade and investment presentations, for example, it is difficult to tell whether or not you are reaching your audience because the Japanese are not in the habit of reacting visibly to what they are hearing. After a presentation, a call for questions is often followed by a long silence which may be embarrassing for the American who is used to dealing with audiences who like to speak up. One of the main reasons for this silence is the ingrained Japanese hesitation to take the lead or to stand out from the group in any way, which is considered bad form. Another reason is that the Japanese prefer to think things over and internalize them before reacting or responding, which leads to a sort of delayed-action response. And, of course, language is a major factor: people the world over hesitate to get up in front of a group and ask a question in a foreign language that they may not speak as well as they would like.

You can get valuable feedback, however, if you make it easier for your Japanese audience. First, eliminate the language barrier by at least having a qualified interpreter on hand. Since the Japanese feel more at ease going through a middleman in almost any situation, it is even better to have a native Japanese moderator on hand to solicit questions in Japanese. The moderator and the interpreter should not, however, be the same person since that is perceived as a mixing of roles. If you have set up the meeting with the assistance of a local Japanese chamber of commerce or industry association, arrange for them to provide a moderator. You can also make the audience feel more comfortable by taking the lead yourself, with the help of the moderator (or through the interpreter if you have no moderator).

Ask whether or not anyone has questions about specific portions of the presentation. Even though the Japanese do not provide as many visual cues as an American audience would, they are not totally poker-faced, so you will have gotten some changes of facial expression or other body language that will indicate points or topics that may need elaboration. Finally, don't let the initial lack of response throw you. Use the silence to review your presentation in your own mind, remember audience response to different items, and formulate suggestions on possible questions.

In discussions or negotiations, you will often find the Japanese following the same policy of remaining fairly silent, listening and taking mental notes. Don't expect immediate answers to questions because the Japanese normally want to think everything over before commenting on it, and they do not want to have to change their position or back out after they have made a verbal commitment to a course of action. In this situation, many foreign businesspeople continue to say more and more in order to fill the gap or get a response, therefore often revealing more than they need to or, at any rate, taking on an excessive burden. It is often more effective to go with the silences, or even to use the Japanese tactic and allow some silences to develop on your side of the table while you ponder the situation.

Another common Japanese habit—one that can drive foreigners to distraction and is even perplexing to many Japanese—is the avoidance of a direct answer or comment. "Yes," for example, more often means "Yes, I understand" than "I agree" or "I will do so." It is fairly rare for a Japanese to say no—partly to avoid being too direct and partly because it would be rude to reject comments, ideas or proposals made by another party. As a result, you will receive responses like "We'll consider it seriously" and "It's a very interesting proposal," which do not imply assent or intention to accept. Instead, they allow the Japanese side to be polite and leave all their options open without any commitment. Again, this tactic is a good one to emulate.

Whom should you approach when dealing with a Japanese company? As a rule, the smaller the company, the higher up the decisions are made. This may seem self-evident (after all, it is true in the U.S. as well, for obvious reasons), but in the case of larger companies, the Japanese decision-making process rarely starts as near to the top as it would in a U.S. company. Instead, an approach should often be made to a middle- or lower-middle manager, who will discuss it with his peers and then pass it up through the chain of command until it reaches the appropriate level for final approval. By the time it gets to this level, of course, approval merely means confirmation of the collective decision of all those who passed on the item on its way up. The "rubber stamp" aspect of high-level approval is particularly important in the many Japanese companies whose titular heads are primarily figureheads whose titles are rewards for long years of faithful service rather than indicators of decision-making ability. After receiving approval from higher-ups, the item will be referred back to the initiating level for implementation.

Since one of the keys to success in dealing with Japanese companies is knowing who the appropriate person to initiate and execute action is and what level that person occupies in the organization, it is important to have a local agent, representative or distributor who can provide that information and make the necessary contact. Otherwise, you run the risk of being referred to someone in the company who has been selected to deal with foreigners primarily because of his ability to speak English, rather than for his expertise or authority in the business matter at hand.

Books on Japanese management and Japanese business practices are full of discussions of duty, obligation, mutual respect, and other fine and noble concepts. The Japanese may apply these in their dealings with each other, but as a foreigner you simply aren't a member of the club. The Japanese are tough competitors among themselves, and with outsiders they are likely to play real hardball. Even a trusted partner can leave you wondering what happened, as the following case history shows.

A major U.S. manufacturer, attracted by the potential of the Japanese market, was determined to make the right moves. It hired a Japanese firm to do market research, and when the positive results were in, it hired a Japanese-speaking expatriate to be the in-country manager. Following the most frequently recommended course for exporters to Japan, the U.S. company teamed up with an experienced, qualified and highly regarded Japanese firm as its distribution agent and—knowing that designing for the market was crucial—signed license agreements with the same company. As a result of this textbook planning and execution, business was good from the very beginning.

Within a year, however, problems began to surface. The Japanese licensee began to be less cooperative, and the American expatriate resident manager complained that the Japanese side was keeping him in the dark on important decisions. Finally, the Japanese announced that they were going to compete with the Americans in the United States, using some of the concepts and designs that the U.S. partner had supplied under their agreement. Almost as a favor, they said that they were willing to continue the business relationship in Japan.

Under these circumstances, the American company sensibly decided to terminate the license agreement, find a new distributor, and continue to market in Japan the products that had been developed for the Japanese market. Then they discovered the bad news. Unknown to them, before they had entered the market, another Japanese company had registered the American company name with the Japanese patent and trademark office (a move that is legal in Japan). Later, the Americans' Japanese licensee had, without advising the American company, signed an agreement with the unauthorized (but legal) registrant which let the licensee use the mark in Japan. When the Americans terminated the license agreement, they found themselves legally unable to market goods in Japan under their own name while their erstwhile licensee now had both their manufacturing technology and the right to use their name without their consent. Much of this nightmare could have been avoided by simply checking to see whether or not the company name had been registered in Japan, but the Americans were too unaware to do so.

INTELLECTUAL PROPERTY RIGHTS

As the preceding example illustrates, foreign firms doing business in Japan often come to grief over intellectual property rights. In fact, some foreign industry sources claim that Japan has the developed world's highest rate of counterfeit products, labels and marks. A ride on a train or subway tends to confirm this opinion, as a wide variety of well-known name brands and designer labels are seen in clearly unauthorized contexts (for example, "For looking the happy, young seek the freshing life" followed by a well-known U.S. sporting goods brand). Some of the counterfeits are made in Japan while others, following the same trend as legitimate Japanese manufacturers in an era of rising Japanese labor costs and a soaring yen, are manufactured in Korea, Taiwan or Hong Kong for import into the Japanese market. Although the Japanese customs authorities and police are sometimes cooperative if requested to take action on a violation (as they should be—after all, bogus goods cheat the Japanese consumer and damage the business of legitimate Japanese importers, wholesalers and retailers), the plaintiff must do all the detective work and provide the evidence. And all too often the police inexplicably fail to take action even in well-documented and properly presented cases.

In the summer of 1985, Japanese officials reacted to international pressure by announcing an "action program" to deal more aggressively with the problem, but although a special police enforcement office was opened in Tokyo on April 1 of the following year (a date which provoked irreverent comments among the expatriate business community), the office is understaffed and still apparently doing too little about the problem.

Even though Japan, unlike Korea or Taiwan, has trademark laws with fairly stiff penalties for violators (a maximum fine of Y500,000—about US$3,000—and a maximum sentence of five years), prosecutions are often desultory. The average fine levied is about Y200,000 (under US$1,200), and considerably less than half the prosecutions result in the imposition of any penalty at all. Because the manufacture or sale of counterfeit goods is such big business (one U.S. sportswear manufacturer estimated losses on one line alone at hundreds of thousands of dollars per year), such light fines are a very acceptable cost of doing business.

As in other Asian countries, there is little awareness of the entire issue of intellectual property rights, and both officials and the public are generally unsympathetic to the problems of legitimate (foreign) owners. Even the relatively cautious steps taken and mild fines imposed by the authorities have on occasion aroused negative reactions in the media, which accuse the police of stifling business and wasting manpower on "victimless" crimes and criticize the intellectual property owners for creating the problem by overcharging (a point of view that is heard often throughout Asia).

In Japan (as in Korea) anyone can legally register any trademark, unless it can be proven that the mark has been in use in Japan and is well known in the country. It is not necessary for the registrant to have used the mark before (or after) registering it, which means that the Japanese can and do register foreign marks that are well known overseas but not yet in use in Japan, figuring that the foreign owner can later be counted upon to ransom the mark in order to enter the Japanese market. Those owners who refuse to do so may find that their attempt to use any similar mark or name is successfully challenged by the holder of their own mark.

The owners of video and audio recordings also face major problems in Japan. A 1986 on-the-spot survey by the Motion Picture Association of America revealed that at least 40 percent of the 5,000 videotape sales and rental outlets in Japan carried pirated tapes. Equally disturbing, about one-fourth of the shops stocking illegal tapes were run by *yakuza* (the Japanese crime syndicate) or similar hoodlums, which makes prosecution more difficult and dangerous.

In the area of on-line computer databases, the Japanese government appears to be moving in a positive direction. After a two-year study, a government body recommended in late 1985 that on-line computer databases be protected under copyright and that other on-line services, including videotex and interactive video services, be given similar protection. Regardless of laws that cover this area of intellectual property, the most important issue is that of wholehearted enforcement.

In Japan, a key test for copyright eligibility is *creativity*, a term which has yet to be given a precise definition. Intellectual property passing this and other tests is protected against unauthorized reproduction for fifty years.

MARKETING IN JAPAN

There is no question that the Japanese government bureaucracy raises many barriers to U.S. and other non-Japanese firms' attempts to market in Japan or that the highly personal and almost ritualized relationships in Japan's multilevel distribution system make it difficult for new suppliers to break in. However, pressure from the U.S. and other foreign governments appears to be having an effect on the former problem, and the use of a qualified Japanese agent, distributor or partner can overcome the latter difficulty. Popular American concepts notwithstanding, the most important considerations when marketing in Japan are related to the intensely competitive nature of the market and the high expectations of consumers and end users in all sectors.

There are a number of market characteristics that must be considered in order to undertake a successful marketing effort in Japan. Some of the most important ones are described below.

High Levels of Support from Suppliers

In virtually every product or service sector, markets in Japan are competitive to a degree unknown in most other countries. As a result, Japanese buyers, agents and distributors at all levels of the distribution chain are accustomed to receiving a greater degree of support than many foreign suppliers are used to providing. In the financing area, this support includes outright financing on favorable terms, buy-back agreements that shift the burden of unsold inventories from the buyer (wholesaler, retailer, etc.) back to the supplier, and extensive use of consignment sales. Suppliers also commonly provide comprehensive personnel services, including actual staffing of retail points of sale and training of the buyer's personnel. In the area of technical assistance, suppliers commonly work with buyers to help develop uses and applications for products and the necessary capabilities (including, in some cases, the design of new equipment) to go with them. In addition, suppliers will often assist in increasing product awareness at all levels by introducing and publicizing different uses for their product, by helping agents, distributors and other middlemen create advertising campaigns, and by engaging in other similar activities.

High Degree of Product Differentiation

Another result of the extremely competitive nature of the Japanese market is the great range of choices available to buyers at all levels. Because large numbers of companies are struggling to increase market share in all sectors, they have become adept at identifying small niches in their sector and being the first (or best) at creating products to meet the specialized demands in those niches. It is not enough to simply maintain (as many American suppliers and advertisers do) that "our product is the best." Instead, it is necessary to show the Japanese (whether agent, distributor, middleman or end user) how the product or service is different from what competing suppliers are offering. In this sense, it can be said that "All Japanese are from Missouri": they have to be shown. To make a sale, it is wise to present a wide variety of possible applications for materials and products, by bringing either samples or catalogues, with the latter written in Japanese.

Designing for the Market

In addition to product differentiation, intense competition makes it necessary to design for the market in Japan. The fragmentation of sectors into a multitude of small, specialized niches and the willingness of Japanese companies to create products to fit those niches mean that suppliers must be ready to work closely with local agents, distributors, middlemen and end users to provide products specifically designed for the market. Because of the size of the U.S. market, American firms can often be very successful at home if they identify a general market, design a product or line that meets the general needs of that market, and undertake a promotional campaign that creates a more specific market demand. In short, they create a market for their product. In Japan, successful suppliers must create their product for a market—the reverse of the common American process.

Small Initial Orders

Small initial orders are a natural outgrowth of competition, differentiation, and the Japanese willingness to design for the market. At all levels of the distribution chain, the companies and people involved with a new product or service must assure themselves that the new item will meet the very specific needs of the niches for which it is designed. If it doesn't, there is probably a competing item that does, and there is no reason to get caught with an oversupply of something that does not conform to demand. Even if the supplier provides a 100 percent buy-back program, the Japanese do not want the embarrassment of having to withdraw the stock and send it back. For those reasons, the Japanese at all levels usually want to begin with small orders and increase them as the product proves its suitability. In addition, the supplier should be prepared to make changes in the product from time to time, to adapt it even more closely to the market or to keep up with market evolution.

Insistence on Quality

The Japanese are accustomed to high quality, and they insist on it—after all, in such a competitive market, there is no reason for them to do otherwise. The concept of quality applies not only to the product but to the presentation of the product. Many U.S. businesses are happy to do business on the basis of "the bottom line," but for the Japanese, who take a more critical look at other factors, price and cost-effectiveness are often not enough. They are price-conscious, of course, but they are also looking for quality and consistent attention to detail in all parts of the business relationship. Do the foreign visitors appear to have done their home-work? Do they know what they are trying to accomplish, or are they on a fishing expedition? Has the foreign company (or state, or economic development group) prepared materials in Japanese? Is the Japanese free of grammatical and typographical errors? Has the foreign firm created a presentation that is clear and to the point, one that provides specific information that will help the Japanese make business decisions? How about samples that are presented—do they represent the very best that the foreign com-pany has to offer?

Need for Organization, Structure and Unity

Americans are justly proud of their individuality, and the Japa-nese are equally proud of their strong sense of unity, organization and structure. When dealing with the Japanese, U.S. missions and business visitors will find that success is much more likely if they adapt to the Japanese point of view. At meetings the "point man" or senior spokesperson for the American group should be made clear, not by direct reference but by his or her position as chairper-son or moderator for the American side in discussions. This does not mean that no one else should speak up at meetings, but that the U.S. group should act as a group, not as a collection of indi-viduals. In keeping with the Japanese desire for structure, business cards printed in Japanese and English should always be available so that the Japanese know the names and positions of those they are dealing with. Mission brochures with pictures, names and titles of the mission members are also very helpful in this regard.

Insistence on Reliability

In Japan, organization, unity and structure lead to a high degree of reliability. To the Japanese, it often seems that Americans lack commitment and are too eager to change their objectives or pursue targets of opportunity. Although Americans often characterize the Japanese as overly cautious or hesitant to commit themselves to a business relationship, this caution is usually due to their awareness that they are taking on a large commitment which they will do everything in their power to honor. The Japanese expect the same from U.S. companies and missions. American commercial officers receive many complaints from Japanese companies that U.S. organizations and businesses fail to answer letters and telexes promptly (and sometimes don't answer at all), don't follow through on promises to send samples, and break appointments with little or no notice. These actions are not only damaging to the business efforts of the U.S. party involved, they also make it harder for other U.S. firms to establish credibility and a reputation for reliability. To succeed in Japan, it is very important for the foreign company to live up to any promises made and to respond promptly to communications from Japanese business and trading partners, especially when problems or business emergencies arise.

Reliability extends to permanence in the marketplace as well. The Japanese need to feel sure that the U.S. business or trading partner will be in this market on a long-term basis, through bad times as well as good. As with other aspects of dealing with the Japanese, it is helpful to pretend that they are from Missouri: don't tell them; show them through your actions.

Tightly Knit Distribution Web

In spite of your best efforts, you may encounter frustration if you don't get good local representation. The Japanese distribution networks for most products are not as complicated as many commentators like to make them sound, but almost any Japanese network can seem like an impenetrable web if you try to get into it without inside contacts. Because everything is based on relationships, it is also hard to take advantage of external factors that should give you an edge. For example, even after the massive run-up of the yen between 1985 and 1987, the retail prices of U.S. imports, which should have come down by a considerable margin (thereby leading to increased sales), failed to budge because no Japanese retailer was willing to undercut the prices of Japanese products supplied by their Japanese wholesalers and distributors.

Foreigners often bemoan the fact that marketing in Japan isn't easy, but then it isn't easy for the Japanese either. The competition in Japan is fierce, and it is necessary to deliver a high level of service, quality and reliability just to keep up. To excel, there is no choice but to make the kind of effort that sportscasters like to call "110 percent."

ESTABLISHING A BUSINESS

The following section, although based on official Japanese government guidelines, is intended only to give you an orientation. The process of establishing a business in Japan is long, arduous, and full of pitfalls. As in the rest of Asia, the bureaucratic system is not transparent (i.e., outsiders are not allowed to see how it works). The authorities often deny permission for activities that appear acceptable, and there may be unexplained delays in granting permits, licenses and other necessary documentation. Any company or individual contemplating the establishment of a business presence in Japan is urged to discuss the possibilities with the commercial and/or economic section of the U.S. Embassy and to hire professional counsel if necessary to obtain interpretation of applicable Japanese laws and regulations. (The U.S. Embassy can provide a list of attorneys, some of whom are knowledgeable and competent in the field of Japanese business and administrative law.)

Other than simply exporting products to an importer, agent or distributor in Japan, there are four basic possibilities for doing business there.

Representative Office

Foreign representative offices, which are extremely limited in their scope of action, are allowed to do market research, facilitate contacts between the home office and Japanese firms, and serve as a general contact point and listening post. A representative office may not engage in any sort of business (taking orders, invoicing, importing, selling, making collections, shipping, and so on).

Since it cannot make money directly, it must be 100 percent funded by the home office. In spite of these restrictions, many companies establish a representative office as a prelude to full entry into Japan. It is a relatively inexpensive move and a relatively easy one since there are no restrictions and it is not necessary to file an application or report with any Japanese government agency.

Branch Office, Branch Retail Store, Branch Factory

This option gives you much more freedom of action because you are allowed to engage freely in trading, retailing, services, manufacturing, or any other business except for a few restricted sectors, mainly in utilities and in the financial area.

It is exceedingly difficult to obtain permission to establish a branch and do business in one of the restricted sectors. To do so, you must first get a special license from the appropriate Japanese government ministry or ministries. Next, you must have a resident agent in Japan file a report ("Report Concerning the Establishment of a Branch . . .") in Japanese with the Ministry of Finance (MOF) and with any other ministries that have jurisdiction. Filing is done through the Bank of Japan (BOJ). You must also register the branch at the registry office in the area where it is to be located. Finally, a report must be filed with the Bank of Japan if the type of branch is changed, if the business objectives are altered, if plans are canceled, or if the branch is terminated.

Equity Position (Stock Ownership) in a Japanese Corporation

Equity may be obtained by establishing a new, wholly-owned subsidiary, by starting a new joint venture with one or more Japanese partners, or by acquiring a minority or majority interest in an existing Japanese company. Basically, you must follow the same procedures as for opening a branch. Within three months prior to acquiring the stock, file a "Report Concerning Acquisition of Stocks" with the Ministry of Finance and other relevant ministries. After filing, you must normally wait at least thirty days before buying the stock so that the ministries have time to review your report. If there are special circumstances, the Foreign Exchange Control Committee may shorten the thirty-day review period to fifteen days or extend it to as long as five months. File the report (in Japanese) through the Bank of Japan. If the investor is not resident in Japan, a resident proxy must file the report. If the MOF or other ministries involved find that the proposed acquisition of stock is not in the national interest, they may, after consulting with the Foreign Exchange Control Committee, require changes in the proposed plan or deny it altogether. The foreign investor must file a report (through the Bank of Japan) with the MOF and other appropriate ministries within thirty days after the acquisition of stock. If a joint venture is involved, the foreign investor must file a report to the Fair Trade Commission within thirty days of executing the joint-venture contract.

The same sectors that are restricted relative to foreign branch activity are also restricted in direct investment. In addition, there is a list of about ten publicly held Japanese companies in which foreigners are barred from holding more than a specified percentage (ranging from 25 percent to 50 percent, depending on the company) of stock outstanding. Most of these companies are involved in the petroleum business; others include aircraft, nuclear energy, silk yarn, and drugs.

Licensing

Licensing is a convenient route for getting your products into the Japanese market. The disadvantage is that you have little control over the activities of the licensee, and you run the risk of having your technology diverted to third parties without your knowledge, or later used against you (either by third parties or by your licensee) in direct competition with your products.

Licensing in Japan may involve three types of items: (1) technical transfer, including intellectual property rights such as patents, designs, utility models and trademarks, (2) nonpatentable specifications, drawings, blueprints and technical know-how, and (3) management know-how.

Once again, you must report (through the Bank of Japan) to the Ministry of Finance and other relevant ministries. The report ("Report Concerning Conclusion of License Agreement") must be in Japanese and must be filed jointly by the licensor and the licensee. Nonresident licensors (including a branch of a foreign corporation) must file through an agent who is resident in Japan.

If the technology under license is not a designated critical technology or if the license is for a designated technology with consideration under 100 million yen, the license agreement may be signed immediately after filing the report. However, if licensing is designated critical technology sectors and if the consideration involved is over 100 million, you must give the authorities thirty days (which may be reduced to fifteen days or increased to four months at the discretion of the ministries) to review your report before you sign the license agreement. Critical sectors include defense, nuclear energy, selected high-tech fields and, surprisingly, leather and leather products.

The reasons behind the inclusion of leather as a critical sector provide a fascinating glimpse into the types of factors that can make some Japanese (and other Asian) decisions so baffling to Western businesspeople. The politics of the leather industry in Japan are byzantine because of its socioreligious roots. Since Buddhist precepts forbid the killing of animals, over the centuries the individuals—and their descendants—involved in activities like the slaughter of livestock and the tanning of hides have come to constitute what amounts to an untouchable caste. The social problems created by this situation have made the leather industry a very delicate issue in Japanese politics; hence the designation of leather and leather products as a critical industry.

If the Japanese ministries determine that the license agreement as proposed is contrary to the national interest, they may refuse to allow it or may require you to modify it. To avoid unnecessary delays, it may be advisable to discuss your proposal with the authorities before submitting it in writing; once a written proposal has been submitted it must often pass through several hands before being returned to you for revision.

Within thirty days of signing a license agreement, the licensor and licensee must file separate reports with the MOF and other relevant ministries (via the BOJ) and with the Fair Trade Commission.

Korea:
Background

The Korean people are a very homogeneous ethnic group. Before the Japanese annexed the Korean peninsula in 1910, Korea was ruled by a traditionalist dynasty that had held power for about five hundred years.

Just before the end of the Second World War, Soviet troops invaded Korea as part of the Soviet offensive against the Japanese on the Asian mainland. Although the Soviet Army had taken and held positions well south of the thirty-eighth parallel, the U.S. and the Soviets reached an agreement whereby the Soviets would withdraw to the thirty-eighth parallel, after which U.S. forces were to administer the physical withdrawal of Japanese troops and personnel south of that line while the Soviets handled the same process north of it. Once this had been accomplished, free elections were to be held and the entire peninsula was to revert to Korean rule under a single, civilian government.

This temporary military administrative arrangement was prolonged when the Soviets refused to abide by the provisions for free elections. The result was a de facto division of the country into a communist north and a noncommunist south. This division was perpetuated when the Korean War (1950–1953) ended in a stalemate that left the opposing sides administering territory divided along a line that extends diagonally from the north side of the thirty-eighth parallel on the east coast to slightly below the parallel on the west coast above Seoul.

By the end of the 1980s there was still no peace treaty between the two sides. Instead, there was an armistice that left two well-equipped armies facing each other across the narrow DMZ with frontline troops within easy rifle range of the other side. Not surprisingly, the armistice was broken by hundreds of firefights and sniping incidents every year. Since 1953 the two sides have held numerous talks at the Panmunjom conference site located in the DMZ, but most of these have been complaints of real or alleged military provocations. Many of the sessions, including those held to discuss nonmilitary issues, have quickly degenerated into mutual recriminations which have caused one or both sides to stalk angrily from the room.

The government of the noncommunist south, now called the Republic of Korea, does not recognize the political division of the peninsula. Many Koreans prefer that their country not be called "South Korea," since this implies a political division of the Koreans into separate countries. They are more comfortable with "Republic of Korea" or simply "Korea."

The United States has about ten thousand troops stationed at or near the DMZ. This force, located along the only major invasion route to Seoul, is responsible for defending only one kilometer (about 1,100 yards) of the border. The U.S. troops are not expected to stop an attack but to serve as a deterrent by constituting a trigger that would ensure U.S. retaliation in the event of an attack by the north.

In 1980 civil disorders in the southern city of Kwangju caused the ROK government to withdraw a combat division from the DMZ and send it to Kwangju, where it retook the city from armed civilian insurgents who held it. These troops killed at least hundreds and perhaps thousands of civilians, many of them unarmed noncombatants. Since the Korean forces were technically under a joint military command structure headed by an American general, many Koreans hold the U.S. responsible for the massacre and some believe that the U.S. military either ordered or authorized it. The U.S. government version is that the Korean general in command of the troops withdrew them from the line and informed the American military only after the fact. The general in command was Chun Doo Hwan, later to become president of the Republic of Korea (1981–1988).

Much of the Korean radicals' hostility toward the U.S. is based on alleged American responsibility for the Kwangju massacre and on U.S. support for Chun Doo Hwan while he was in power. The Kwangju massacre has become the most important event in post-war Korean politics, and it will continue to affect the viability of the U.S. presence in Korea for years.

Republic of Korea (ROK)

The Republic of Korea faces two major issues: relations with the north and the communist world, and the legitimacy of the ROK government. These issues are closely related to the politically sensitive problem of the presence of about 40,000 U.S. troops on the peninsula, which in turn affects Korean perceptions of U.S. business activity in their country. The periodic euphoria (triggered by such events as north-south sports talks to contacts between the ROK and the Soviet Union) that causes predictions of peaceful reunification of the peninsula before the end of the century does not alter the fact that the two Koreas are still armed, dangerous, and technically at war. On the domestic front, despite the generally fair election that resulted in a peaceful transfer of power when former president Chun Doo Hwan stepped down in 1988, radical factions continue to identify the government with militarism and dependence on the U.S. and periodically take to the streets in highly disruptive and violent antigovernment demonstrations with anti-American overtones.

The potential for conflict with the north causes a significant drain on national resources, including the necessity of maintaining a large standing army (some 650,000 men). It also contributes to the problem of legitimacy. The Korean military, although much less politically visible than in the past, will probably have to be satisfied with whoever runs the country; at the same time the so-called "ruling military clique" is one major target (the U.S. is another) of criticism from students and other opposition groups in spite of the fact that free and fair elections have finally become a part of the Korean political scene. This polarity generates high-energy tension that shows signs of becoming institutionalized. Widespread civil disorders that broke out in the spring of 1987 and continuing periodic violence (much of it aimed at American cultural centers) involving hundreds of students are disturbing reminders that elections have not resolved the domestic political situation.

Another problem is the overconcentration of population (about 25 percent) in Seoul, which is only a few miles from the DMZ and the Democratic People's Republic of Korea (DPRK). This demographic imbalance, which has worsened despite attempts by the government to limit the growth of the capital, has caused uneven economic development. Not only are there more business and career opportunities in Seoul, a degree from a university in Seoul virtually guarantees a better job, and the centralized nature of Korean society means that the rest of the country is dominated by public and private sector institutions (including everything from trade and industry associations and corporate headquarters to universities and R&D centers) in Seoul. The result is that other commercial and industrial centers suffer a continuous drain of human and financial resources.

Even though the PRC's entry into the Korean War on the communist side prolonged the war and added to the suffering of the Korean people, Koreans identify with mainland China in many respects, and the ROK government has long sought good relations with the PRC. The government's eagerness became apparent as early as 1984, when the hijacking of a mainland airliner to the ROK gave the Seoul regime a chance to extend red-carpet treatment to passengers, crew and PRC negotiators sent to arrange for the plane's return. Recognizing that the PRC is a natural market and business partner in many sectors, both the ROK government and major Korean conglomerates send businessmen and officials there, and additional contacts are made in Hong Kong, Japan and elsewhere. Although the ROK is careful to preserve its fraternal relationship with the Taiwan (Kuomintang) government, the KMT can see the writing on the wall; articles by government officials in the Taiwan press have been preparing people on Taiwan for the eventual loss of their strongest Asian ally.

Koreans feel very different about the Japanese. They harbor considerable ill will toward Japan because of Hideyoshi's invasion of Korea (1592–1598), the reduction of Korea to a Japanese colony from 1910 to 1945, the profits garnered by the Japanese from the Korean War, and the position that the ROK presently occupies as an involuntary first line of defense for Japan against (increasingly unlikely) threats from the Soviets, the DPRK or the PRC. Although the military situation is caused to a great extent by geography, the Koreans tend to attribute it solely to Japan's unwillingness to assume a fair share of responsibility; at the same time they would strongly oppose any Japanese moves toward rearmament and would doubtless reject Japanese military aid. At any rate, there is resentment against Japan over the significant disparity in percentage of GNP spent by the two countries on defense. (The ROK spends about 12 percent, Japan less than 1 percent.) Japanese treatment of the some 800,000 Koreans living in Japan is also a sore spot, as is the perennial trade imbalance in Japan's favor and the persistent Japanese refusal to sell advanced technology to Korean industry. Korean students tend to blame Japan (together with the U.S.) for many of the country's ills. Nevertheless, Japan, while keeping a very low profile (it is impossible to find a Japanese billboard in Korea and the Japanese embassy is virtually indistinguishable from the buildings around it), has the lion's share of foreign trade and investment in the ROK. Despite setbacks caused by the Japanese texbook controversy mentioned above (the offending sections have since been modified to make it clear that Japan was an aggressor in Korea), relations with Japan improved dramatically in the 1980s, especially since the Japanese emperor's formal apology (grudgingly accepted in 1990) for wrongs committed in the past. Future relations will depend largely on conditions on the Korean peninsula; both Korean politicians and radical leaders tend to turn to Japan-bashing when Korea's internal problems become too pressing.

MAJOR TRADE AND BUSINESS OBJECTIVES

After the Korean War (1950–1953), Korea's main objective was survival. By the 1960s, however, the authoritarian but forward-looking Park Chung Hee was putting the country on the path to rapid industrial development. After Park's assassination in 1979, the government of ex-general Chun Doo Hwan was generally able to continue the trend, moving beyond the heavy industrial (steel, cement, shipbuilding, chemicals) orientation of the Park years to everything from automobiles and consumer electronics to biotechnology, semiconductors and computers. This movement has continued, with Korean companies moving aggressively into world markets formerly dominated by the Japanese.

It is impossible to separate the ROK's stance on business, trade and development from the legacy of the past (under Japan) and the present (under the onus of political division between north and south). Koreans of all political persuasions seem united in their determination to surpass the Japanese and prove once and for all that Koreans, rather than being backward country cousins, are a nation of high-tech go-getters who deserve the same respect and status that they once had as the bearers of Chinese (and local) culture to the Japanese. Many Koreans believe that the Japanese are so determined to prevent a Korean renaissance that they have obtained America's commitment to keep the peninsula divided.

Another powerful motivation is peninsular politics: the ROK has sought to facilitate reunification by outstripping the north and becoming so much more prosperous, economically powerful and internationally accepted that the rival communist regime would see the wisdom of cooperation. In this regard, the example of a pragmatic, market-oriented mainland China has raised many hopes, for if the PRC could in just ten years go from the left-wing radicalism of the Cultural Revolution to the fostering of private enterprise and foreign investment, the DPRK might also be capable of major changes.

The ROK has used trade and business to put itself in a stronger political and economic position. In 1989 it quickly leveraged a still-recent trade agreement into full diplomatic relations with Hungary, and at about the same time it launched a well-publicized series of business and trade discussions with both the Soviet Union and the PRC. Undoubtedly prodded by these ROK successes in dealing with the DPRK's communist allies, the North Koreans made several important conciliatory gestures, including the signing of a joint venture agreement to develop a tourist resort at a mountain site located in the north and the opening of the northern capital of Pyongyang to Korean-Americans wishing to visit family members.

Realistically, however, these modest steps are a long way from the Korean dream of reunification, and even as they were being taken, the north continued to lambaste the south for alleged military provocations and shooting incidents along the DMZ. Korean politics tends to be a winner-take-all proposition and it is unlikely that there would be a place in either system, northern communist or southern capitalist, for leaders of the other side. An example of this all-or-nothing mentality could be seen in the DPRK's response to the historic meeting between ROK president Roh Dae Woo and Soviet president Gorbachev in 1990; instead of responding favorably to the reduction of international tension implicit in the meeting, the Korean communist regime reacted with dark threats of permanent hostility if the ROK became too friendly with the USSR.

Some sort of Korean confederation might be possible, but many Koreans in the south are in no hurry because they believe that time is on their side. After all, they are on increasingly good terms with the north's most significant allies, and their economy—growing at over 10 percent in some years while the north is hard put to attain 2 percent growth—is pulling far ahead of the economy of the north. Accordingly, they may choose to wait until they can obtain a solution on southern terms. Centuries of Korean history indicate that the most likely alternatives to the present stalemate are absorption of one side by the other or periods of hostility punctuated by occasional temporary alliances of convenience.

So far, the ROK has done a good job of meeting the objective of economic expansion. For years real growth has averaged over 7 percent, and there are no serious economic obstacles on the horizon. The rapid rise of the Japanese yen between 1985 and

1987 was a real boon to the Koreans, whose currency rose far more slowly: as the dollar and the Korean won went down against the yen, Korean exports rushed into the gaps left when newly expensive Japanese products failed to hold market share in the U.S. and elsewhere; and Korean goods, now much cheaper than local products, began appearing in volume on the shelves of Japanese stores. Meanwhile, Korean companies had already been challenging the Japanese in some of their strongest export sectors (steel, ships, consumer electronics, automobiles) with great success.

The two dark spots in the picture are labor and politics. Korea, like most newly industrialized countries and most of the nations of Asia, has an authoritarian labor environment in which most strikes are illegal (workers' attempts to organize are still met with employer violence), and workers have virtually nothing in the way of workers' compensation, unemployment insurance, and other benefits. At the same time, the average annual per capita income (less than one-fourth of that of Japan) is simply not high enough to allow the vast majority of Korean workers (blue- or white-collar) to enjoy many of the consumer items they are producing. At some point, the labor environment is going to have to open up, and what will happen to the economy when it does is anybody's guess. If wages are allowed to rise too rapidly, as some businesspeople fear they might under a liberal regime, Korean products could become too expensive to compete in world markets. If wages are not significantly raised, prolonged walkouts (legal or not) could be even more damaging to the economy than higher-priced export goods.

On the political front, any radical shift may well be opposed by the military (who still enjoy significant privilege under the present system) and by at least some of the business establishment who prefer a less than ideal, but still very functional and productive, system to the possible economic upheaval and risk of North Korean aggression or subversion that could accompany major changes. The conservative case was strengthened in the spring of 1987 when domestic violence caused many Western businesspeople to reconsider plans to invest in Korea or to source products there. At the same time, pressure for some sort of basic restructuring of the political system continues to build, mainly among students but with some middle-class support. At this point, one of the main restraints on radicalism is the fact that every year most Koreans are better off than they were a year or two earlier. However, the Korean economy is highly leveraged and heavily dependent on exports. Two or more bad years in a row in the world economy or retaliatory trade restrictions caused by the ROK's own protectionist policies could enlarge existing cracks in the nation's political and economic order.

To protect access to foreign markets, many Korean industries are taking manufacturing offshore. At home, the ROK government is deemphasizing traditional (and troubled) industries like textiles and providing incentives to favored industries including auto parts, electronics, components, consumer durables, and others. The government has also increased support for R&D in a number of scientific and high-tech fields. Banks, although private, are tightly controlled, as is foreign exchange. In the future, the main question in business (as in labor and politics) will be how to loosen the government's grip without things falling apart. Here the experience of the PRC should provide interesting and valuable lessons.

THE PERSON ACROSS THE TABLE

Just as a knowledge of the national and regional history of Asian countries can help you do business there, an awareness of the history experienced by the person with whom you are negotiating or doing business can give you a big advantage by helping you understand some of that individual's motives and underlying psychology. The following section, organized by approximate date of birth, provides an overview of the general background and experience of a person you might face across the negotiating table in Korea.

* * *

1925: Childhood and college spent under Japanese colonial occupation. Forced to learn and speak Japanese in school. May have gone to a Japanese university, may have served in the Japanese

Army. Entered the work force during the turbulent period of the late 1940s. At age twenty-five, life was disrupted by the Korean War (1950–1953). Probably served in the ROK Army, probably lost relatives. May still have relatives unaccounted for in the DPRK. At war's end, was ideally positioned for entrepreneurship during rebuilding period.

1935: Elementary school was under the Japanese Empire. Attained minimum military age (sixteen or eighteen) during the Korean War, probably served. First major exposure to any foreigners was U.S. and U.N. troops. Had a good chance to rise with the ROK economy as it went from oxcarts to electronics.

1945: Childhood marred by the Korean War (1950–1953) and resulting misery, hunger and poverty. Up through age twenty or so, saw overwhelming U.S. influence, huge USAID mission literally running the economy. Entered the work force with many major Korean companies well established (mid-1960s), if sometimes on a low technological level. Has probably been in ROK Army, may have served with ROK forces in Vietnam. Entire career has been spent in a rapidly developing and constantly expanding economy. Well positioned to be part of Korea's first generation of international trade managers.

1955: Entire life has been in an economy taking on a new industrial character after the destruction of the Korean War. The war itself, as past history, means little. By high school age, the ROK was still heavily agrarian but definitely destined to grow and modernize. Entered the work force under the industrializing regime of Park Chung Hee. Many of his generation have U.S. college degrees. Is strongly motivated to overtake Japan, eager to open business with the PRC, wants to see Korea universally recognized as a world-class business and economic competitor. A member of Korea's first generation of internationalist technocrats, well positioned to help guide Korean moves into electronics, durable exports, offshore investment.

DEALING WITH THE KOREANS

Korea is a tough place to do business, so much so that many foreigners (including Western business executives active in Korea) ask why Western businesses want to be active there at all. There are several answers to this question, many of which involve future possibilities more than present returns. The Korean economy is dynamic, and Korea represents a very good potential market for Western goods and services. It is a growing market that cannot be ignored; therefore, many Western companies have made the decision to enter it with an eye to the future. Some of these companies have had to make painful and expensive readjustments (including disinvestment), and others have had problems that absorbed undue amounts of corporate resources, including time and energy. Although there is good potential in Korea, foreigners should look carefully at both the pros and cons of doing business there before making a commitment.

Even though the Koreans get down to business faster and get moving quicker than the highly structured Japanese or the bureaucrats in the PRC, you need as much or more patience to do business in Korea because it is so difficult to create a lasting agreement. Often, almost everything you have agreed upon seems to be subject to further negotiation as the Korean side tries to extract further advantages. For Westerners trying to understand the dynamics of contract negotiation and resolution in Korea, the relationship between the two halves of the divided peninsula is instructive: a cease-fire in place; no final peace treaty (and no significant progress toward the stated goal of peaceful reunification); and an endless round of negotiating, mutual recriminations, probing for weak spots, and jockeying for a superior strategic position (both military and diplomatic). In a sense, this political situation is a metaphor for many Korean business relationships.

Some foreign businesspeople come away from Korea complaining that Koreans are untruthful, but this generalization is unfair. As we noted earlier, Asians—and perhaps especially Chinese and Koreans—have the attitude that everything in life and business varies according to the circumstances of the moment. Therefore, although they may agree in all sincerity to a given set of terms and conditions, they feel no qualms about abandoning the agreement if circumstances change. Changed circumstances warranting such a switch in posture are not limited to Western concepts of force majeure, but include such factors as the desire to increase profit margins in one business activity or sector to make up for poor performance in another.

A related factor in dealing with Koreans is their desire to give you good news regardless of whether or not good news is in stock at the time. They practice what you might call relative truth: they tell you not just what you want to hear, but what they would like to be true, or what they hope has a chance of being true. This seems to be what they mean when they talk about "sincerity," a concept that is ill defined but very important throughout Asia.

A variation on relative truth hinges on an anticipated result: if things work out as desired, there is no harm in providing an imaginative account of how it happened. In fact, the imaginative account may as well be created first since it will give the foreign business partner the incentive to push forward. In one such case, for example, the officers of a Korean company told a would-be foreign joint-venture partner that necessary ministerial approvals were a sure thing because the Korean company president had a close personal relationship with key ministers involved in the approval process. Of course, if the project had been approved, the U.S. side would have been totally contented, and the joint venture would have gotten under way with considerable goodwill toward the Korean partner. Unfortunately, however, the project was not approved—in part because there was in reality no personal relationship between any minister and anyone in the company. One of the most revealing things about the whole situation was the attitude of the Americans' Korean contact, who cheerfully admitted his deception with the justification that he had been sure the deal would be approved and had wanted the Americans to feel confident.

Perhaps because they have always bounced back after having been down so often in the past, Koreans have an apparently boundless faith that things will turn out well. Their tendency to focus on the end result may be one reason that Western notions of truth get pretty blurry in the process. Your Korean contacts (including employees) will often make commitments, agree to take action, or even tell you that vital steps have been taken when in fact nothing has been done. Furthermore, they may be incensed (and show it in no uncertain terms) if you act independently to verify the accuracy of their claims or ask for details or some sort of tangible proof. Don't be dissuaded by displays of injured pride or indignant professionalism. Be gently but firmly insistent, and remember that in Korea seeing is believing.

In some situations, your Korean contact will say nothing because he can come up with no good news (real or fabricated). This can lead foreigners to unwarranted conclusions of dishonesty, as it did one U.S. company that sent some industrial equipment to Korea for a trade show. After the show, their new Korean agent, who was supposed to return the equipment, failed to do so. When he also failed to respond to their telexes, the Americans, convinced that he had absconded with the equipment, asked the U.S. Embassy for help in bringing him to justice. As it turned out, the man had simply been embarrassed by his failure to sell the equipment at the show and had been carting it the length and breadth of the peninsula looking for a buyer. To him, it was more important to wait until he could report a sale than it was to reassure the U.S. company by answering their frantic telexes.

Another common way for Koreans to influence Americans' perceptions and actions is to show them a good time. Incredible as it sounds, there are still plenty of U.S. businesspeople (and, it should be added, politicos and State Department types) who suspend any semblance of good judgment or objectivity after a couple of days and evenings in the company of smiling, charming Koreans who show them the time of their lives. It is hard to pinpoint the qualitative differences, but the Koreans probably outdo any other people on the face of the earth in their ability to send people home happy, optimistic, and full of warm and friendly feelings. Many an agreement has been signed under these conditions, only to unravel later in the cold, hard light of implementation. You are well advised to put personality aside to verify the probability of success through independent sources and to examine carefully the actions of your Korean associates to be sure that they match their words. Finally, don't allow yourself to be rushed into long-term, exclusive commitments. You are far better off to base the continuance of business relations on performance by the Korean side.

The reverse side of charm and, for want of a more diplomatic word, manipulation, is often a coldly efficient method of imposing their own terms and conditions on the actual business transacted. Remember the story recounted earlier about the U.S. manager who had been continually frustrated by the seeming incompetence of his smiling, friendly staff and his Korean counterparts in a joint venture. He only learned the truth the weekend before leaving the country, when he went out for an evening of drinking with the Korean manager he worked with. After a few drinks, the Korean confided ("confess" would imply a sense of remorse) that since his company had learned all they needed from the joint venture, top management had instructed everyone that nothing requested by the American manager—all the way down to such details as keeping the bathroom supplied with toilet paper—was to be done properly or on time. The purpose was to exceed the American side's level of tolerance for frustration and induce them to withdraw on terms favorable to the Koreans, who would then have the market to themselves. This type of situation is difficult to deal with, but you will have an easier time if you have reserved the right to turn to other Korean companies rather than getting prematurely locked in with just one.

A variation on these hardball tactics involves the exploitation (sometimes unwitting, sometimes not) of the authority of the government. In one well-publicized case of the early 1980s, a major U.S. company, after repeatedly failing to get Korean government permission for activities needed to make the joint-venture's operations profitable, disgustedly withdrew, taking a loss of tens of millions of dollars in the process. Within a few months, the Korean partner (who had bought the American interest at a fire-sale price) was granted full permission to do everything that had remained out of reach while the U.S. company was involved. Of course, not every Korean company has the connections needed to stage this kind of coup, but even the smallest company can manipulate government authority by simply withdrawing the sponsorship necessary for the foreign manager and any foreign staff to get their visas renewed. It is hard to stay in the market without anyone to run your side of the operation. This sort of government manipulation is rare and only happens if the stakes are high, but if you encounter or suspect it, inform the embassy and your congressional representative early on.

The case mentioned above is a reminder that although it is unwise to believe anyone who claims that his political access can solve your business problems, politics does have a major influence on corporate activities in Korea. Much of this influence is exercised indirectly, through the Korean banking system. Korean companies are heavily leveraged (the average debt to equity ratio is an almost unbelievable 400 to 1) and thus rely heavily on domestic banks. The banks, in turn, are closely controlled by the government, which tells them how much they can lend to whom. This means that Korean corporations with good access to the right government officials can obtain the financing they need for expansion or to weather a crisis while other companies may find it difficult or impossible. Likewise, a company may find itself out in the cold if changes in the bureaucracy remove its government contacts from positions of financial influence. This is another reason that wholesale political change could be destabilizing to the entire economy.

First-time business visitors to Korea are invariably impressed with the vibrant rush and bustle evident on all sides. In many respects, Korean business life resembles that of Hong Kong, with plenty of initiative, creative entrepreneurship, and a willingness to experiment and take risks. This same spirit also lends itself to a short-term business philosophy, a frequent lack of planning, and a tendency to rush into attractive-looking projects with the confidence to say "can do" but without the prudence to ask "what if ...?" All too often the results are problems that could have been avoided and the disillusionment of foreign partners or associates who end up feeling deceived or used.

To avoid this type of situation and the others discussed above, you must be prepared to second-guess your Korean counterparts.

Start by taking the time to make a list of all the homework they have agreed to do or can reasonably be expected to do. Then get ready to do much of it yourself, as a fail-safe measure. Duplication of effort is far preferable to failure. For example, it is not enough to be told that your Korean agent has done all that is needed to protect your trademark in the country. Take out some "insurance" by hiring an in-country attorney to check with the patent office and be sure that the trademark is registered to your company and that no protests have been filed against the registration. Large and internationally experienced U.S. exporters and offshore manufacturers have suffered delays of months and expenses of tens or hundreds of thousands of dollars because they couldn't bring themselves to buy a few hours of objective in-country expertise to discreetly backstop their Korean associates.

In addition, the same open, freewheeling character of many Korean businessmen and officials that makes them accessible, adaptable, and amenable to last-minute changes also keeps them from having a strong sense of commitment in many cases. Employees, agents or partners may drop a job or a business relationship on a moment's notice if there is a better deal to be had elsewhere. In manufacturing, suppliers may turn out extremely high quality on samples or even initial production runs; but if a new order from a different buyer comes along, they may give it their full attention and let the quality of established customers' orders fall to disastrously low levels. Other problematic tendencies include dropping customers without warning and copying goods to make unauthorized sales on the side. Your best defense is eternal vigilance and a willingness to inspect, reject, and monitor by having your staff or a qualified consultant make frequent visits to suppliers. It also helps to diversify sources of supply whenever possible.

When dealing with Koreans, one often gets the impression that they view life as a "zero-sum game," where every situation has a winner and a loser, and compromise leads only to defeat. Such an attitude is understandable, given the Koreans' history of scarcity and foreign domination and their collective experience that a second-place finish spells disaster. This is probably one cause for their extreme competitiveness and their tendency to continually push for a better deal. There is not enough wealth or power for everyone to get a fair share, and even the amount available today may be reduced tomorrow; so many Koreans feel an inner need to get all they can on a daily basis. One side effect of this worldview is that your Korean business contacts or employees may withhold information from you: since knowledge is power, they often tend to keep it to themselves, thinking that if they told you all they know, you would no longer have any need for them. You may find it advantageous to play to their sensitivities by keeping them reassured that they are in a strong position.

In an economy of scarcity, virtually anything that can be produced can be sold, and the scarcity that has marked much of Korean history—and particularly recent history—has favored aggressive sales activity at the expense of marketing sense. In a similar way, Korea's chronic instability has reinforced the primacy of the quick sale over the development of solid business relations between supplier and user, which sometimes (as was noted above) leads to a rapid deterioration in quality once a large order has been booked. Instability has also created a short-term outlook that makes it difficult for anyone to make sales to Koreans on the basis of cost-effectiveness. The Korean tends to look at the price without regard for the useful life of the product, a tendency that can hurt your chances of selling more expensive products, regardless of quality.

Like other Asians, Koreans tend to change the rules to fit the circumstances, but many Western businesspeople claim that Koreans carry it farther than other Asians. A common theme in the complaints reaching the U.S. Embassy and AmCham is that contracts are not honored and that agreements made and reaffirmed by both parties are continually violated in both letter and spirit. Some observers believe that many such problems are caused by the Koreans' desire for control, which in turn stems from their historical experience of foreign domination, combined with a tradition of authoritarianism and a hierarchical society. It may be helpful to build business relationships and structure agreements in such a way that this need for feeling in control is met. One of the most satisfied U.S. manufacturers ever to operate in Korea apparently solved the problem by having no American management or staff in-country; the lack of a foreign presence or obvious foreign control seems to have ensured the success of the operation. (In this regard there is a parallel to the striking success of McDonald's in the difficult Japanese market; the Japanese franchise holder has encouraged Japanese consumers to believe that McDonald's is a Japanese company.) After a careful analysis of any proposed business activity in Korea, you may find it wiser to minimize your control (or at least the obvious aspects of it) than to wage a constant defensive battle against the control drive of your Korean business partner or agent.

One thing that adds to Westerners' confusion is the lack of Western logic that, while prevalent throughout Asia, reaches sublime heights in Korea. Korean thought tends to be holistic, not structured, so that discussions are often not limited to the thin line of linear progression or to cause and effect. Add to this the common tendency to interpret events in terms of desire (rather than fact), throw in a dash of relative truth and situational ethics, and you have the stock for the kind of mutually exclusive statements that Koreans can make—and hear—without so much as a raised eyebrow. Here, as elsewhere, be patient, resist the urge to set the record straight or take some sort of moral high ground, and hew gently but firmly to your position. This is especially advisable if you are trying to reach a compromise. Although compromise based on logical considerations and an underlying belief in cooperation and fairness is part of Western tradition, it is far less important and less readily understood in Asia. Rather than persuading your associates, you may get the results you want because they are humoring you. Your objective should be results, so don't be too insistent on having your Korean associates see things your way.

DEALING WITH THE KOREAN GOVERNMENT

Although Korea is a hotbed of freewheeling capitalism and aggressive entrepreneurship, its highly leveraged economy is tightly controlled. Koreans (including those in government) are very partial to debt financing, in part because it does not dilute their control over the business in question. As a result, the Korean economy depends for its survival on very highly leveraged businesses, which in turn makes the government acutely aware of foreign exchange flows and balances. This concern for the conservation of foreign exchange creates many of the government limitations and restrictions imposed on imports (others arise from the desire to protect local industry). Another consequence is the government's tendency to continually raise local content requirements and export requirements for foreign manufacturing operations in the ROK. Foreign exchange concerns are also behind the Koreans' reluctance to pay a fair price (or any price at all in many cases) for imported technology and are definitely a contributing factor in widespread violations of foreign intellectual and industrial property rights. Understanding the ROK government's concerns can be helpful in discovering ways to obtain its cooperation, or at least acquiescence, when structuring proposals.

The government is divided on the issue of foreign trade and foreign investment. Government officials have had extensive, positive contacts with foreigners in general and with Americans in particular, and both in the government and in the private sector there are significant numbers of Koreans with degrees from American universities. In spite of this, at all levels of government there is a large group that favors protectionism and restrictions on foreign business activity. In addition, each ROK ministry has powerful private-sector constituents with a vested interest in reducing foreign competition, and the ministries themselves are constantly jockeying for greater overall influence. All this can have serious effects on your business plans.

The best way to approach this minefield is to use the U.S. Embassy, AmCham, and your Korean agents, representatives, distributors or customers to identify the Korean government agencies and officials most likely to be receptive to your proposals. Take the time to meet with these officials and discuss your plans in terms of their objectives and concerns. This will be much easier if you understand the country's social, economic and political priorities and if you have done some research on the Korean government's

objectives in your product or service sector. As is true when dealing with any nation's bureaucracy, you may find that a project
opposed by one agency may be supported by another. For example, the Ministry of Finance may oppose the import of expensive
hospital equipment because it would involve large expenditures
of foreign exchange while the Ministry of Health might back the
same project if it helps improve public health care.

Be prepared to spend some time laying this type of groundwork. Often, this is a time-consuming process, and you may experience considerable frustration, especially if your project falls into
an area for which there is an official party line, which you may
hear repeated almost verbatim at every stop and which may get
in the way of serious discussion. But if you are anticipating or
having problems, you simply must take the time to build the necessary support for your project. The U.S. Embassy should only be
called in for assistance and support (i.e., an expression of interest)
if all else fails. Koreans, like most nationalities, are sensitive about
national sovereignty, and they resent the premature or excessive
use of embassy officials to push foreign business interests.

INTELLECTUAL PROPERTY RIGHTS

Intellectual and industrial property rights are a major problem
in Korea. The Korean copyright law that prevailed from 1957 to
1987 offered no protection for foreign authors. Although Korea
produced more comprehensive copyright legislation in 1987, the
market is still full of pirated editions of English-language books
(mostly textbooks), records, audiotapes and videotapes; and foreign plays are routinely staged without payment of royalties to the
authors or their agents. Although software is not yet a major problem (few Korean businesses are computerized, and the number of
personal computers is minuscule), there is little doubt that it soon
will be if protective legislation is not backed by effective enforcement decrees and aggressive enforcement. There is already a burgeoning business in counterfeit computer hardware.

The Korean government's aggressive drive to acquire technology is a major contributing factor to intellectual property rights problems in Korea. Foreign firms have repeatedly charged that research institutes funded by the ROK government have access to a wide range of proprietary information and materials received by ROK government agencies as part of the required approval process that foreign firms must go through to introduce their products into the country. The government also encourages so-called "shuttle research," whereby major Korean companies and research institutes recruit scientists and technical experts (often ethnic Koreans working in the U.S. or Europe) at high salaries or consulting fees for short periods of time in order to acquire the latest technological information from their places of employment.

Korea is a good market for pharmaceuticals, and for years foreign pharmaceutical manufacturers waged an unsuccessful struggle to obtain product patents for pharmaceutical compounds. Process patents were available, but they provided no protection against Korean labs that could easily analyze a compound and recreate it using processes that varied only slightly from the original. In 1987 the Korean government succumbed to international pressure and approved legislation that extended patent protection to pharmaceutical processes, but foreign companies claiming infringement may still have an uphill battle to get satisfaction.

One of the main roots of the counterfeiting problem is the Korean attitude toward intellectual property. Since the Koreans (like other Asians) have great difficulty in internalizing the rationale behind the concept of intellectual property, even areas protected by law are rife with counterfeiting. In consumer products, for example, foreign trademarks and designs can be and are duly registered by their rightful owners, but shops and stalls are still full of unauthorized imitations, and Korean companies have been known to reprint entire catalogues of U.S. products, merely stripping in their own company name in appropriate places. Therefore, even if the Korean government passes theoretically meaningful copyright legislation or puts other intellectual property rights laws (complete with effective enforcement decrees) on the books, enforcement may not be vigorous enough to solve the problem.

As in Japan and China, anyone can legally register any trademark in Korea unless the mark can be proven to have already been in use in the country and to be well known. It is not necessary for the registrant to have used the mark before registering it, which means that Korean companies can—and do—register foreign marks that are well known overseas but not yet in use in Korea, figuring that the foreign owner can later be counted upon to ransom the mark in order to enter the Korean market. Those owners who refuse to do so may find that their attempt to use any similar mark or name will be successfully challenged by the holder of their own mark.

Korean government restrictions on imports may make the situation even worse, turning it into a catch-22. Korean officials can reject a foreign trademark registration application which is connected with a product that cannot be imported on the grounds that it would be manifestly impossible for the applicant to make use of the trademark in Korea. And since the applicant's product cannot be sold in Korea, it is also impossible for the foreign company to make its product sufficiently known to protect its trademarks or trade dress (general appearance of a product or package or significant parts thereof) under the public awareness doctrine. Japanese companies have gotten around this problem by doing extensive advertising for products that they cannot market in Korea but do sell to the many Koreans making the short (ninety-minute) and relatively inexpensive trip to Japan on business or to visit relatives among the over 800,000 Koreans living there. Most foreign companies not only find the expense unjustifiable, but also resist on Western grounds of absurdity and unfairness.

Like other Asian counterfeiters, Korean companies are often aggressive in marketing counterfeited products overseas, so that the original manufacturer finds itself not only shut out of the Korean market but also competing with cheaper Korean imitations in other world markets. Some U.S. firms, especially those whose products have good potential in Korea, might be well advised to swallow their pride, emulate the Japanese, and start advertising there even though their products are not yet importable.

MARKETING IN KOREA

Since most Korean company headquarters are in Seoul and since about one-third of the nation's value-added manufacturing takes place there, U.S. firms dealing in industrial products can make a high percentage of sales without ever leaving the capital city. However, several other major cities are traditional centers for certain types of manufacturing, and the Korean government's attempts to disperse industry should contribute to this trend. Major Korean industrial cities and their principal industrial bases are Pusan (food processing, shipbuilding, plywood, rubber products), Ulsan (chemicals and petrochemicals, shipbuilding), Masan (free trade zone), Gumi (electronics), Changwon (machinery), and Yochun (chemicals and petrochemicals). In addition to its overall role as the nation's headquarters city, Seoul has a heavy concentration of production in the apparel, paper, and printing industries.

In some ways the Korean market is not especially demanding— rising incomes and an emphasis on exports keep customers eager to buy—but it is essential to have good local representation. The Foreign Commercial Service of the U.S. Embassy can provide assistance in identifying potential agents and distributors.

When making industrial sales, it is often advisable to be sure that the Korean customer is aware of new developments in equipment and technology. Because of Japan's geographic proximity, similar language (which means that many Japanese sales and marketing agents speak fluent Korean), and extensive market penetration (which dates from Japan's 1910–1945 colonization of Korea), many Korean manufacturers will "buy Japanese" almost from force of habit unless they learn of better products from the U.S. Technical seminars, promoted by the U.S. Embassy Trade Center and presented by you and your Korean agent, are an effective way of demonstrating the advantages of your product without resorting to a hard sell which might be counterproductive.

It is also important to have a frequent American presence and frequent contact with both major and potential customers, partly because of the general Asian tendency to require more personal contact and human relationships in business and also because the

Japanese are just a short plane trip away. Korean end users need to feel that you will be there if they need you, and the only way to give them that feeling is to be there before they need you. Even with good local representation, someone from the U.S. should visit several times a year to give presentations, go on factory visits, and generally become acquainted with customers, their operations and their needs.

As the Korean market and industry develop and become sophisticated, it is increasingly difficult to make sales to Korea on the basis of price and quality alone. More and more U.S. firms are finding it desirable to help their Korean reps develop a stocking and servicing capability. This is especially important if one is successfully to compete with the Japanese, who can make extremely rapid deliveries and send personnel for on-site inspection and servicing on a same-day basis if necessary. At a minimum, you should service your Korean accounts on a priority basis. They may prefer to do business with the U.S., but they simply cannot afford to if delays are too great. Minimum ocean-shipping times from the U.S.—twenty-one days from the east coast (via land bridge) and fourteen days from the west coast—often force them to buy Japanese unless an American supplier or his Korean distributor is willing to maintain stock (including spare parts) and service capabilities in Korea.

Since Koreans tend to be more concerned with price than with cost-effectiveness, some U.S. equipment suppliers find it advantageous to produce special no-frills, stripped-down models for the Korean market, or to sell main products at a reduced cost linked to a spare-parts and replacement-parts contract and the eventual purchase of accessories and auxiliary equipment.

Another major factor is credit: a shortage of credit in the Korean financial system makes commercial loans expensive and difficult to obtain. Since most Korean companies have a high debt-to-equity ratio, U.S. suppliers find themselves in a bind: they may not be able to make a sale without extending credit, but the risk makes them reluctant to do so. One solution is to obtain a foreign currency guarantee from the Korea Exchange Bank, under which the Korean purchaser receives a won-denominated guarantee from a

Korean commercial bank in exchange for a first or second mortgage on the firm's assets. The Korea Exchange Bank will then issue a foreign currency guarantee. This procedure effectively secures the credit to the buyer but involves additional time and expense and may not go through if the buyer fails to qualify for the guarantee. In addition, other foreign suppliers (including the Japanese) may be more willing than U.S. firms to extend credit on the basis of the Korean firm's track record.

As is true in Japan, the Korean distribution system is fairly complex. Especially for consumer products, there is a high degree of fragmentation at the final-sales outlet level. As a result, many sectors are dominated by wholesalers, who may even have considerable influence over manufacturers. A knowledgeable Korean agent or distributor is essential if you wish to give your product the widest and most effective distribution.

TRADE AND TRADE REGULATIONS

You should note that the following guidelines, although based on material furnished by the ROK government, are unofficial, and neither the author nor the publisher is responsible for their accuracy or completeness. Since Korean government regulations are subject to revision at any time, you will need to contact both the U.S. Department of Commerce (either in the U.S. or through FCS Seoul) and the Korean government for current regulations. Korean government rulings are often based on special laws, separate regulations, internal administrative guidelines (not available outside the bureaus that create them), and the ROK's evaluation of the merits of the specific case under consideration. You should obtain legal counsel (the U.S. Embassy can furnish a list of attorneys, and AmCham and FCS can give informal recommendations from the list) during the early planning stages of any project, and consult with counsel before entering into any binding agreement. You should also contact the Ministry of Finance, Foreign Investment Promotion Division, regarding proposed agreements and visit the MOF to discuss the proposal before submitting it.

Tariff and Nontariff Import Controls

The ROK has several different tariff rates: general rates, temporary rates, General Agreement on Tariffs and Trade (GATT) rates, and emergency rates. Emergency rates are to protect vital industries and to control surges of imports in any sector. An additional 2.5 percent defense tax is assessed on all imports, and imports of items subject to value-added tax (VAT) are subject to an additional 10 percent VAT duty (which is calculated on CIF *plus* customs duty—a tax on a tax). The ROK government may also impose import surcharges of up to 30 percent as a further brake on imports. The existence of this surcharge legislation has the potential to render the formal tariff schedule meaningless, a good example of the role of form and function in Asian societies in general.

The ROK is committed to a gradual and general reduction of tariff rates, which should mean new opportunities in increasing numbers of product sectors. The ROK government has created a comprehensive list (available through the U.S. Embassy, the U.S. Department of Commerce, or any USDOC district office) with both present and future rates. Most tariffs are ad valorem (CIF basis at the time of filing of the import declaration) and must be paid in won before the goods clear customs.

Although advertising materials and samples are exempt from customs duties, many U.S. firms have problems clearing these items and replacement parts shipped under warranty. Although the ROK has agreed to honor carnets, in practice ROK customs officials rarely, if ever, do so. To avoid last-minute problems, contact the U.S. Embassy Trade Center before you ship or travel with these items. All goods entering Korea for exhibition purposes must be stored in a bonded area: either the U.S. Embassy Trade Center or the Korea Exhibition Center.

Every import transaction must be made under an import license from the Korea Exchange Bank, and no letters of credit may be issued until the license has been obtained. Licenses are granted automatically for all commodities except for restricted items on the so-called "negative list." This list, revised annually by the Ministry of Trade and Industry, is published as the "Annual Trade Plan" and takes effect every year on July 1. Import applications for restricted items are approved on a case-by-case basis after screening by relevant government agencies and Korean manufacturers' associations. Historically, the ROK government provided protection from foreign competition whenever local industry became capable of providing goods of a suitably high standard of quality for the local market. However, current policy calls for selective protection of industries that the government has decided to promote and less protection for marginal industries or those in which local industry enjoys significant natural advantages. This means that the number of product categories on the negative list is being reduced somewhat. Check with the U.S. Embassy regarding items that are to be moved to automatic approval status in the future.

Licensed Traders

Under Korean law, only trading companies and import-offer agents registered with and licensed by the Ministry of Trade and Industry are authorized to import and export goods. Since many Korean companies that manufacture for export or buy foreign products do not want the bother of becoming a licensed trader, foreigners who buy Korean goods or sell to the Korean market may have to deal through a licensed middleman. The commissions charged for this service are very low, so the extra layer means little in terms of cost. However, since the licensed trader holds title to the goods at one point in every transaction, it is important to be sure of the reliability and financial strength of the trading company or import-offer agent through whom you and your Korean supplier or buyer are working. If a deal goes sour or financial losses are incurred because of the licensed middleman's actions, the Korean principal is not responsible.

There are several types of licensed trading companies in Korea. The principal ones are general trading companies, ordinary trading companies, special trading companies and local trading companies, each of which must meet specific requirements to obtain a license. One advantage of this regulatory system is that it allows for a wide range of size and volume and gives the foreign businessperson a clear picture of each trading company's capabilities. The FCS of the U.S. embassy can provide you with assistance in selecting a trading company.

INVESTING IN KOREA

Following a period (early 1980s) of minimal cooperation with foreign investors, during which many foreign firms diverted new investment to Taiwan, Hong Kong, Singapore and other areas in the Pacific, the ROK government became more willing to pay attention to the needs and problems of the foreign business community. However, the government's continued use of a case-by-case approach in many areas (including tax holidays, accelerated depreciation, and customs and other tax exemptions for the import of capital goods) leaves large areas of uncertainty. For guidance and information, investors may seek assistance from the Investment Promotion Division of the Ministry of Finance; it is also advisable to contact the FCS and to retain local counsel during the early stages of any investment project.

The ROK evaluates all foreign investment in terms of three national criteria: the ROK's balance of payments position, the development of key industries and public utilities, and the overall development of the national economy and social welfare. Obviously, projects that have the most potential in these areas will have the best chance of obtaining approval. The minimum foreign investment allowed is US$100,000.

The basic law governing foreign investment is the Foreign Capital Inducement Law (FCIL, amended 1983) and its Enforcement Decree (1984). Under earlier regulations foreign investment was limited to the following categories:

1. Large-scale, capital-intensive facilities that domestic enterprises are not yet capable of creating, operating or managing without foreign participation
2. Industries for the production of electric, electronic, or chemical products

3. Energy-related industries
4. Export-oriented projects where foreign participation is deemed necessary for effective penetration of foreign markets
5. Projects for the development or utilization of domestic natural resources
6. Manufacture of foodstuffs and pharmaceuticals
7. Distribution of commodities (wholesale and retail) and selected service industries
8. Other projects as determined by the Ministry of Finance

Although modification of the FCIL in 1983 created a new system for categorizing investment, the above list is valuable as an indication of ROK priorities. The system in force since 1983 is a so-called "negative list system," which means that all areas not appearing on the negative list are open to foreign investment. There are four categories under this system: *open* (foreign investment permitted across the board), *partly free* (foreign investment limited to specific lines of business), *restricted* (temporarily off-limits, but with future possibilities or present participation with special MOF approval), and *prohibited* (sectors in which the Korean government does not want foreigners involved). The list is revised every six months to reflect new priorities resulting from changes in the ROK's economic development and monetary position.

The "restricted" category generally includes areas and projects which involve Korean government assistance, are likely to cause pollution, are dependent on energy and other imported materials, or involve investment in underdeveloped sectors of the Korean economy that require ROK government protection. This category specifically includes dairy operation; livestock breeding; electric power generation; and the wholesaling of fruits, vegetables, and bakery and confectionery products.

The "prohibited" category includes the operation of irrigation, postal, transport or communications systems; the manufacture of cigarettes or coal briquettes; the operation of casinos; publishing; real estate brokerage and property rental; liquor wholesaling; and agricultural production.

The MOF may approve foreign investments without consulting other ministries (this is defined as *automatic approval*) under the following conditions:

1. Foreign equity investment of US$1 million or less
2. Foreign equity ownership of 49.9 percent or less

The 49.9 percent provision is waived if the foreign-invested company exports 60 percent or more of total production or if the joint venture produces an item that would otherwise be imported, is subject to a basic duty rate of 10 percent or less, and is free of import licensing restrictions.

Application for approval of a foreign-invested project must be submitted to the Foreign Investment Promotion Division, International Finance Bureau, Ministry of Finance. Supporting documentation includes project plan, certification of nationality, articles of incorporation of the new firm, proxy authorization, and joint-venture agreement (if applicable). Although the MOF prefers that applications be submitted in the Korean language, joint-venture agreements themselves should be in English.

It is very important to include in the application any possible future expansion or diversification of the proposed company's business. Korean bureaucrats are extremely reluctant to allow changes once a project has been approved. To spare yourself the frustration of watching your business lag behind the market or grind to a halt because you cannot get necessary changes approved, think as far ahead as possible before filing the initial application and get as much as you can going in. Do *not* rely on assurances from either your partner (in the case of joint ventures) or the ROK government that it will be easy to make modifications later. It won't be. Koreans can be very persistent and persuasive. Get everything—including all agreements regarding ROK government concessions and exemptions—in writing and get it signed by appropriate ROK government officials. Major points to cover include local content ratios, export ratios, repatriation of profits and capital, and reinvestment of profits.

Because the ROK places a high priority on foreign exchange, be sure to clarify all matters pertaining to overseas remittance or repatriation of dividends, profits and capital. All such remittances must be approved via application to a foreign exchange bank; approval is subject to conformity with the original investment approval, status of tax obligations, and "legitimacy" of the remittance.

Reinvestment of profits is allowed, but prior approval from the MOF is required if the proposed reinvestment exceeds the foreign equity ratio permitted in the original investment approval or if investment is to be made in another project. Reinvestment is simply reported to the MOF if it is in the same project and keeps total investment below the limit established in the original approval.

ESTABLISHING A BUSINESS OFFICE IN KOREA

Since 1982 branches of foreign corporations that intend to make remittances of profits to head offices overseas must be licensed by the Bank of Korea (BOK). Other foreign branch offices need no license but must file a "Report on Establishment" with the BOK. There are other regulations for specific industries; since Korean government regulations are subject to revision at any time, foreign firms should contact both the U.S. Department of Commerce (either in the U.S. or through FCS Seoul) and the Korean government for current regulations.

LICENSING IN KOREA

Note: the following guidelines, although based on material furnished by the ROK government, are unofficial, and neither the author nor the publisher is responsible for their accuracy or completeness.

Many U.S. exporters make their initial entry into the Korean market via licensing and technical assistance agreements. This tactic can increase the risk of losing intellectual property rights through piracy, but the Korean authorities appear to be taking steps to improve the situation. After extended urging by U.S. interests, Korea agreed to join an international industrial property convention, and it has for several years protected patents and trademarks that are registered in Korea. Although in 1987 legislation was passed to create product patents for pharmaceutical and chemical compounds, problems still exist. Although the Korean government pledged to provide effective copyright protection for foreign authors, the government is not enthusiastic about the concept and it will probably be some time before full and effective protection becomes available.

Korean regulations governing licensing provide a good indication of the Korean government's priorities: conservation of foreign exchange, export of finished goods, and acquisition of up-to-date technology.

The ROK views with disfavor licensing agreements that provide principally for the use by Korean firms of foreign designs, brands, trademarks or exclusive (Korean government regulations use the word *monopolistic*) sales rights. Government officials are also inclined to reject contracts intended primarily to promote the sales of raw materials and/or components, and contracts which contain "unfavorable or unduly restrictive" terms (e.g., limitations on licensee access to export markets). Where technology is concerned, the Korean government will not approve contracts for "outdated, low-grade, or declining" technology or for technology that is reserved for development by Korean companies. Licensing, like other business activity, takes place in a regulated and protected environment.

In technology transfers, the assessment of the value of the technology is made without regard to whether compensation takes the form of equity or a percentage of sales. In all cases attempts are made to evaluate the technology separately from any equity investment, but if a foreign company realizes a substantial return on equity investment, the Koreans have been known to attempt to reduce royalty payments on the grounds that the foreign firm has realized an adequate return. Final agreement on the proposed technology transfer usually involves an initial payment and a royalty based on a percentage of net sales.

Democratic People's Republic of Korea (DPRK)

F ew Westerners have occasion to deal directly with the DPRK, often referred to in the West as North Korea. Nevertheless, the influence that the DPRK has on South Korean affairs, Chinese policy, and overall political risk in northeast Asia is so great that it is essential to have some understanding of this small, isolationist and militantly Stalinist state. Western businesspeople in Macao and other places who encounter agents of North Korean trading organizations should also be aware that these agents are widely regarded as being operatives of North Korean political and intelligence services.

North Korea, perhaps the world's toughest intelligence target, has been compared to Romania under Ceauşescu. The parallels are startling: a leader, Kim Il Sung, with absolute control of the populace, the official title of "Glorious Leader" and a personality cult bordering on religion; an economy foundering in spite of ambitious industrialization schemes; and rumors of decadence and luxurious living, especially by Kim's heir apparent, Kim Jong Il. It is uncertain how much power is already exercised by the younger Kim, a plump, middle-aged playboy with little experience in external politics or world affairs. Rumors abound that Kim Jong Il has alienated powerful northern clans with strong military connections, which could mean that any regime he heads will fall prey to a military coup. The actual situation is difficult to determine because North Korea is one of the world's most secretive countries. The experiences of the late Shah of Iran and Haiti's Duvalier family indicate that the pampered son may lack the ruthlessness and cunning to keep the power acquired by his father.

North Korea's self-imposed isolation (based in large measure on the doctrine of total self-reliance, or *juche,* and echoing ancient Korea's reputation as the "hermit kingdom") has caused North Korean leaders to lose touch with international realities. As a result, North Korean officials have become involved in counterproductive escapades, including smuggling and drug dealing by DPRK diplomats, that have resulted in numerous diplomatic expulsions and a very negative international image. The north's truculence, lack of sophistication, and fierce rivalry with the ROK culminated in an attempt to assassinate South Korean president Chun Doo Hwan in the 1983 Rangoon bombing that killed several Burmese and most of the ROK cabinet. International reaction to this ill-conceived action caused the north to back off from such extreme and obvious violence, at least for a while.

In 1987 the crash of a Korean Air Lines jumbo jet with the loss of hundreds of lives was immediately blamed on the north by the regime in Seoul, which quickly produced a pair of culprits to prove it. To seasoned Korea watchers the speed with which the accusations were made, the circumstances under which the alleged perpetrators surfaced, and the details of the story were reminiscent of other cloak-and-dagger incidents that skeptics believe have been fabricated by the ROK government. Their suspicions were reinforced by the breathless performance and somewhat inconsistent testimony of the young, attractive, headline-grabbing female member of the sabotage team. Although she was convicted and sentenced, the numerous book and film proposals that she received (in addition to offers of marriage from dozens of infatuated Korean men) indicated that many Koreans, although outraged about the alleged sabotage and loss of life, were unconvinced of her participation in the bombing.

Regardless of the DPRK's alleged involvement in the airline disaster, the northern regime did make vague, dark threats to wreck the 1988 Olympics (held as scheduled in Seoul) unless it was named co-host, an unprecedented arrangement to which the DPRK attached patently unacceptable conditions. In mid-1987, no compromise solution had been found, and in the midst of massive antigovernment riots in Seoul and other South Korean cities, Pyongyang (the North Korean capital) announced plans for a new, Olympic-class sports facility to provide a venue for the Olympics if Seoul became too dangerous for athletes and spectators. Some South Korean government figures took this announcement as an indication that Pyongyang may have had some hand in instigating the unrest in the ROK. At the very least, the North Koreans did their best to create uncertainty about the stability of the South Korean regime and the success of the Olympics, which fortunately were held without incident.

Unlike other players in the capitalist-communist rivalries that abound in Asia, the North Koreans seem to have little use for defectors. Although the PRC, Taiwan and the ROK all welcome defectors with open arms, give them extensive media coverage, and reward them with prestigious jobs, cash (in Taiwan the prevailing prize for PRC pilots who escape with a plane is over a million dollars), and a fast-lane social life involving political leaders and beauty queens, the DPRK follows a totally contrary policy. For example, of the eight American military men known to have defected to the north since the Korean War, all are dead. (The most recent American defector, Private Joseph White, who crossed over the DMZ in 1982, was claimed to have drowned in a flood in the summer of 1985; the North Koreans waited until December of that year to announce his death.) South Korean soldiers who defect simply disappear.

The DPRK's GNP is about one-fourth the size of the ROK's, which means that per capita GNP is about half. Much of the north's GNP (an estimated 20 percent) goes into the military, resulting in a much larger military force than that of the ROK. The DPRK's emphasis on military affairs has made it active in international military training, especially in Africa. In addition, North Korean troops (both combat and training) have been reported in several hot spots in Africa and elsewhere.

Judging by the North Koreans' warlike preparation and their infrequent public statements, their major goal is reunification of the Korean peninsula by military means, and defectors report that the population is kept in a constant state of readiness for combat. According to the best U.S. intelligence estimates (which include photos taken from satellites and high-flying XR-71 reconnaissance aircraft), the DPRK army, with some 830,000 troops, outnumbers the ROK's 600,000-man force by a substantial margin. The DPRK also has a significant numerical edge in mobile heavy weaponry: 2-to-1 in combat aircraft, tanks, artillery, and armored personnel carriers and 3-to-1 in surface ships, as well as twenty submarines (against no subs in the ROK). In addition, the north has a 100,000-man special forces (commando) group, the largest in the world. Some of this manpower, which is deployed in an aggressive forward posture, is constantly engaged in hostile activities like nocturnal, seaborne sabotage missions to the south (a practice that has placed ROK beaches off-limits after dark) and the digging of invasion tunnels under the DMZ. One such tunnel, discovered by the ROK Army, had been hastily painted black, sealed shut, and abandoned by North Korean sappers; when the issue was brought up as a complaint in talks at Panmunjom, the DPRK claimed the ROK probers had stumbled on an abandoned Japanese coal mine.

Since Seoul, reportedly targeted by multiple missile batteries located just north of the DMZ, is only about fifteen air miles from the DPRK, in the event of full-scale hostilities the north's military apparatus could devastate the ROK capital within hours, seriously disrupting the ROK's ability to counter any invasion. This is one of the reasons the U.S. long maintained about 40,000 military men and women (including fighter squadrons) in the ROK, backed up by additional forces in nearby Japan. Nevertheless, as ROK military readiness and technology improved and Eastern Europe and the Soviet Union adopted a new international posture at the end of the 1980s, the U.S. announced in 1990 that it would begin withdrawing substantial numbers of troops (seven thousand the first year) with the goal of a total withdrawal within a few years.

A reduction in America's military role in Korea, however, does not imply approval of the DPRK. The U.S. government still has regulations that can be used to keep most Americans from doing business with the DPRK. ("Except as authorized by the Secretary of the Treasury, Foreign Assets Control Regulations, 31 C.F.R. Part

500, prohibit persons subject to U.S. jurisdiction from dealing in any property in which North Korea has any interest of any nature whatsoever, direct or indirect.") Even though this prohibition is no longer strictly enforced, the north has little hard currency and is a generally unattractive place to do business. In spite of symbolic DPRK announcements that efforts will be made to attract foreign investment, neither the economy nor the existing sociopolitical structure (including juche) is geared to accommodate any sort of foreign business or industrial presence, and anything like an "open door policy" is probably decades away. Finally, almost all commercial activity with the U.S. has been limited to Korean-Americans and Korean expatriates residing in the U.S.

Luckily, the PRC, which gave fairly unquestioning support to Kim Il Sung from the Korean War until the early 1980s, has realized that the ROK has more to offer and that any military adventurism on the part of the North Koreans could damage China in any number of ways. Although the elder Kim is good at playing off the PRC and the Russians, most observers believe that the Koreans' mistrust of the Soviet Union and their long history of fraternal relations with the Chinese will keep them from entering completely into the Russian camp. And although assistance extended by Russia to the DPRK has at times raised the specter of a North Asian Vietnam, complete with a Russian naval base, fleet, and airpower, the budding development of commercial ties between the Soviet Union and South Korea make such fears appear unfounded. Nevertheless, since the DPRK has amassed enough spare parts and supplies (including petroleum) to fight for about ninety days without outside assistance, there is little that either the Soviets or the PRC could do to restrain the north if it decided to attack the south on its own.

There are encouraging signs of north-south detente, including talk of business dealings and the north's new willingness to let Koreans residing in the U.S. enter the DPRK to visit relatives. But the visits are confined to designated meeting sites in the capital, and the postwar record of relations between the two halves of the peninsula shows that northern gestures of friendliness have often gone hand in hand with sabotage.

Singapore

S ingapore is an unusual place. Smaller by far than the major
cities of most of its Asian competitors and with less than half
the population of Hong Kong, it has nevertheless managed
to be highly successful over the long term, posting annual economic growth rates near 10 percent in the 1970s and early 1980s.
Part of this success must be credited to the stability and developmental awareness of the government, which has had a free hand
thanks to the parliamentary monopoly (formerly 100 percent; sev-
enty-seven out of seventy-nine seats since 1984) enjoyed by its
dominant political party, the Political Action party (PAP). Although
Singaporeans appear inclined to continue along more or less the
same path, two issues—a deep economic slump which shocked
the economy in 1984 and the question of freedom of the press—
may create further openings for the opposition, whose share of the
vote rose from 25 to 37.1 percent in the 1984 elections.

Paradoxically, the recession (which caused two years of economic contraction followed by weak tentative expansion) has been
attributed to excessive government influence. The Singaporean
government has direct control of, or exerts significant influence
on, over six hundred companies—a significant number in Singapore's circumscribed environment. Although the government responded to the 1984 recession by modifying previous policies of
high wages, high taxes and a mandatory savings and pension plan,
the persistence of a bureaucratic presence in the private sector is
believed to have slowed recovery. The government is taking steps

to reduce its business participation by selling shares in government-invested companies.

One of the most difficult things for Westerners to adjust to in Singapore is the government's tight rein on the news media, a control which in many ways is even tighter than Korea's was in the 1980s, when the threat of communist invasion or internal subversion was often used to justify restrictions on the media. Discussions of policy or criticisms of the government, which have always been frowned upon, became even more risky for foreign publications under a 1986 foreign-press bill. Under the bill, the Minister of Communications and Information has the authority to limit or ban sales of foreign publications deemed to be intruding into Singapore's domestic politics. Foreign publications have no right of appeal from such action. In addition, the bill provides for fines of up to S$10,000 (US$4,490) and prison terms of up to two years.

Major foreign publications, including *Time* magazine and the *Asian Wall Street Journal,* have already experienced the results of offending the government in print. In October 1986 the government cut *Time's* circulation in Singapore in half because of a dispute over the magazine's stance on government rebuttals to a *Time* article; a few months later the Singaporean government further reduced circulation to a trickle of two thousand until the restrictions were lifted in the middle of 1987. While *Time* was laboring under this enforced curtailment, the *Asian Wall Street Journal's* circulation was slashed by more than nine-tenths for allegedly "engaging in the politics of Singapore." Although there is nothing unique about Asian countries restricting freedom of expression (in 1986 the Republic of Korea refused reentry to an American attorney, resident in Korea, because of remarks he had made in Tokyo allegedly criticizing the Korean government), in cases involving the press it is fortunately more common for an offended government to restrict or expel the journalists involved rather than to punish the publication and, indirectly, the businesspeople who depend on it for business information.

Apart from government confrontations with the press, Singapore, with its educated, Mandarin-speaking population and good commercial relations with the PRC, is a favorable location for foreign companies, including those seeking an Asian channel for the transfer of technology to the PRC. Compared to Hong Kong, it has several distinct advantages: the use of Mandarin Chinese (the official language of the PRC) rather than Hong Kong's Cantonese, a higher percentage of English-speaking people, no significant political uncertainty (Hong Kong's rendezvous with 1997 is just around the corner), and much cheaper rental property rates (in 1986 prime office space in Singapore averaged US$13.25 net per square meter per month against Hong Kong's US$35.90). The availability of inexpensive rental property should continue for several years; the vacancy rate for 1990, for example, was estimated at about 25 percent for offices and shops, 33 percent for factories, and 30 percent for warehouses. One of Singapore's major concerns is to wean the economy from excessive reliance on the construction industry (which accounts for about 30 percent of GDP and between 10 percent and 13 percent of total employment) and to develop strength in new business areas, especially services.

MAJOR TRADE AND BUSINESS OBJECTIVES

Singapore, which gained independence in 1965, is a very tightly run ship. Prime Minister Lee Kuan Yew, who with the PAP has been in command ever since independence, is an innovative leader with strong and often controversial ideas about how to create a model society. In the late 1960s and early 1970s, for example, Lee's aversion to long hair led Singapore authorities to bar overly shaggy (mostly young) foreign travelers from the city-state and to force occasional involuntary haircuts on local youths (a practice which, it must be noted in fairness, was also observed in the ROK during the same period). Other campaigns have included extremely strict enforcement of antispitting and antilittering laws (few complaints there) and unique plans (which included an officially sponsored Asian version of a real life "love boat") to encourage marriage and childbearing by college-educated—and therefore presumably more intelligent—women.

Today, however, business is at the center of Singapore's attention. In the 1960s and 1970s, foreign business was eager to take advantage of Singapore's stability, favorable business climate, low operating costs, and low-cost labor. In 1979 (about the same time that the PRC announced its "open door policy" to foreign business), the government decided to upgrade its industrial base—at the expense of foreign companies—by pushing up wages to drive out low-skill, labor-intensive industries. Coupled with soaring property values and increases in other costs, these moves made Singapore a very expensive proposition, and soon new investment was dropping and existing foreign firms cutting back or leaving.

In 1985, business activity plummeted, dragging the economy down to a 1.8 percent contraction; 1986 was little better. After two decades of heady economic expansion at about 9 percent average annual growth (including 8.2 percent in 1984), the shock of two bad years in a row, compounded by overbuilding in office and residential markets and a surplus of hotel capacity, led to more intense scrutiny of priorities.

One major effect has been a movement away from strongly centralized control under which the government gave tax advantages and low-cost loans to targeted industrial sectors. Under new policies, market forces (aided by overall tax cuts and wage restraints) have a greater role. To stimulate investment and overcome skepticism created by earlier policies, the government offered foreign companies attractive packages to relocate in Singapore.

Formerly interested in promoting a wide variety of manufacturing industries (which accounted for 25 percent of GDP in 1986), Singapore, which has a well-developed transportation and telecommunications infrastructure, now believes that the best strategy is to become a center for multinational companies' Asian regional headquarters and to focus on the servicing and supervising of operations elsewhere in the region. Sectors and activities attracting favorable government attention include personnel development; fund management and treasury functions; business planning and administration; technical support services; research and development; product development; marketing and sales promotion; and sourcing of materials, parts, components and products.

The idea is for Singapore to become a business center where

foreign companies can develop both products and more efficient regional management capabilities. Technology transfer and secure on-site use of proprietary technology is essential for the attainment of these goals, and in 1986 the Singapore government, aware of industrialized nations' concerns for unauthorized uses and leaks of technology, introduced import and export controls as a means of creating the climate of confidence necessary to attract technology-intensive companies.

For a number of years Singapore has also entertained the idea of becoming a major regional banking and financial center in competition with Hong Kong. Although progress in this direction has been uneven (partly because of the same types of financial wheeling and dealing that also abound in Hong Kong), Singapore's plans to induce multinationals to install their regional fund management and treasury functions to the city-state can, if successful, make an important contribution to this objective.

First, however, some housecleaning is in order. Singapore, like Hong Kong, has very lax controls on financial and credit activities, and banking secrecy laws make it very hard to find out what is going on behind the scenes. One result of this has been the spread of questionable financial activities that have had negative effects on Singapore's economy. For the last few years, for example, brokerage firms have made extensive use of letters of hypothecation ("hypos") in financing their business operations. Hypos, which theoretically secure loans through the pledge of stock shares, are in fact mere listings of shares owned. In the absence of any guidelines from the Monetary Authority (Singapore's guardian of financial affairs) or the Stock Exchange of Singapore, borrowers using hypos often change portfolios without notifying lenders and, in some cases, use the same shares as collateral for more than one loan. The bankers, in turn, have generally been too busy and too trusting to actually verify the accuracy of the lists. Fortunately, it appears that one effect of a major 1985 financial disaster involving hypos will be the end of this form of camouflaged unsecured credit.

Another problem of the banking industry is its excessive reliance on property financing. With commercial property values still well below their 1981 peaks and with banks still carrying their real estate collateral and investments on the books at acquisition cost rather than current value, some observers fear that major bank failures could occur. One mitigating factor is the financial strength of Singapore's leading banks, which are much larger than those in Hong Kong. However, the heavy concentration (about 70 percent) of commercial deposits in the four largest Singapore banks (United Overseas Bank, Overseas Chinese Banking Corporation, Overseas Union Bank, and the government's Development Bank of Singapore) means that a failure in any one of the four would have a profound effect on the entire economy. Aware of this fact and mindful of the bank problems revealed by Hong Kong's property market crash in 1982, Singapore's central bank and watchdog agency, the Monetary Authority of Singapore, has undertaken a policy of close supervision that should be sufficient to avoid similar difficulties.

INTELLECTUAL PROPERTY RIGHTS

Until the second half of the 1980s, Singapore was one of the worst infringers on intellectual property rights, being a major production center for pirated textbooks, videocassettes, and computer software, and holder of the dubious distinction of being the world's largest exporter of pirated music cassettes. A 1986 copyright bill was intended to change all this. Covering virtually all forms of intellectual property (including computer software, which has proven resistant to classification and protection in a number of countries around the world), the bill has sharp teeth: maximum fines per offense of S$100,000 (US$45,000), prison terms of up to five years, and forfeiture of counterfeiting equipment (recorders, etc.), regardless of whether or not the offenders are found guilty.

The bad news is that the bill, like similar bills and laws elsewhere in Asia, does not offer much protection to foreigners. In the first place, works can only be copyrighted if they are created by Singaporean citizens or residents or by locally incorporated companies, or if they are published in Singapore within thirty days of their original appearance overseas. Even worse, convictions for copyright infringement appear almost impossible to obtain since under the new law the copyright owner would be required to prove that the pirate knew the work in question was protected. As in much of Asia, foreign creators and owners of intellectual property are well advised to check with reliable in-country sources (including appropriate embassies and foreign chambers of commerce) and obtain competent in-country legal assistance before getting into an exposed position.

DOING BUSINESS IN SINGAPORE

Foreign companies investing in Singapore can take advantage of financial incentives introduced in 1986. Companies that locate regional offices in Singapore are eligible for special tax rates of 10 percent on domestic income (rather than the normal 33 percent rate); the reduced rate applies for ten years and may be extended. In addition, foreign source income of operational headquarters will also qualify for tax relief, with conditions and terms negotiated by the company and the Economic Development Board on a case-by-case basis. For firms setting up manufacturing operations, the Economic Development Board still offers a "pioneer certificate" that grants new manufacturers a minimum of five years' exemption from income tax, with a possible five-year extension.

To further lower the cost of doing business in Singapore, the government has also limited corporate contributions to the Central Provident Fund, a mandatory savings and pension program. Effective April 1, 1986, employer contributions to the fund were reduced from 25 percent to 10 percent of total salaries. The 2 percent payroll tax has been suspended, and compulsory contributions to the Skill Development Fund (a training program) have been cut by half, to 1 percent. Finally, wages have been frozen for at least two years, and rental and tax rates have been reduced for companies operating in government-owned facilities.

Traders will be affected somewhat by the import and export regulations established in 1986 to monitor technology flows and prevent unauthorized diversions of technology. Products listed on import certificates must be imported directly, and diversions or reexport must have prior governmental approval. In addition, the name of the end user must appear on the import certificate.

Conclusion

From tiny, tightly run Singapore to the vastness and bureaucratic confusion of the People's Republic of China, Asia offers Western businesses myriad opportunities inextricably bound up with a host of unfamiliar problems and challenges. Although each country in Asia constitutes a unique business environment, both the success of Western business activity and the future of the Asian business world are conditioned by a set of factors (including Confucian tradition, historical isolationism, and a winner-take-all or zero-sum-game philosophy) that prevents all the countries of the region from becoming Westernized in spite of their adoption of Western technology and trappings.

The differences between the business environments of Asia and the West are especially evident in the area of government intervention and control. Asian governments can easily obtain business compliance with government trade and industrial policies and can shape business activity to support long-range economic planning. Industries deemed vital to the economy can be supported in a variety of ways; and research, development and productive capacity can be channeled in such a way as to make selected industries in any Asian country highly competitive with those of the West. Host-country businesses and the country's overall international trade competitiveness also benefit from government controls on wages, prices and other factors that influence profitability.

Because of extensive intervention by Asian governments, Westerners competing in Asia find themselves disadvantaged by what appears to be a well-trained team of government agencies and business competitors and by a playing field rendered uneven by host-country government influence. In addition, a multitude of subtle factors (including general aversion to foreign penetration; a widespread philosophy that business exists to contribute to state policies; and well-established and deep-rooted political and economic ties between business and government leaders) puts foreign businesses on the defensive and forces them to spend considerable amounts of time and energy trying to obtain an equitable business environment.

The position of Western business in Asia is far better than it often seems, however. In the first place, within every Asian nation there is intense competition—some political, some between bureaucracies, some restricted to the business arena—that can be exploited by Western businesses that take the trouble to understand more than the outer layers of the business environment. Moreover, Asian nations compete fiercely with each other and this competition creates further opportunities for Western companies that understand how to take advantage of it. Meanwhile, the increasing complexity of the Asian business world and its relationship with the global economy have revealed the problems inherent in governmental intervention in the marketplace. Government technocrats are not infallible, and even when their theories and plans are appropriate, implementation may be stymied by bureaucratic incompetence, inertia and infighting. In addition, many Asian economic strategies and trade and industrial policies have placed a heavy price on labor and on small- and medium-sized businesses, a process which has generated internal pressure for changes in the system. Finally, Asian markets have so much potential and Asia offers so many advantages as a manufacturing base or source of supply that Western companies find it worthwhile to persevere.

The environment for foreign business in Asia is improving, as is the ability of foreign business to operate in that environment. Asian governments (perhaps influenced by a century or more of enforced contact, unequal treaties, lopsided trade flows and outright occupation that have characterized much of their experience with the West) may still seem insensitive to Western business needs, but in many cases they are willing to reassess troublesome policies. They are motivated not only by changes in the international economic order but also by increasing competition from other Asian nations and from countries outside Asia and, increasingly, by the evolution of their own economies. Copyright and patent laws have been passed, trade barriers are slowly coming down, restrictions on foreign investment are being eased, and foreign companies are being allowed more freedom in their business operations. Progress has been slow, uneven and incomplete, but it appears to be irreversible. Asians are learning that Western attitudes and practices (including such concepts as the level playing field, the primacy of the private sector, the intrinsic legitimacy of business as an activity, and the desirability of open markets as a goal) are valuable and that historically they have produced higher levels of prosperity, stability and well-being than the contrary tendencies that have generally dominated business in Asia.

At the same time, Western businesspeople are becoming more sensitive to the historical and cultural factors that have created Asians' attitudes toward business in general and toward foreign business in particular. They are also beginning to realize that in many areas the differences between Asians are as great or greater than the traits Asians have in common, and that many of the common traits—including a desire to excel, a willingness to adapt, and a tendency to put work and thrift before self-indulgence—can be valuable additions to the Western business repertoire. This continuing development of mutual awareness and respect promises to create increased business opportunities, smoother business relations, and greater prosperity both for Western business and for Asian national economies.

Western businesses should be prepared for new and stiffer competition created by changes in the Asian political environment. Although the Russians historically have been relatively unsuccessful in their efforts to penetrate Asia, the doctrines of glasnost and perestroika, coming as they have on the heels of economic liberalization in the PRC, have had perhaps even more effect there than in the West. Suddenly, both the specter of communist domination and the image of the Soviet Union as an unwelcome predator have lost much of their impact—officials from Taiwan visit the Soviet Union and the Chinese mainland, Korean businessmen fly to Moscow and Beijing in search of trading partners, Japanese firms cut joint-venture deals with the Russians in the Soviet Far East, and the Russians talk of opening Vladivostok to give themselves a major commercial port on the Pacific Ocean.

The reshuffling of economic and political relations in Asia is beneficial, but it can create problems for Western business in two ways. As the Asian economies (including the eastern part of the Soviet Union) become more integrated, Western countries will find it increasingly difficult to compete in pricing, financing, distribution and after-sale service. In addition, greater rapprochement between communist and noncommunist regimes will make nationalism more attractive to moderates and outright xenophobia more viable for Asian radicals. American firms may actually encounter less anti-Americanism in the PRC than in historical allies like Japan, Taiwan and Korea. Throughout the region U.S. business would profit if the U.S. abandoned its posture as a high-profile, aggressive front-runner and cultivated more of the soft-spoken humility that many Asians respect.

Each Asian national group is very different, of course, and the different orientations and stages of development of the players in Asia are reflected in their activities and concerns. For example, consider articles on China (PRC), Japan and Korea that appeared in a single issue of a major U.S. newspaper. The China piece dealt with the PRC's struggle to resolve the conflicting demands of liberalizers, technocrats and conservatives without sacrificing desperately needed economic growth. One article on Japan analyzed the increasingly visible role of women in Japanese society; another discussed the international transfer of technology in computers, aerospace and related fields. A pair of articles on Korea detailed internal trends, including nationalism, the dream of unification and the desire to reduce foreign influences. Of course, the choice of topics for these articles was partly determined by the orientation of the Western journalists who wrote them and the Western readers for whom they were written. There is no question, however, that each Asian country and culture brings unique concerns to its dealings with the West and with Western business. Your understanding of these concerns can determine the success or failure of your activities in Asia.

Directory
of Key Contacts

All data in this directory are based on information supplied by the governments and organizations listed. The author and publisher are not responsible for accuracy or completeness, and we recommend verification with the appropriate authorities as a first step in planning contacts and business activities. We would appreciate your advice on errors and omissions. The best way to verify information or to obtain the location of the most appropriate contact office is to telephone the nearest U.S. Department of Commerce office, the nearest appropriate foreign consulate, or the appropriate foreign embassy in Washington, D.C. Overseas contact points include the U.S. Embassy or American Chamber of Commerce in the applicable foreign capital, or the U.S. Consulate if one exists in a city where you have business. Foreign government agencies generally are not prepared to deal with cold calls by Western businesspeople.

PEOPLE'S REPUBLIC OF CHINA (PRC)

Contacts in the U.S.

Embassy of the People's Republic of China, 2300 Connecticut Avenue NW, Washington, DC 20008. Tel: (202) 328-2500. **Commercial Section,** Tel: (202) 328-2520. **Visa Section,** Tel: (202) 328-2517.

China International Tourist Service, Inc. (CITS), 60 East 42nd Street, Suite 465, New York, NY 10065. Tel: (212) 867-0271. CITS is the official tourist agency for the PRC.

National Council for U.S.-China Trade (NCUSCT), 1050 17th Street NW, Suite 350, Washington, DC 20036. Tel: (202) 331-0290. NCUSCT is a private, nonprofit organization for trade with the PRC. With over four hundred member firms, it has close working relations with all the major PRC organizations and agencies involved in international trade. It publishes several publications, including *China Business Review* (bimonthly) and *China Market Intelligence* (monthly).

Contacts in the PRC

U.S. Embassy, Xiu Shui Bei Jie 3, Beijing; or Department of State, Washington, DC 20520; or FPO San Francisco 96655. Tel: 52-3831. Telex: AMEMB CN 22701.

HONG KONG

Since Hong Kong will be a British colony until 1997, all international affairs are handled by the U.K. until that date.

Contacts in the U.S.

British Embassy, Office of the Counselor for Hong Kong Commercial Affairs, 3100 Massachusetts Avenue NW, Washington, DC 20008. Tel: (202) 898-4591. Telex: 023440484 HKWSH UI. Cable: PRODOME WASHINGTON.

British Consulate General, Office of the Commissioner for Hong Kong Commercial Affairs, Tower 56, 17th Floor, 126 East 56th Street, New York, NY 10022-3642. Tel: (212) 355-4060. Telex: 025 961075 NYHKO HK.

Industrial Promotion Office, Crocker Plaza Building, Suite 2130, 1 Post Street, San Francisco, CA 94104. Tel: (415) 956-4560. Telex: 023 340192 HK IND SFO.

Hong Kong Tourist Association, 548 Fifth Avenue, New York, NY 10036. Tel: (212) 869-5008.

Hong Kong Trade Development Council:
  California: 350 South Figueroa Street, Suite 520, Los Angeles, CA 90071. Tel: (213) 622-3194. Telex: 194288 HKTDC LA LSA. Cable: CONOTRAD LOS.
  New York (main office): 548 Fifth Avenue, 6th Floor, New York, NY 10036-5091. Tel: (212) 582-6610, 730-0777. Telex: 58550 CONZH CH.

Contacts in Hong Kong

U.S. Consulate, 26 Garden Road, Box 30, Hong Kong; or FPO San Francisco 96659-0002. Tel: 5-239011. **Commercial Section,** U.S. Consulate, St. John's Building, 17th Floor, 33 Garden Road, Hong Kong; or FPO San Francisco 96659-0002. Tel: 5-239011, ext. 294/228/333, 5-211467. Telex: 63141 USDOC HX.

American Chamber of Commerce in Hong Kong, Room 1030, 10/F Swire House, Charter Road Central, Hong Kong. Tel: 5-260165. Telex:

83664 AMCC HX. Cable AMCHAM HONG KONG. AmCham has an Executive Office Center with temporary executive offices and support services for transient businesspersons. A fee is charged and reservations are recommended.

Hong Kong General Chamber of Commerce, United Centre, 22nd Floor, 95 Queensway, G.P.O. Box 852, Hong Kong. Tel: 5-299299. Telex: 83535 TRIND HX. Cable: CHAMBERCOM. This office provides a variety of assistance, including identification of potential joint-venture partners, response to trade inquiries and the issuance of certificates of origin.

Chinese General Chamber of Commerce, 24-25 Connaught Road Central, Hong Kong. Tel: 5-256385. Cable: CHICHACOM HONG KONG. The main focus is promoting trade with the PRC and other countries.

Hong Kong Productivity Council, World Commerce Center, 12th Floor, Harbor City, 11 Canton Road, Kowloon. Tel: 3-723-5656.

Hong Kong Government Offices

Business Registration Office, Inland Revenue Department, Windsor House, 3/F, 311 Gloucester Road, Causeway Bay, Hong Kong. Tel: 5-79593145.

TAIWAN, REPUBLIC OF CHINA (ROC)

Contacts in the U.S.

Coordination Council for North American Affairs (CCNAA), 5161 River Road, Bethesda, MD 20816. Tel: (301) 657-2130. Since the U.S. has no diplomatic relations with the ROC, the functions of the ROC Embassy and consulates in the U.S. have been transferred to an ostensibly private organization (CCNAA) established for the purpose. Contact the office listed for the branch office in your area.

American Institute in Taiwan (AIT), 1700 North Moore Street, 17th Floor, Arlington, VA 22209. Tel: (703) 525-8474. Since the U.S. and Taiwan have no formal diplomatic relations, AIT performs the functions formerly assigned to the U.S. Department of State and the U.S. Embassy in Taiwan.

Visitors' Association, 1 World Trade Center, New York, NY 10048. Tel: (212) 466-0691. This office is a source of travel and general information.

Trade and Investment Information

Coordination Council for North American Affairs (CCNAA), Economic Division, 4301 Connecticut Avenue NW, Suite 420, Washington, DC 20008. Tel: (202) 686-6400. Telex: 440292 WASHINGTON DC. Cable: SINOECO WASHINGTON DC.

Contacts in the Republic of China

Taipei:

American Institute in Taiwan, 7 Lane 134, Hsin Yi Road, Section 3, Taipei. Tel: 709-2000. Telex: 23890 USTRADE. Since the U.S. and the ROC have no diplomatic relations, AIT Taiwan fulfills many of the functions formerly handled by the U.S. Embassy.

AIT Commercial Section and Trade Center, 600 Min Chuan East Road, Taipei. Tel: (02) 713-2571/6. Telex: 23890 USTRADE.

AIT Cultural and Information Section, 54 Nan Hai Road, Taipei. Tel: 303-7231.

American Chamber of Commerce in the Republic of China, N-1012, Chia Shin Building II, 96 Chung Shan North Road Section 2, P.O. Box 17-277, Taipei, Taiwan. Tel: 551-2515. Telex: 27841 AMCHAM TPF. Cable: AMCHAM TAIPEI.

Kaohsiung:

American Institute in Taiwan, 88 Wu Fu 3rd Road, Kaohsiung. Tel: 251-2444.

JAPAN

Contacts in the U.S.

Embassy of Japan, 2520 Massachusetts Avenue NW, Washington, DC 20008. Tel: (202) 234-2266. **Visa Section,** Suite 900, Watergate Office Building, 600 New Hampshire Avenue NW, Washington, DC 20037. Tel: (202) 234-2266. Consult your local telephone directory or contact the Japanese Embassy for the Japanese consulate nearest you.

The Japan External Trade Organization (JETRO). JETRO, which provides import and export information and assistance, has no office in Washington, D.C.; consult your local telephone directory or contact the Japanese Embassy or consulate for the nearest JETRO office.

Japan National Tourist Organization, 630 5th Avenue, New York, NY 10017. Tel: (212) 757-5640. This organization has offices in major cities throughout the U.S.

Contacts in Japan

U.S. Embassy, 10-1, Akasaka 1-chome, Minato-ku (107), Tokyo, Japan; or APO San Francisco 96503. Tel: (03) 583-7141. Telex: 2422118. **Foreign Commercial Service,** Tel: (03) 583-7141.

American Chamber of Commerce in Japan (ACCJ), Fukide Building Number 2, 4-1-21 Toranomon, Minato-ku, Tokyo 105, Japan. Tel: (03) 433-5381. Telex: 23736 KYLETYO. Cable: AMCHAM TOKYO.

The Japan External Trade Organization (JETRO), 2-5, Toranomon 2-chome, Minato-ku, Tokyo 107, Japan. Tel: (03) 582-5511. **Trade Information,** Tel: (03) 582-5171/5173. **General Affairs,** Tel: (03) 582-5522. **Import Promotion,** Tel: (03) 582-5543.

REPUBLIC OF KOREA (ROK)

Contacts in the U.S.

Embassy of Korea, 2370 Massachusetts Avenue NW, Washington, DC 20008. Tel: (202) 483-7383. Cable: KORIC WASHINGTON DC/USA. **Information Office,** 1414 22nd Street NW, Suite 101, Washington, DC 20037. Tel: (202) 296-4256. **Financial Attache,** 460 Park Avenue, New York, NY 10022. Tel: (212) 972-1670.

Office of Supply of the Republic of Korea (OSROK), 460 Park Avenue, New York, NY 10022. Tel: (212) 752-1700. OSROK handles all sales to the ROK government.

Korean Traders Association (KTA), Hahn Kook (USA), Inc., 460 Park Avenue, New York, NY 10022. Tel: (212) 421-8804. KTA is a private but official organization for trade. Emphasis is on Korean exports.

Contacts in Korea

U.S. Embassy, 82 Sejong-ro, Chongro-ku, Seoul; or APO San Francisco 96301. Tel: 732-2601/18. Telex: AMEMB 23108.

U.S. Agricultural Trade Office, 63, 1-ka, Eulchi-ro, Choong-ku, Seoul.

U.S. Trade Center, c/o U.S. Embassy.

American Chamber of Commerce in Korea, Chosun Hotel, Room 307, 87 Sokong-Dong, Chung-Gu, Seoul 100, Korea. Tel: 753-6471, 752-6516, 752-3061. Telex: K28432 CHOSUN. Cable: AMCHAMBER SEOUL ATTN AMCHAM-K.

SINGAPORE

Contacts in the U.S.

Embassy of the Republic of Singapore, 1824 R Street NW, Washington, DC 20009. Tel: (202) 667-7555.

Singapore Trade Office, 745 Fifth Avenue, New York, NY 10151. Tel: (212) 421-2207.

Singapore Tourist Promotion Board, 342 Madison Avenue, New York, NY 10017. Tel: (212) 687-0385.

Contacts in Singapore

U.S. Embassy, 30 Hill Street, Singapore 0617; or FPO San Francisco 96699. Tel: 338-0251. **Foreign Commercial Services and Library,** 111 North Bridge Road #15-05, Peninsula Plaza, Singapore 0617. Tel: 338-9722. Telex: RS25079 (SINGTC).

U.S. Regional Export Development Office, 111 North Bridge Road #15-01, Penninsula Plaza, Singapore 0617. Tel: 336-3100. Telex: RS25079 (SINGTC).

U.S. Agricultural Trade Office, 541 Orchard Road, 08-04, Liat Towers Building, Singapore 0923. Tel 737-1233. Telex: RS55318 USDA.

American Business Council, 354 Orchard Road, #10-12 Shaw House, Singapore 0923. Tel: 235-0077. Telex: 50296 ABCSIN; or Charles E. Krukiel, Monsanto Company, 101 Thomson Road #19-00, Goldhill Square, Singapore 1130. Tel: 250-2000 (15 lines). Telex: MOSIN RS 21118.

U.S. GOVERNMENT OFFICES FOR EAST ASIA AND SINGAPORE

U.S. Department of State, Washington, DC 20520. **Office of Security,** Division of Foreign Operations. Tel: (202) 632-3122. This office provides current information on security conditions to U.S. citizens planning overseas travel. **Office of Business and Export Affairs,** Bureau of Economic and Business Affairs. Tel: (202) 632-0354.

American Institute in Taiwan (AIT), 1700 North Moore Street, 17th Floor, Arlington, VA 22209. Tel: (703) 525-8474.

U.S. Department of Commerce (USDOC), International Trade Administration (ITA), 14th Street & Constitution Avenue NW, Washington, DC 20230. Tel: (202) 377-2000. **Foreign Commercial Service (FCS),** Tel: (202) 377-2000. **Office of Export Administration,** Tel: (202) 377-4811. **Office of Japan,** Tel: (202) 377-2425. **Korea Desk,** Tel: (202) 377-4399.

Office of PRC and Hong Kong, Tel: (202) 377-3583; 377-2462. **Taiwan Desk,** Tel: (202) 377-4957. **Singapore Desk,** Tel: (202) 377-3875.

Textiles (Export or Import) Information

Office of Textiles and Apparel (OTEXA), Room 3100, U.S. Department of Commerce, Washington, DC 20230. Tel: (202) 377-5078; or **International Agreement and Monitoring Division,** OTEXA, Room 2814, International Trade Administration, U.S. Department of Commerce, Washington, DC 20230. Tel: (202) 377-2000.

Export License Information

Exporter Services, Office of Export Administration, International Trade Administration (ITA), Room H1099, U.S. Department of Commerce, Washington, DC 20230. Tel: (202) 377-4811.

Import Information

Office of Investigations, Import Administration, International Trade Administration, U.S. Department of Commerce, Washington, DC 20230. Tel: (202) 377-5497.

U.S. Food and Drug Administration (FDA), Registration and Listings Branch, 5600 Fishers Lane, Rockville, MD 20857. Tel: (301) 443-6597. Controls the import of new drugs and importer registration.

U.S. Food and Drug Administration, Industry Programs Branch, 200 C Street SW, Washington, DC 20204. Tel: (202) 245-1191. Controls the import of canned foodstuffs and related items.

Major Projects Information

Office of Major Projects, Room 2007, U.S. Department of Commerce, Washington, DC 20230. Tel: (202) 377-5078.

U.S. DEPARTMENT OF COMMERCE (USDOC) DISTRICT OFFICES

USDOC district offices are the recommended starting point for international business and trade activity. To locate the nearest office, check the U.S. government listing section (under "Department of Commerce, International Trade Administration") of your telephone directory. If there is no listing, or for further information, call USDOC in Washington, D.C.

Additional Reading

In recent years there has been a deluge of books on every facet of Asian culture and business. Because of the volume of literature on the subject, the suggestions below are necessarily limited to a tiny fraction of the materials available. Background reading will be far more successful if it is used as a foundation for understanding current newspapers and magazines, and if you are serious about doing business in Asia, a subscription to one or two relevant periodicals is a good investment. Even if newspapers are out of date by the time you read them, you can use them to get a subjective feel for the countries in which you have a business interest and for the way people in those countries interpret and react to events.

BUSINESS BULLETINS AND REPORTS

The U.S. Department of Commerce, International Trade Administration publishes reports that provide good overviews of business, trade and economic conditions in various countries. These reports, which are updated fairly frequently, can be obtained from USDOC offices in the U.S. and from the U.S. Embassy in each country. There are two types of reports: *Foreign Economic Trends* reports (FETs), which tend more toward economic analysis, and *Overseas Business Reports* (OBRs).

American Chamber of Commerce chapters overseas publish regular journals that contain a wealth of information on business conditions in each country.

NEWSPAPERS AND MAGAZINES
(d) daily, (w) weekly, (m) monthly

General and Regional
Asian Business (m), c/o Far East Trade Press Ltd., 15th Floor, Lockhart Centre, 301 Lockhart Road, Hong Kong. Tel: 5-8934331. Telex: 83434.

Asian Wall Street Journal (d), P.O. Box 9825, Hong Kong. Tel: 5-737121. Telex: 83828. The AWSJ is probably the most useful reading you can do.

Far Eastern Economic Review (m), Centre Point, 181-185 Gloucester Road, P.O. Box 160, Hong Kong. Tel: 5-8936688. Telex: 75297.

People's Republic of China (PRC)

China Daily (d), 2 Jintai Xilu, Beijing. Tel: 581-958. Telex: 22022.

Hong Kong

Hong Kong periodicals devote considerable space to events in the PRC.

Hong Kong Economic Journal (d), 4th Floor, Block A, North Point Industrial Building, 499 King's Road. Tel: 5-626221.

Hong Kong Economic Times (d), 3rd Floor, Cheong Kong Building, 661 King's Road. Tel: 5-651833.

South China Morning Post (d), Tong Chong Street, P.O. Box 47. Tel: 5-652222. Telex: 86008.

Hong Kong Trader (m), 31st Floor, Great Eagle Centre, 23 Harbour Road. Tel: 3-8334333. Telex: 73595.

Taiwan, Republic of China (ROC)

China Post (d), 8 Fu Shun Street, Taipei. Tel: 596-9971.

China Times (d), 132 Da Li Street, Taipei. Tel: 308-7111. Telex: 26464.

Commercial Times (d), 132 Da Li Street, Taipei. Tel: 308-7111. Telex: 26464.

Economic Daily News (d), 555 Chung Xiao East Road, Sec. 4, Taipei. Tel: 768-1234. Telex: 27710.

Japan

Daily Yomiuri (d), 7-1, 1-chome, Ohtemachi, Chiyoda-ku, Tokyo 100. Tel: (03) 242-1111.

Japan Times (d), 5-4, 4-chome, Shibaura, Minato-ku, Tokyo 108. Tel: (03) 453-5311. Telex: 2422319.

Mainichi Daily News (d), 1-1-1, Hitotsubashi, Chiyoda-ku, Tokyo 100. Tel: (03) 212-0321.

Mainichi Daily News (d), 1-6-20, Dojima, Kita-ku, Osaka 531. Tel: (06) 343-1121.

Korea

Business Journal, 120-2 Kwonnong-dong, Chongno-ku, Seoul. Tel: 744-6827.

Business Korea, 26-3 Yoido-dong, Yongdeungpo-ku, Seoul. Tel: 784-4010.

Korea Herald (d), 1-2, 3-ka, Hoehyondong, Chung-ku, Seoul. Tel: 756-7711. Telex: 26543.

Korea Times (d), 14 Chunghak-dong, Chongno-ku, Seoul. Tel: 722-4151. Telex: 23644.

Singapore

Business Times (d), Times House, 390 Kim Seng Road, Singapore 0923. Tel: 737-0011. Telex: 21239.

Singapore Business (m), Times Periodicals Pte Ltd, Times House, 390 Kim Seng Road, Singapore 0923. Tel: 737-0011. Telex: 21239.

Straits Times (d), Times House, 390 Kim Seng Road, Singapore 0923. Tel: 737-0011. Telex: 21239.

Sunday Times (w), Times House, 390 Kim Seng Road, Singapore 0923. Tel: 737-0011. Telex: 21239.

BOOKS

General and Regional

Rabushka, Alvin. *The New China: Comparative Economic Development in Mainland China, Taiwan and Hong Kong.* Boulder, CO: Westview Press, 1987.

People's Republic of China (PRC)

De Keijzer, Arne J. *The China Business Handbook.* San Francisco: China Books and Periodicals, 1986.

De Mente, Boye. *Chinese Etiquette and Ethics in Business.* Lincolnwood, IL: National Textbook, 1989.

Mann, Susan. *Local Merchants and the Chinese Bureaucracy.* Stanford, CA: Stanford University Press, 1987.

Teng, Waizao, and N.T. Wang, eds. *Transnational Corporations and China's Open Door Policy.* Lexington, MA: Lexington Books, 1988.

Tsao, James T. *China's Development Strategies and Their Effects on U.S. Trade.* Lexington, MA: Lexington Books, 1987.

Hong Kong

American Chamber of Commerce in Hong Kong. *Doing Business in Today's Hong Kong.* London/New York: Oxford University Press, 1988.

Bennett, Martin (Alison Lanier, originator of Update series). *Update Hong Kong.* Forthcoming. Yarmouth, ME: Intercultural Press, Inc.

Taiwan, Republic of China (ROC)

Leppert, Paul A. *How to Do Business with Chinese: A Taiwan Handbook for Executives*. San Diego, CA: Patton Pacific Press, 1985.

Japan

Condon, John C. *With Respect to the Japanese*. Yarmouth, ME: Intercultural Press, Inc. 1984.

Czinkota, Michael and Jon Woronoff. *Japan's Market: The Distribution System*. New York: Praeger, 1986.

De Mente, Boye. *Japanese Etiquette and Ethics in Business*. Lincolnwood, IL: National Texbook, 1986.

Deutsch, Mitchell F. *Doing Business with the Japanese*. New York: New American Library, 1985.

Hoopes, Aaron (Alison Lanier, originator of Update series). *Update Japan*. Forthcoming. Yarmouth, ME: Intercultural Press, Inc.

McCreary, Don R. *Japanese-U.S. Business Negotiations: A Cross-cultural Study*. New York: Praeger, 1986.

Shane, Scott. *Marketing in Japan*. Forthcoming. Yarmouth, ME: Intercultural Press, Inc.

Zimmerman, Mark. *How to Do Business with the Japanese: A Strategy for Success*. New York: Random House, 1985.

Korea

Bridges, Brian. *Korea and the West*. Chapman & Hall, 1987.

De Mente, Boye. *Korean Etiquette and Ethics in Business*. Lincolnwood, IL: National Texbook, 1988.

Kang, T.W. *Is Korea the Next Japan? Understanding the Structure, Strategy and Tactics of America's Next Competitor*. New York: Free Press, 1988.

Moskowitz, Karl, ed. *From Patron to Partner: The Development of U.S.-Korean Business and Trade Relations*. Lexington, MA: Lexington Books, 1984.

Whitehill, Arthur M., ed. *Doing Business in Korea: Challenge in the Morning Calm*. New York: Nichols Publishing, 1987.

Singapore

Chew, Soon Beng. *Small Firms in Singapore*. New York: Oxford University Press, 1988.

Dentsch, Antal, and Hanna Zowall. *Compulsory Savings and Taxes in Singapore*. Aldershot, Hampshire, England: Brookfield, VT: Gower Publishing Company, 1988.

Mirza, Hafiz. *Multinationals and the Growth of the Singapore Economy*. New York: St. Martin's Press, 1986.

Index

D

E